D1551173

Blacks and the Quest for Economic Equality

James W. Button   Barbara A.Rienzo   Sheila L. Croucher

Blacks and the Quest for Economic Equality ★ The Political Economy of Employment in Southern Communities in the United States

THE PENNSYLVANIA STATE UNIVERSITY PRESS

UNIVERSITY PARK, PENNSYLVANIA

LIBRARY OF CONGRESS
CATALOGING-IN-PUBLICATION DATA

Button, James W., 1942–
Blacks and the quest for economic equality : the political
economy of employment in southern communities in
the United States / James W. Button, Barbara A. Rienzo,
Sheila L. Croucher.
p.   cm.
Includes bibliographical references and index.
Summary: "An analysis of economic issues and political
conditions for black Americans, based on quantitative
and qualitative data from six Florida cities"
—Provided by publisher.
ISBN 978-0-271-03555-0 (cloth : alk. paper)
1. African Americans—Employment—Florida.
2. African Americans—Florida—Economic conditions.
3. Florida—Race relations.
I. Rienzo, Barbara Ann.
II. Croucher, Sheila L.
III. Title.

HD8081.A65B87   2009
331.6'396073075—dc22
2009006740

*To our grandchildren, who we hope will create and
live in a more egalitarian society.*

~ J.B. *and* B.R.

*And to the many women and men, present and past, whose courageous
quests for equality have created a better world for us all.*

~ S.C.

Contents

Illustrations

★

TABLES

FIGURES

Preface

Thirty years ago, I began the exploration of race, politics, and change in six southern (Florida) communities. In *Blacks and Social Change: Impact of the Civil Rights Movement in Southern Communities* (Princeton University Press, 1989), I detailed transformations that resulted following the 1960s political mobilization of blacks, including the election of African Americans to public office, improvements in municipal services, and the desegregation of schools and public accommodations. Now, in the latest investigation of these six cities, Barbara Rienzo and I look at the issue of most importance to African Americans more recently—the betterment of economic (primarily employment) conditions.

In my first book, I surmised that greater black political participation helped African Americans in the South by removing legal barriers, providing greater status, and enhancing basic public services such as street paving, recreation, and police protection. I also suggested, however, that the larger and more complex battle would be the quest by blacks for economic equality with whites. In the words of Martin Luther King Jr., "Jobs are harder and costlier to create than voting rolls" (King 1976, 6). Thus, the focus of this work is to explore the employment situation of blacks in the new millennium and the factors that have influenced how blacks are faring economically.

This study is unique in several respects. First, it blends both quantitative and qualitative data that triangulate our findings. The more than four hundred personal interviews (we completed the vast majority!) provide a rare entrée into blacks' and whites' perspectives as they deal with the issue of race and employment within southern communities. Second, we closely look at the policies and problems not often investigated in context yet related to jobs and African Americans, including the salient issues of affirmative action, interminority competition, inequities in public education, and cultural diversity programs.

Third, this study focuses on typical communities in the South. While this region encompasses more than half the African American population, race and economics in the South are sorely neglected by both scholars and policy-makers. Finally, unlike most academic tomes on race-related issues, this study concludes with a discussion of prescriptions for change that, based on our findings, have the best chance of improving the economic status of African Americans through employment opportunities.

This study could not have been completed without the funding bestowed by The Russell Sage Foundation. For this, we are most grateful. We would also like to acknowledge the work of two graduate research assistants who assisted with a portion of the fieldwork for this study: Shannon Tynes Michael and Phil Gold.

Jim Button
May 2005

1

Race Relations and Economic Progress

> The dilemma facing blacks today is how to achieve economic parity with whites
> when they aren't given the same opportunities or resources as whites.
> — BLACK LEADER, DAYTONA BEACH, 2001

AS THE UNITED STATES ENTERS THE NEW MILLENNIUM, race in the South continues to be the distinctively American Dilemma that Gunnar Myrdal (1944) identified sixty years ago. While African Americans have made substantial progress in politics in the South since the 1960s civil rights movement, particularly following the passage of the Voting Rights Act of 1965, similar advancements in economic have lagged behind. As historian Harvard Sitkoff (1981, 237) concluded in his investigation of the black struggle for equality since the *Brown* decision of 1954, "A Third Reconstruction, aiming for economic justice, is imperative if civil rights are to be meaningful to the poor and unemployed, to all those [blacks] still in despair."

One of the major problems in the quest for economic equality for African Americans is that many Americans (mostly white) believe that racial equality has been achieved. According to a 2001 *Washington Post*/Kaiser Foundation/ Harvard University survey, 50 percent of whites think the average black is about as well off as the average white in terms of employment. However, most blacks maintain that there is "a lot" of discrimination against them when seeking jobs (Bobo 2001b). African Americans are more than twice as likely as whites to be employed in lower-paying, less prestigious service jobs. Blacks' unemployment rate is double that of whites, and they are three times as likely as whites to live in poverty. The median income of black households is $27,000, compared with $42,000 for white households. Perhaps the most

poignant economic statistic of racial disparity is total household wealth—
the average net worth for whites is $84,000, whereas it is approximately
$7,500 for blacks (Raines 2002). In the South, blacks have traditionally oc-
cupied the lowest rung on the socioeconomic ladder and southerners in general have suffered from poverty more so than persons in other regions of the
country (Scher 1997).

Racial Attitudes in the South

Another major factor that has differentiated the South from the rest of the
country is white racial attitudes. Southern culture and traditions were based
on the belief that blacks were inferior. Yet much has changed in the South
over the past several decades since the civil rights movement of the 1960s. Indeed, some analysts have claimed that a "new South" has emerged in which
bigotry against blacks has declined and racial prejudice exhibited by southern whites does not differ from nonsoutherners' racial prejudice (Firebaugh
and Davis 1988; Schuman and Bobo 1988). Other academics challenge this
notion, arguing that white southerners' massive shift from the Democratic
to the Republican Party was due primarily to race, since blacks were joining
the Democratic Party in large numbers (Carmines and Stimson 1989; Huckfeldt and Kohfeld 1989). Similarly, a recent study using unobtrusive measures
of racial attitudes designed to alleviate social desirability effects found that
antiblack attitudes were markedly greater in the South than the non-South
(Kuklinski and Cobb 1997). While racial prejudice has declined to some
degree in the South, large numbers of white southerners still harbor feelings
of racial hostility. Going beyond attitudes, national audit studies in which
members of different racial groups with matched qualifications applied for
jobs found that blacks (and Latinos) are less likely than whites to attain an
interview or to be offered a job (Fix and Struyk 1993).

Evidence of the persistence of employment discrimination is most clearly
depicted in the scope and dispensation of racial discrimination lawsuits,
many of them occurring in the South. In the 1990s, a number of highly visible corporations, each with thousands of employees, were successfully sued
for racial and gender discrimination in employment, training, promotion,
tenure, layoff policies, and work environment (Darity and Mason 1998).
The most publicized case was the $176 million settlement reached between

Texaco and black employees after disclosure of taped antiblack comments by white corporate officials provided evidence of severe racial discrimination in employment. Texaco executives used the words "niggers" and "black jelly beans" and mocked the black cultural festival Kwanzaa, while black employees complained of being repeatedly passed over for promotions and being called "orangutans" and "porch monkeys" to their faces (Solomon 1996).

Other major southern-based firms that settled multimillion-dollar racial lawsuits included Winn-Dixie, Publix Super Markets, Cracker Barrel, Wal-Mart, and Shoney's. Since 1990, racial harassment charges have increased by 100 percent, whereas the number of minority workers has grown by only 36 percent. Such suits became easier after Congress passed a 1991 civil rights law that allowed jury trial and compensatory and punitive damages in race cases. Yet the rise in lawsuits may actually reflect improved race relations in the United States as more minorities are convinced that our society will no longer tolerate blatant bigotry. Others blame blue-collar white men who believe that affirmative action has given blacks an unfair advantage while their own wages have lagged behind inflation, and who thus take out their anger on minorities (Bernstein 2001).

Economic Conditions of Blacks

Black poverty and white racism have combined to affect blacks economically. Initially, following the 1960s civil rights movement in the South, black leaders were generally optimistic that political power would improve economic conditions. In many major metropolitan areas, affirmative action, better education, and the growth of the postindustrial economy had opened new employment opportunities for blacks (Moss and Tilly 2001). African Americans elsewhere in the South, however, never experienced any major changes in their economic and social lives. In smaller cities and rural areas, segregation and discrimination were no longer as open or legal. Nonetheless, as southern historian David Goldfield (1990, 207) puts it, "The sensitivity of both races to patterns of etiquette and custom built up over the decades enabled a subtle, unofficial residue (of racism) to continue." While southern and northern whites noticed the growing movement of urban blacks into the economic mainstream, poorer African Americans in the rest of the South remained invisible and neglected.

Other factors have influenced black economic progress, particularly in employment. The rapid growth of Hispanics and white females (and Asians to a lesser extent) in the labor market has created greater job competition for African Americans. Moreover, employers often prefer other minorities and immigrant groups, even when blacks have somewhat greater skills (Holzer 1996). In addition, of the occupations held by large numbers of blacks, only those in the low-paying service sector are expected to increase significantly in the next decade or two because of deindustrialization (Leigh 1998). Even in jobs filled by less-educated workers, employers are seeking laborers with higher-level cognitive and social skills due to technological and organizational changes (Holzer 1996). All of these labor market changes, occurring both in the South and non-South, have had negative consequences for black workers.

Furthermore, school desegregation, often viewed as a panacea for disadvantaged blacks in the South, has proved to be less than successful in many communities. Resistance from whites made desegregation difficult and disruptive for black youth, with large numbers of white students exiting to private schools or to other less-integrated school districts. School desegregation also brought blacks a loss of power and influence in school systems as the number of African American teachers, counselors, and administrators declined significantly. White teachers often did not know how to relate to or deal with black students, who in turn became discouraged or dropped out. As a result, growing numbers of African Americans, along with many whites, have become ambivalent about school desegregation. These attitudes, along with a decline in federal government pressure to maintain racially mixed schools, have led to an increase in resegregation of public education (Hochschild and Scovronick 2003). For growing numbers of black communities in the South, resegregated schools have meant fewer resources and less positive environments for learning, leaving black youth without the quality education necessary for economic success.

While this pessimistic view of black employment and economic improvement has tended to dominate social science thinking, there is a more positive perspective on black progress. As a whole, African Americans in the South and elsewhere have continued to make great strides in the job market over the past several decades. As blacks moved into larger cities and as industry relocated to the South, more and better labor opportunities appeared for minorities (Hogan and Feathermann 1977). Furthermore, as African Americans improved their levels of education, their occupational status and wages rose apace (Smith and Welch 1989). In 1995, for example, 93 percent of blacks with a college degree were employed, while only 57 percent of those without a high school diploma held jobs (Leigh 1998). Similarly, antidiscrimination laws and affirmative action programs have often been key factors in boosting employment opportunities for blacks (Heckman and Payner 1989; Leonard 1984).

Political scientist Frederick Wirt (1997), who closely investigated the political and economic changes in poor, largely black, rural Panola County in Mississippi from the mid-1960s to the 1990s, found that local business and public leaders developed a progressive approach to economic development. Urged on by federal and state laws and programs, the new progressive regime sought to expand local business and to transform the job market from farming to industry. Industrial recruitment strategies were successful by the 1980s, securing many new jobs in the process. Black leaders in both the private and public sectors worked closely with white progressives to ensure that black workers filled a large share of the new employment opportunities. While wages are relatively low and blacks complain of discrimination in promotion, the new economy, based increasingly on industrialism, has clearly offered a better quality of life for formerly destitute blacks. Other Delta towns and rural areas elsewhere in the South have emulated this economic development approach, which, in the process, has changed many traditional norms to the new cultural realties that form the New South.

In a similar longitudinal study of political and economic changes since 1960 in six Florida cities, it was reported that black employment in both the public and private sectors was influenced greatly by local black elected officials (Button 1989). Since the passage of the Voting Rights Act of 1965 and the dramatic increase in black voting, the number of southern blacks elected to office has increased from less than 200 before the act to 2,601 in 1982; by 1993, the figure had reached 4,924 (Scher 1997). Two-thirds of these black officeholders were found in local governments, city councils, county commissions, and school boards. Black officials had their greatest effect on public employment for blacks, particularly on police departments, which traditionally symbolized white authority and injustice toward blacks. In addition to putting political pressure on city and county governments to employ more blacks, African American elected officials strongly supported affirmative action in hiring. On the "supply" side, black officials actively encouraged minorities to apply for public and private sector jobs. A more recent study of black elected officers throughout Florida indicated that, compared with the 1970s, minority officials in the 1990s were more likely to focus on employment, housing, and economic development as services they were emphasizing for their constituents (Button, Richards, and Bethune 1998).

School desegregation in the South, while initially resulting in intense hostility between whites and blacks, ultimately benefited African Americans. Compared with racially isolated black students, those in desegregated schools were found to have higher job aspirations, a greater likelihood of college attendance, and better chances of gain white-collar and professional jobs (Hochschild 2004). Integrated public education has clearly helped to provide greater economic opportunities for southern blacks.

Another major force in promoting blacks in the workforce and thus creating greater economic advantage has been renewal of corporate America's embracing of "diversity management." In the 1970s, businesses adopted a variety of antidiscrimination and affirmative action practices to fulfill federal initiatives. But as federal efforts waned in the 1980s, many employer commitments to these practices did not end. Instead, human resources managers, who had originally been hired and trained to carry out Equal Employment Opportunity Commission and affirmative action mandates, developed new rationales for these programs (Lynch 1997).

By the late 1980s, these personnel specialists touted the competitive advantages of diversity policies. Demographic changes were altering labor markets, increasing minorities and immigrants as the number of white male workers declined. It was necessary to attract minority workers using the same strategies as before: antidiscrimination policies, diversity training programs, and special recruitment efforts. Helping minorities feel comfortable and appreciated on the job would increase their productivity and that of the organization. In addition, consumer markets were also changing, and a culturally diverse workforce would help to develop new products and marketing approaches as well as offer greater appeal to new consumers. Finally, the globalization of markets required doing business in many countries, and this meant having employees who could deal with business leaders from other cultures. Because of these relatively recent demographic and business trends, diversity programs became common in the 1990s, first in large corporations and then spreading more broadly (Henderson 1994; Kelly and Dobbin 2001). Thus, antidiscrimination and affirmative action policies did not die but have been reformulated without the most controversial practices. "Diversity management" is a program that has improved the employment opportunities of blacks, women, and other minorities.

Focus and Methods of This Study

Clearly, African American employment, particularly in the South, has not been fully explored. As a result, there are many unsubstantiated claims about the plight of black economic development in the land of Dixie. What is needed are data that go beyond U.S. Census figures to provide a complete picture of the kinds of jobs blacks are filling, how employers recruit and screen applicants, what skills employees need, the ways in which employers view black applicants, and how black and white workers respond to and view employment issues. Moreover, it is necessary to investigate interminority competition for jobs since new immigrants and more white females in the job market have created unique labor conditions. Antidiscrimination laws and affirmative action policies, while less well enforced than previously, may also play a role in black jobholding and advancement. Finally, the major increase in black elected and appointed city officials should affect not only African American municipal employment but perhaps private sector jobs as well.

These are the major and most important questions we investigate in this study, and to do so fully, we look at black employment in both the private and public sectors, surveying businesses as well as focusing on city departments of police, fire, recreation, and public works. To obtain sound quantitative and qualitative information, we interviewed not only employers but workers. Furthermore, to ensure complexity and comprehensiveness, we carried out these studies in six representative southern communities. Because James W. Button had studied these cities for more than twenty-five years, we are also able to describe the political, economic, and racial contexts of black employment.

The selection of cities for this study was important. We wanted to vary two contextual variables that seemingly would influence black jobholding. One factor is the relative size of the black population and therefore the potential for black applicants (Matthews and Prothro 1966; Keech 1968). The other variable is political culture, the Deep South–Border South dichotomy (Key 1949; Scher 1997). Florida provided cities with such variations and allowed us to control for state-level politics. North Florida is representative of the rural, agricultural Deep, or Old, South with comparatively large numbers of African Americans and a history of a plantation system where cotton and slaves once dominated the economy. In contrast, south Florida, particularly the coastal cities, is part of the more urbanized, fast-growing New, or Border, South. This region is more economically diversified, middle class, and progressive. Virtually unsettled until the early 1900s, racial antagonisms have been less apparent in this area (Button 1989).

Considering both the magnitude of the black population and the form of political culture, six cities were selected along a continuum of African American population size, ranging from relatively small in Crestview and Titusville (10–25 percent), to medium sized in Lake City and Daytona Beach (30–45 percent), to relatively large in Quincy and Riviera Beach (more than 50 percent). Two communities (one in the Deep South and one in the Border South) were chosen in each category. The Deep South cities include Crestview, Lake City, and Quincy, and the New South is represented by Titusville, Daytona Beach, and Riviera Beach. Table 1.1 depicts this typology of cities and their basic demographic characteristics. While these cities are generally representative of these regional and black population variations, they were not selected randomly, and therefore, we do not claim generalizability to the entire South.

In terms of data-gathering approaches, we used multiple methods to capture a complete and more accurate picture of black employment. First, to investigate city employment, we carried out lengthy interviews with high-level city officials (city managers, mayors, city council members, and personnel

TABLE 1.1 Types and Characteristics of Communities (2000)

Characteristics	Deep South	Border South
Low percent black	Crestview	Titusville
Population	14,818	40,662
% black	19	12
Per capita income	$15,479	$18,901
Medium percent black	Lake City	Daytona Beach
Population	9,951	64,070
% black	38	32
Per capita income	$14,697	$17,530
High percent black	Quincy	Riviera Beach
Population	6,923	30,414
% black	65	68
Per capita income	$15,133	$19,847

Source: U.S. Census Bureau, "American Fact Finder," http://factfinder.census.gov. Accessed May 18, 2004.

directors), city department heads, and a sample of black and white employees in each department. We also perused city records, particularly affirmative action plans and reports. Second, in the private sector, we selected a random sample of businesses in each city and interviewed the primary person charged with hiring and promotion decisions, typically the owner, manager, or human resources director. Focus groups were used to gain the perceptions of black and white workers. Finally, local and regional newspapers, including the black press, along with interviews with key black and white community informants, provided contextual information. Appendix A presents further details of these approaches.

Chapter 2 presents an overview of race, economics, and politics for each of the cities from 1985 through 2002 (for further historical information, see Button 1989). Chapter 3 describes African American employment in the private sector, including views of employers and workers. Minority city employment in the departments of police, fire, recreation, and public works is the focus of chapter 4. Interminority competition for business and city jobs and promotions is addressed in chapter 5. Chapter 6 explores affirmative action policies and their effect on black workers in the public and private sectors. The final chapter summarizes major findings and proposes prescriptive programs and policies that would likely improve the plight of African American employees.

Harvard professor Robert Putnam (2003), in his presidential address to the American Political Science Association, strongly urged social scientists to perform a visible public role. Putnam contends that one of the most crucial issues facing society is social justice. He said, "The most important contemporary example in this domain, I believe, comes from the simultaneous increase in the United States (and some other advanced nations) of ethnic diversity and social and economic inequality. . . . Perhaps the most fundamental problem facing America, and most other advanced democracies, over the next several decades will be to reconcile the demands of diversity, equality, and community" (Putnam 2003, 253). At the core of this American dilemma is the economic condition of blacks in the South, where traditions of racial bigotry and social class still run deep. Thus, one of the ultimate tests for our democracy is whether greater political power can be translated into improved economic status for a disadvantaged racial minority.

2

The Economic, Racial, and Political
Contexts of the Cities

THE POLITICAL AND ECONOMIC ENVIRONMENTS in which African Americans seek employment are important to understand. We have posited that two major contextual factors that influence black progress are political culture and relative size of the black population. Political culture, as exemplified in our Deep South–Border South dichotomy, includes the history and basic traditions of a community, particularly those that have contributed to the current racial climate. The northern counties of the panhandle region of Florida are representative of the rural, predominantly agricultural Old, or Deep, South. With relatively large numbers of African Americans, this region was developed before the Civil War, when cotton, slaves, and the plantation system were mainstays of the economy. The "southern way of life," including Civil War memories and the race issue, continue to influence this traditional subculture, much as it does the neighboring southern states of Alabama and Georgia (Scher 1997; Key 1949).

In contrast, most of the coastal counties of central and south Florida are typical of the urbanized, fast-growing, and relatively progressive New, or Border, South. Virtually unsettled until the twentieth century, this region is more cosmopolitan, affluent, and economically diverse than the Deep South. Because the New South has no history of a plantation economy and black slaves, and because of the in-migration of many northerners after World War II, race relations there are less hostile than in the Old South (Black and Black 1987). Moreover, south Florida communities tended to actively encourage economic growth, soliciting new industry, the immigration of diverse populations, and an increasing tourism trade.

Nonetheless, over the past two to three decades, the lines of economic and political demarcation between Deep and Border South have blurred. The federal expansion of military establishments and financial assistance for infrastructure improvements, such as airports and interstate highways, encouraged economic growth throughout the South. Additionally, national civil rights laws and court decisions, along with the influx of northerners with relatively progressive racial attitudes, eroded traditional southern norms of race relations. As a result, many local business and political leaders began to endorse the idea of the "new" South, where economic development and population growth supplanted an agrarian society, with blacks providing the necessary cheap labor (Scher 1997; Wirt 1997).

Current socioeconomic characteristics of whites and blacks in our six cities attest to the attenuation of distinctions between the Old and New South (table 2.1). High school graduation rates for blacks (and whites) are about the same in the Deep South communities (averaging 69 percent) as in the Border South cities (66 percent). Median household incomes and poverty rates are also similar for blacks and for whites who live in the Old and New South cities. Just two decades earlier (1980), black and white educational and economic status were different, depending on whether these groups inhabited Deep or Border South communities (Button 1989).

The continuing and sizable gap between whites and African Americans in each socioeconomic indicator in every city is also clear. This racial difference is greatest in the percentage of whites and blacks living in poverty, with whites averaging 12 percent and blacks averaging 33 percent, or almost three times the rate for whites. Even though each of these measures of black living standards has improved, and the gap with whites has narrowed in the past several decades, a high level of black poverty persists in these cities and in the South in general. As southern scholar Richard Scher (1997, 51) recently concluded, "Just as the economic system of the South has improved for most southerners, so have many southerners been left behind as the new South economic engine runs in high gear. In both cases, those left out, those at the lowest end of the socioeconomic ladder, are more likely to be black than white."

The relative size of the African American population is the other important condition that affects white relations with blacks. The influence of this factor has become an axiom among scholars of the South (Keech 1968; Key 1949; Mathews and Prothro 1966). Specifically, "as the proportion of blacks in southern communities increases, so do the racial anxieties and fears of

TABLE 2.1 Socioeconomic Characteristics of White and Black in Six Cities

City Name	High School Graduates (age 25+), 2000 (%)		Median Household Income, 1999		Income Below Poverty Level, 1999 (%)	
	White	Black	White	Black	White	Black
Deep South						
Crestview	80	75	$34,869	$22,905	13	35
Lake City	82	66	$29,673	$19,898	12	33
Quincy	83	66	$40,903	$22,700	10	24
Average	82	69	$35,148	$21,834	12	31
Border South						
Titusville	86	68	$37,487	$20,201	9	37
Daytona Beach	84	66	$27,140	$20,525	17	35
Riviera Beach	89	64	$43,405	$26,907	9	29
Average	86	66	$36,010	$22,544	12%	35%

SOURCE: U.S. Census Bureau, *Census 2000*, Summary File 3.

southern whites" (Mathews and Prothro 1966, 117). Typically, the threshold of white fear of and resistance to blacks is the point at which the African American population is somewhere between 30 percent and 50 percent of the population. Even when blacks compose the majority—up to about 65–70 percent—white opposition to black progress is great (Button 1989). Only when blacks become the majority of the population (80–90 percent or more) are they able to control or to influence political and economic institutions to the point that they can overcome white resistance.

While the size of the black populace affects the degree of racial hostility, we found pervasive and persistent white racism in every community. Most contemporary racism is institutional, as evidenced in the hiring and promotion processes of some businesses and municipal departments; in the second-generation discrimination practiced in schools; and in the lack of adequate and affordable housing for many blacks. Clearly, a racial chasm continues in each of these cities today.

What follows is an overview of each of the six cities, beginning with those of the Deep South and succeeded by a look at Border South communities. In each setting, we explore the nature of economic and political developments since the mid-1980s. Political activity does not determine economic conditions, but it clearly has an effect. Moreover, as we emphasize black employment in both the private and public sectors, it is essential to understand local politics. Race relations in each community are also a focus, with the expectation that the relative size of the African American population and the differing political cultures (Deep South–Border South) may influence white-black relationships.

Crestview

A small, rural community in the northwest panhandle region of north Florida, Crestview is a typical southern city where religion and sports pervade the local culture. Eglin Air Force Base, one of the largest military bases in the world, dominates the area and provides employment for many of the city's residents. Nonetheless, poverty plagues the city as the lumber industry and agriculture, mainstays of the economy for many years, have faded in recent times. Little industry was found here, especially after a major textile factory closed in the 1970s.

Beginning in the early 1990s, however, the Crestview area experienced dramatic growth. Military retirees and residents of south Florida and the increasingly crowded Gulf Coast communities relocated to this haven of beautiful forests, cheap land, and low taxes. The city's population more than doubled in a decade. New restaurants and retail stores, including the state's first Wal-Mart Supercenter, developed to accommodate new residents. In addition, with its proximity to Eglin, military-related industry grew along with other technology firms. This economic boom fueled local job opportunities.

The black population of the city has always been relatively passive and small, less than 20 percent of Crestview's residents. Despite their size and the existence of white racism common to the Deep South, blacks experienced moderate progress in race relations following the civil rights movement of the 1960s. Desegregation of schools occurred relatively early and proceeded smoothly, as did the integration of public accommodations. The city elected its first black council member and hired a black police officer sooner than most cities in north Florida. Such progress was possible because the small black population rarely threatened white dominance and therefore did not arouse white resistance. In addition, black military personnel and retirees from Eglin air base proved to be a major force in achieving desegregation of public institutions, thus serving to ameliorate potential race conflict (Button 1989).

While Crestview experienced unparalleled growth in the 1990s, second-generation and other forms of race discrimination began to surface. In June

1988, three white men burned a cross in the front yard of a newly arrived black family. The men were convicted of a hate crime—the conspiracy to intimidate—after federal investigators were brought in to work on the case (Furry 1991; *Okaloosa News Journal* 1989). In a similar case in 1991, a white man firebombed a mobile home owned by a black family (*Okaloosa News Journal* 1991). A year later, racial tensions spilled over to the local high school. A fight occurred between white and black students; police were called in, and nine students were suspended (Furry 1992; Wolf 1992). Six months later, even more serious interracial fighting took place at the school; ten students were arrested, several were injured, and police initiated patrols of the school (Smith 1992a, 1992b). High school administrators and community leaders claimed that the racial conflicts were precipitated by arguments over inter-racial dating and over the Confederate flag emblazoned on the shirts and cars of white students. Amid these conflicts, the Ku Klux Klan, not very orga-nized nor active previously, held a rally outside of Crestview, and about two hundred people attended (Holland 1992).

Because of the racial turmoil at Crestview High School and in several other county high schools, the school board appointed a Cultural Coalition Task Force to address minority issues. The task force and a parents' group, Parents Against Inherent Racism, filed a complaint of discriminatory school prac-tices with the U.S. Department of Education's Office of Civil Rights. The complaint claimed that the school district discriminated by subjecting black and other minority students to different treatments and disciplinary sanc-tions than white students; by not hiring more black teachers, administrators, and counselors; and by allowing hate groups, Confederate flags, racial slurs, and noose-hanging in the schools (Wolf 1993). The Office of Civil Rights investigated the complaints and suggested a conflict-resolution program and greater dialogue between school district officials and community members (Lennard 1994).

Racial antagonism continued in Crestview schools, however, when a black female teacher was appointed principal of an elementary school in 1994. She was the first black in the district to be named to such a position, and al-though she had won a teacher of the year award previously, she received a number of complaints of harassment and unfair treatment of students and staff from parents and teachers. District administrators originally found no basis for the complaints, and the local NAACP and blacks rallied to the black principal's defense, claiming that whites were carrying out a concerted effort to get rid of her (Forst 1995). The black principal was reassigned to another administrative position, angering blacks who organized a protest "march against racism" with about one hundred participants (Associated Press 1995). The black principal accused the school district of racism; yet a Justice Department investigation of the complaint and other allegations of discrimination in employment found no fault with the district administrators. The black ex-principal was later denied a teaching position in the schools (Associated Press 1999).

In addition to discrimination in the schools, police treatment of blacks has also been a contentious issue. After several years of alleged police brutality toward blacks, a race riot occurred in 1994 following a police drug sweep of black neighborhoods. About twenty police officers were pelted with rocks and bottles by a crowd of approximately seventy-five blacks (Martinez 1994). The riot resulted in several town hall meetings with black residents who confronted city officials with a list of grievances, including the charge that police indiscriminately searched black men. City council members responded that the police were addressing high crime rates in the black neighborhood and that they would encourage the hiring of more black police (Golden 1996b). As of 2001, the police department employed only one black officer of thirty-one sworn personnel, and allegations that the police treat blacks differently from whites continue.

In the mid-1990s, the flying of the Confederate flag at a public memorial site alongside a major highway near downtown emerged as another controversy in Crestview. For many blacks, the flag is a vivid reminder of slavery and the attempt by southerners in the Civil War to maintain this system of brutal subjugation. For southern whites, the flag symbolizes a valued part of southern heritage and an honorable tribute to ancestors who fought or died defending the Confederacy. Blacks in Crestview took issue with the city's displaying the flag and, with the support of the Southern Christian Leadership Conference (SCLC), brought the complaint to the city council. After several heated meetings, the council voted 3–2 to keep the flag hanging above the Confederate memorial site. The close vote and final decision did little to ease racial tensions (Gilsenan 1996).

Despite lingering black-white conflicts, the population growth and economic development of the 1990s brought increased job opportunities. Many of the new jobs are in the service industry, however, offering low pay and typically no benefits (Heinz 1995). Moreover, many employers argue that blacks are often not qualified for higher-paying management positions because of lack of education or of job experience. Some black leaders agreed, claiming that many African Americans have problems, including drugs, criminal records, and semiliteracy, that deter them from obtaining decent jobs. Other blacks contend that often they are not hired because of their race. According to a longtime NAACP official in Crestview, "You are still hired by who you know, and whites tend to hire whites. . . . They go to the same country clubs and churches and know each other well. And they will not promote blacks because whites don't want a black supervising them." This black leader went on to say that most businesses and government agencies will hire a "token" black or two to show they hire blacks and that they do not discriminate. He also claimed that employers often hire white females over blacks because they believe that white females are compliant and less likely to challenge white males.

As an example of "tokenism," the city of Crestview had 139 full-time employees in 1999. Only 11, or 8 percent, of these employees were African American, although blacks made up 19 percent of the city's population. In comparison, American Indians, who made up less than 1 percent of the city's population, held 10 positions, or 7 percent of the city's workforce. Twenty-six white females, or 19 percent of the workforce, were city employees, and 18 of these women served as secretaries or clerical workers. Among the 38 city employees classified as administrators or professionals, only one was black. All department heads and top-level administrators were white males, except for the white female city clerk.

The most contentious issue regarding minorities among city workers occurred when a black female in the fire department quit her job and filed a sex and race discrimination lawsuit against the city in 1996. The city's first and only female firefighter (and second black ever in the department) claimed that employees created a hostile work environment and that the fire chief unjustly failed to promote her. The chief, however, responded that the black woman was treated fairly, that she was provided with separate sleeping and bathing facilities, and that she had the lowest score of the five applicants who took the independently administered promotion exams. In addition, the city's black councilman, an advocate for black workers, disagreed with the female firefighter's contentions, as did other black leaders and organizations such as the NAACP and SCLC. After a bitter trial before six white jurors, she lost the discrimination suit (Buccino 1998a, 1998b; Golden 1996a).

Despite the racial conflicts of the 1990s and blacks' poor employment record with the city, recent economic growth has meant greater job opportunities for Crestview's African Americans. Lack of education and pressing poverty, however, continue to be significant economic barriers for many blacks. In 2000, only 75 percent of blacks twenty-five years old or older had graduated from high school, while 35 percent of blacks lived in poverty (compared with 13 percent of whites). Moreover, lingering white racism limits workplace opportunities, especially in higher-level positions. Yet both blacks and whites agree that racial animosity has lessened. As a white businessman expressed it, "I'm from the North originally, and there are southerners who don't like blacks here. But relations have improved a lot due to the military coming in here. Redneck ways have subsided." A longtime black leader agreed: "Race relations are not as conflict-oriented as in the past. Blacks and whites accept each other for the most part, and there is less racial tension today. Blacks no longer feel they have to 'sleep with one eye open'; they trust whites more."

Lake City

Lake City is an isolated, rural community located sixty miles west of Jacksonville, Florida, just south of the Georgia border. Adjacent to Interstate 75, a major north-south highway, it is the "gateway" to Florida and a major stopping point for travelers and tourists. As a result, the city boasts of its growing commercialism, as shown by motels, restaurants, outlet and shopping malls, a new medical center, and several technological firms. Rich farmland surrounds Lake City, along with rolling hills and scenic lakes that have attracted a small but steady growth in county residents, many of whom have migrated north from overpopulated south and central Florida.

Despite the city's sleepy southern image of civility, Lake City has a history of racism and brutal subjugation of blacks found only in the rural Deep South. Blacks have always totaled one-third or more of the city's population and have thus provided a visible threat to white economic and political dominance. Many whites responded to this perceived vulnerability with fear and resistance that historically produced an active Ku Klux Klan and numerous lynchings and beatings of black residents. During the post–Civil War period, the Ku Klux Klan was active and notoriously violent in Lake City. That activism lasted in some form for the next one hundred years, including a series of well-publicized Klan rallies in Lake City in the early 1960s and a rally held in 1981 that drew more than two hundred people (Button 1989, 49–45). In the 1970s, Lake City grudgingly desegregated its schools and other major institutions, making it one of the last communities in north

Florida to do so. Even today, a Confederate memorial stands in the center of the city, and the reenactment of the Battle of Olustee, a Civil War conflict in which the Confederate army was victorious, is an annual ritual (Button 1989). As a longtime white businessman describes contemporary race relations, "Deep-seated racial animosity still exists in this community. Whites own and manage everything, and blacks are generally oppressed."

Over the past decade or so, the most serious racial conflicts have involved public school issues. In 1990, the local NAACP filed a complaint with the U.S. Office for Civil Rights (OCR) charging the school board with racial discrimination for failing to hire and promote more blacks to supervisory and teaching positions. Even though the OCR had cited the school board for discrimination in employment in 1980, the NAACP claimed little progress had been made (Kuhn 1990). At about the same time, the school superintendent appointed a white man to replace the county's only black principal, who had been terminated. Blacks had strongly advocated the appointment of a black principal (there were three among the position applicants) to the school, which had always had a black principal, was named for a black educator, was located in the black community, and was built on land donated by a black resident. The superintendent responded that she had appointed the best-qualified candidate for the job, and her decision was supported by the predominantly white school board (Swirko 1991b).

Several hundred black residents protested this decision at subsequent school board meetings and with a march through downtown Lake City (Swirko 1991a). The NAACP and the Interdenominational Ministerial Alliance, representing more than twenty black churches, called for black athletes to boycott sports, selective picketing of white-owned businesses, and a black student boycott of the first week of classes. When the student boycott of classes was called off for fear it might hurt black students academically, a dozen black protesters, including the city's lone black council member, blocked entrance to the black school on the first day of classes, stepping aside after a confrontation with the police. The superintendent responded by naming a black assistant principal at another school, but this move did little to assuage anger over the county's lack of a black principal. The superintendent called off all negotiations with the NAACP and demanded the arrest of the protesters. The police refused to arrest the peaceful demonstrators, who were violating no laws (Swirko 1991c).

Although the OCR absolved the school district of most charges of racial discrimination, including hiring the white principal, the lack of minority employment remained a problem. An affirmative action plan adopted by the school board in 1979 called for the district to achieve a ratio of 20 percent minority and 80 percent white teachers by 1985. Despite the appointment of a Minority Teacher and Administrator Recruitment Advisory Council that actively sought out and recommended minority applicants, the ratio in 1995 was 13 percent black and 86 percent white teachers (with 1 percent Hispanic or Asian). Indeed, the proportion of black teachers had actually declined from 20 percent to 13 percent between 1984 and 1994 (black students composed 24 percent of all students in 1994). While the recruitment advisory council presented twenty-six minority applicants to area principals in 1994, only three were hired (Beeler 1994b). Many blacks blamed the conservative superintendent and white principals for not taking determined action. In the words of a black teacher and member of the council, "We're going into 1995 now and nothing's been done . . . it makes me feel like minorities are being slapped all over the place. I really feel the minorities here are being treated truly unjustly—there is more discrimination here than anyplace I have lived" (Beeler 1994a, 6). By 2002, the number of black teachers in the school district had declined further, down to just 11.8 percent of all teachers.

Racial friction in the schools was exacerbated when in 1994 and 1995 the marching bands of the two largest schools in the county declined to join in the annual Martin Luther King Day parade. Many blacks were angered by what they perceived as a sign of separation, if not racism, on a holiday that celebrates unity and racial equality (Roberts 1995). In addition, black students at the local community college, an important venue of educational opportunity for many minorities who cannot afford or are not yet prepared for a four-year college, encountered racial issues as well. An editorial in the local newspaper criticized the president and the almost all-white staff of the community college for not better integrating blacks into extracurricular activities and for generally being "insensitive to the needs of black students" (Kenon 1992, 4). The NAACP and many blacks were also incensed by the college's decision in 1992 to suspend the basketball program for budget reasons. Most of the basketball players were black, and their athletic scholarships enabled them to attend the community college. At the same time, the college retained the mostly white softball and baseball programs, the only other organized sports (Martin 1995).

While racial discrimination plagued the educational system, several black educators voiced concern over the lack of preparedness and poor attitudes of many black students. "Decent jobs require an education, and blacks simply don't ready themselves . . . like staying in school. No one is giving black youth the message that education matters," claimed a black school administrator. Another longtime black teacher and principal observed that "black attitudes toward education are poor . . . kids skip school, drop out early, and many just assume they will not do well in school and that influences them." Among local high school graduates who took college entry-level placement tests in 2000, only 59 percent of blacks passed the reading exams (compared with 82 percent of whites), and an even lower 41 percent of black students passed the math tests (71 percent of whites passed; Florida Department of Education 2001).

Despite problems in the school system, the city embarked on a plan to increase black hiring and advancement in city departments. In 1993, the city council adopted an affirmative action plan with specific goals and timetables. Strongly supported by a progressive city manager and a black activist on the city council, the plan was necessary for the city to receive federal grants. The goal of the plan was to hire at least twenty-three minorities (mainly blacks) in from 1993 to 1998, thus achieving proportional representation of African Americans. At that time, blacks made up 34 percent of the population but only 24 percent of city employees (Moore 1993). To implement the affirmative action plan, the city manager stressed minority recruitment in staff meetings and had departmental representatives participate in "career day" at local high schools and at the community college. The city also advertised positions more widely in regional newspapers, trade publications, and on the Internet. Despite these efforts, few African Americans applied for city jobs; yet the city was able to hire several blacks in recreation and public works. By 2002, after much controversy and claims by some city officials that the community was not yet ready, a black (formerly the assistant chief) was appointed fire chief, the city's first black department head.

Nonetheless, throughout the 1990s, as in previous decades, African Americans in Lake City were harassed, intimidated, and faced physical violence from extremist antiblack groups and individuals. In 1991, the Grand Dragon of Florida's Ku Klux Klan spoke at an annual rally in the downtown park claiming, "race mixing is against the laws of God" (Kuhn 1991, 2). In 1992, four white boys were suspended from Lake City Middle School for writing "KKK" on a piece of paper and spreading rumors that a Klan group was forming at school (Callahan 1992b). Two years later, county road department workers, many of whom were black, were ordered off a job site that bordered on a Ku Klux Klan member's home, which had a twenty-foot charred cross in the front yard. Many of the workers were upset and fearful, suspecting satanic worship or Klan activity in the area (Kuhn 1994). In 1997, a chapter of the National Association for the Advancement of White People was formed to promote and preserve "white culture." In the most serious racial incidents, eight homes inhabited by black families in mixed-race neighborhoods were targets of drive-by gunfire in 1992; no persons were hurt, but police were unable to apprehend any suspects (Callahan 1992a). A few years later, a single black woman had a rock thrown through the window of her home with a message attached: "Fucking niggers get the hell out of Five Points [subdivision]" (Ward 1997, 1A). Several days later a group of white men appeared outside her home cursing, yelling racial epithets, and throwing rocks and beer bottles against her house. Police investigated the incident but again claimed they could find no culprits. The woman involved and other blacks stated that police did not actively pursue the criminals (Ward 1997).

The most recent racial confrontation occurred in late 2000 when the NAACP asked the city council to remove the Confederate flag from the city logo, which appears on Lake City's government stationery, city vehicles, and municipal buildings. The NAACP claimed the flag, shown in one corner of the logo, is a "hurtful and racist symbol that should not be the official logo at this time in history" (Thompson 2000b, 1B). When city officials refused to alter the city seal, the NAACP staged a protest during the Olustee Battle Festival. Police were called in to prevent violence when more than 150 counterprotesters, waving Confederate flags, confronted NAACP members (Thompson 2000a).

In a response aimed at appeasing black residents, city officials changed the disputed logo to showcase both the Union and Confederate flags. Nonetheless, the NAACP criticized the new logo because it still included the Confederate colors (Thompson 2001). With support from the state and national conferences of the NAACP, another, larger demonstration took place during the next year's Battle of Olustee parade. An estimated seven hundred protesters and counterdemonstrators arrived from various parts of the state. The head of the local NAACP, who had been arrested by police before the protests (but subsequently released) for illegally posting flyers on city utility poles, burned a Confederate flag in public (Rowland 2002). A day earlier, the Sons of Confederate Veterans had dedicated a permanent monument above which flew a large Confederate battle flag. The monument and flag cost $40,000 and was located just north of the city, adjacent to well-traveled Interstate 75 (Ouder and Arndorfer 2002). These events further intensified the anger among antagonists. "My tax dollars shouldn't pay for a flag that kept me a slave," stated a black protester. But a supporter of the logo countered by claiming that the Confederate flag is part of the city's history, not a message of hate or racism (Rowland 2002, 10B). Despite the protests, the issue of the city logo remains unresolved.

The pervasive racial conflicts in Lake City have affected economic opportunities for blacks. A professional survey of the city's residents in 1990 showed that blacks considered employment to be "the most important problem facing the city," ranking this issue higher than did whites and as more serious than crime and education. "Economic injustice is our number one issue, since opportunities for employment and housing are racially biased," stated a black leader and educator. "Blacks get only the lowest-paying jobs, and those with the education to gain higher-level positions are denied them. . . . It's the 'good ol' boy' system here."

In terms of racial discrimination in employment, dozens of class action and individual complaints by blacks were filed with the Equal Employment Opportunity Commission (EEOC) during the 1990s. The Lake City VA Medical Center was the source of more than thirty charges of race discrimination in hiring, promotion, and on-the-job treatment of blacks (Ives 1999b). At Cracker Barrel restaurant, two black employees filed suit for alleging that the better-paying positions, such as hosts, waitstaff, and cashiers, were given to whites while blacks were relegated to "back of the house" dishwasher jobs (Ives 1999a). Black residents filed other employment discrimination claims against Burger King, a mobile home company, the city police department, the county sheriff's department, and the local correctional facility. Many of those claims were settled in favor of black complainants, resulting in monetary awards or job improvements.

Allegations of racism have been commonplace as blacks have learned to fight back against injustices and file formal complaints. White employers, however, have become more conscious of treating blacks fairly because of the increase in lawsuits and the fear of discrimination accusations. Larger as well as nationally affiliated businesses realize that blacks are a sizable and growing portion of their market and share a commitment to employment diversity that is based on both economics and social philosophy. Nonetheless, many employers of smaller service-oriented establishments, which are the majority of business firms, are strongly influenced by deep-seated racial prejudice. In the words of a business leader, "White employers are still intimidated by blacks; some . . . think that blacks who walk in are going to steal something.

There's lots of racial profiling and stereotypes." And as another white employer added in agreement, "There's lots of prejudice here . . . lots of jokes about blacks . . . their hair, laziness, interracial dating. Whites here have not seen blacks in affluent, professional positions. Most blacks are kept down, are menial laborers, and that's all people see."

Beyond racial prejudice, however, blacks suffered from a high rate of poverty (33 percent in 1999), almost three times the rate for whites. According to the director of a local job-training agency, poverty often creates a number of conditions that limit economic opportunity, including lack of transportation (there is no public bus system), dependence on low-paying public assistance, need for childcare, lack of job experience, and lack of motivation to work. Racism combines with black poverty, social disadvantage, and lack of education to create serious economic inequalities for blacks.

Quincy

A large, golden-domed courthouse dominates the city square in the center of this poor, rural community just south of the Georgia border. It symbolizes the Deep South heritage; slavery and a plantation economy based on shade tobacco once reigned here. Even after tobacco production declined in the mid-1970s, the city's population, equally divided between whites and blacks, remained stable, and the Old South mentality continued. Civil War memories and the issue of race still permeate the culture, and white control over blacks has been central to the continuance of this traditional way of life.

Even today, Interstate 90, which runs through the middle of the town, divides the city's population. To the north are many millionaires and antebellum mansions owned by white families, some of whom bought Coca-Cola stock years ago and became rich. To the south lie the black neighborhoods, where some roads remain unpaved and many homes are small and made of wood or cinderblock.

While farming of tomatoes, other vegetables, and mushrooms replaced tobacco as the economic base in Gadsden County, poverty and unemployment among blacks remain high. Even though the county, with Quincy as the largest city and county seat, is 60 percent black, only 3 percent of black adults were registered to vote in 1960. The civil rights movement, spurred by Congress of Racial Equality and SCLC activism, sparked a rise in political awareness among blacks, and by 1972 the county's black electorate had expanded to 50 percent, approximately 12 percent below that of whites. Political and economic change were slow, however, as whites in Quincy resisted the desegregation of public accommodations and schools.

In 1970, frustration and discontent among blacks exploded in a riot and a series of protests after a policeman shot a disabled black man. Sixteen white-owned stores were damaged, and twenty-two blacks were arrested. The riot served to galvanize blacks, who carried out new voter registration drives and demanded that local businesses and government hire more blacks. Quincy had never experienced such mass protest, and whites in power realized they could no longer control blacks as before. Local businesses hired more blacks, as did the city, especially the police department (*Gadsden County Times* 1970).

Politically, blacks gained their first taste of power in Quincy's government in 1975 when two blacks were elected to the city commission. Two years later, one of those blacks became mayor by a vote of the commissioners. In addition, blacks gained a seat on the school board in 1978, and by 1982 blacks had won two more positions on the board to attain majority control. A black superintendent of schools was elected shortly thereafter (Bracey 1982; *Gadsden County Times* 1975, 1977). Blacks were learning to use their numbers and power at the polls.

Despite electoral success, blacks found it difficult to translate that power into ameliorating the most pressing problems affecting the black community. The crime rate increased dramatically in the mid-1980s, especially among young blacks, much of it due to "crack" cocaine (DuPont-Smith 1987a). Crime and drugs tended to originate in large public housing complexes with concentrated poverty (DuPont-Smith 1987b). At about the same time, drugs and violence invaded the schools, which were largely black, as most whites had abandoned the public schools shortly after school desegregation (Carey 1986). In addition, federal courts ruled that the local hospital had discriminated against a black worker in job promotions and that the county jail was in such poor condition as to be unsuitable for inmates (Carey 1987b, 1988). At Higdon Grocery Company, one of the largest employers in the county, twenty-five blacks walked off the job complaining about low pay, terrible working conditions, and uncaring managers. Attempts to unionize workers and discuss issues with supervisors at the company failed, and all workers who walked out were fired (DuPont-Smith 1987c; DuPont 1986). In city hall, the longtime city manager was fired partly due to his "dismal" record of hiring blacks (DuPont-Smith 1988b). The department of public safety (combined police and fire services), for example, had only fourteen African Americans among sixty full-time employees (DuPont-Smith 1988c).

While the problems for blacks appeared overwhelming, black leaders, both in and outside public office, began to address the issues. A special drug unit was developed by the public safety department, and a law enforcement officer was assigned to each public school to deal with drugs and violence. Alarmed by the high rate of juvenile crime among blacks, the Gadsden County Men of Action, a group of approximately forty community-minded black professionals, was formed to provide assistance. The group, concerned about the lack of positive male role models for many young blacks, mentored, tutored, and provided scholarships for black youth (Carey 1987a). The police antidrug unit implemented Drug Abuse Resistance Education, a school-based program that about six hundred fifth graders completed in the first two years. The Men of Action also proved helpful in getting the community involved in education and crime prevention. By 1991, drug trafficking had declined in the housing projects and other black neighborhoods (DuPont-Smith 1991).

Despite these efforts, serious problems confronted black youth in school. Fights and violence among students were common in the late 1980s. In 1990, two teachers were physically assaulted by students at Shanks High School, the only public high school in Quincy (DuPont-Smith 1990). The school was 90 percent African American as white students continued to transfer out of the public schools. Because of the increased violence, teachers found it difficult to teach and parents feared sending their children to school (Harper 1991b). Student scores on statewide standardized tests were consistently among the lowest in Florida while student dropout rates were high. Many of these problems were due to pressing poverty, as more than half the students lived below the poverty line (DuPont-Smith 1993b; Harper 1991a). Increasingly, mainly white, middle-class parents chose to educate their children outside the county's public schools, while black and poor students remained.

As blacks and whites increasingly competed for public office and jobs, racial conflict became more apparent. In 1992, the white supervisor of the public works department, which was largely black, was suspended and ultimately fired for misuse of departmental equipment and employees. At the time of his suspension, his son angrily threatened employees with a bullwhip, saying that if his father was fired he would "get the KKK to come down here and straighten these niggers out" (Snowden 1992, 1). A year later, the longtime county manager was fired by a 3–2 vote of the commissioners, with three blacks in the majority. The county manager had summarily fired the black planning director, the only black in the county administration, refusing to listen to black citizen comments on the dismissal and thus angering many blacks. This resulted in black protests and voter rallies that produced the black majority on the county commission (DuPont-Smith 1993a).

A watershed in race relations occurred in 1997 when blacks became a majority on the city commission for the first time and were able to vote as a cohesive group. Almost immediately, the black majority fired the city attorney and city manager, both white, and demanded changes in city policies toward the black community. Both city administrators were replaced by blacks. Not long after, the white police chief was also fired and a black chief was named with orders to hire more black police (Ensley 1998a, 1998b; O'Halloran 1998). Most other department heads were also replaced by blacks. These major changes brought some criticism from both races, with contentions that the new appointees were not always the most qualified and that their decisions were guided by vindictive feelings toward whites. Many blacks, however, supported the shift toward greater equality and fair treatment for African Americans (Pfankuch 1998). In the words of one black commissioner, "I was sick and tired of the white folks dictating how things should be for black folks . . . they're [African-Americans] tired of living like trash, and they want to be treated like true citizens of Quincy" (Pfankuch 1998, 8B).

In the private sector, a similar kind of revolt by blacks was occurring. At Quincy Farms, a major mushroom-growing business with about six hundred workers (approximately half black and half migrant-working Hispanics), laborers had long complained of poor working conditions and low wages. In March 1996, sixty employees, angered because farm officials would not listen to them, demonstrated, and a week later 150 farmworkers joined the protest. The laborers asked for better wages (average pay was $6 an hour), job security, safer working conditions in a hazardous job, health care, and a grievance procedure. Of those who protested, twenty seven were arrested and ninety more were fired (DuPont 1996a, 1996b). The United Farm Workers, a large farmworker union, agreed to assist by calling for a boycott of Quincy Farms in seventeen states with the greatest markets (Navarro 1996). Although 75 percent of the farmworkers voted to have the union represent them, management refused to bargain with the United Farm Workers since farmers were excluded from labor laws that govern most other workers. Protests by farm laborers continued, and other organizations joined in support, including

SCLC, NAACP, National Organization for Women, black state legislators, and other labor unions in Florida (*Gainesville Iguana* 1997). As the boycott of mushrooms grew increasingly effective, officials at Quincy Farms agreed to a settlement that reinstated most fired workers and provided benefits such as a 401(k) savings plan and limited health benefits (DuPont 1996c).

Whites were not willing to lose political and economic control without a struggle. As the new police chief urged white police officers to retire or, in some cases, fired them and replaced them with blacks, white officers began to file expensive lawsuits against the city. By 2000, seven white policemen had filed suits based on race (or "reverse") discrimination (DuPont 2000). Meanwhile, increased public spending in black neighborhoods led to a $1.3 million deficit for the city. Black officeholders were blamed for the fiscal crisis and labeled incompetent by whites.

Not surprisingly, most white wrath focused on the controversial black chief of police. When the chief announced his candidacy for county sheriff, historically the most visible and powerful symbol of white authority, whites retaliated. The white sheriff, who had been in office for twenty-nine years, longer than any other such officer in the state, was considered the dean of Florida sheriffs. Before the primary election, the police chief was arrested and suspended from his job on charges of ticket fixing and corruption. Blacks protested and rallied to the chief's defense, blaming politics and white racism for the arrest (Royse 2000). Although the police chief lost the election for sheriff, he was ultimately found not guilty of all legal charges and reinstated to office (DuPont 1991). A year later, however, the chief resigned under allegations of sexual harassment (DuPont 2002).

Political and racial turmoil, lack of decent schools, and little business growth have reduced the city's population over the past decade. Almost seven hundred whites left Quincy during the 1990s, while the black population remained stable, making up 65 percent of the city's population. By 2003, the city's industrial park had only one small business. Tomato packing continued to expand, but there still continued to be no major industrial growth and too few decent-paying jobs. Racial conflict continued to discourage people and businesses from relocating to Quincy, and workers with skills and transportation found jobs in Tallahassee, the state capital located twenty-fives miles away. According to a longtime black leader, "Deep down inside, both races do not *trust* each other and don't have a feeling of *care*. Blacks are still aware of slavery and its effects . . . they're still holding on to past injustices and feel they are owed something." He went on to say, and most white leaders concurred, that until blacks get beyond this feeling and demonstrate their competence, racial prejudice will not be overcome.

Titusville

The space program of the 1960s brought an economic boom to this formerly quiet community located on Florida's east coast. Although the boom ended with the demise of the Apollo program in the 1970s, the development of the space shuttle in the 1980s and 1990s has brought new, but fewer, economic opportunities to the area's Kennedy Space Center. Manufacturing industries centered around space-related activities have become a mainstay of the local business community. Shuttle launches and the space center have also given rise to a tourist economy of motels, shopping centers, and restaurants. Nonetheless, the lack of oceanfront development on federally owned land adjacent to the space center has deprived the city of potentially valuable growth and development opportunities.

The black population of Titusville has always been relatively small, poor, and segregated. By 2000, African Americans constituted 12 percent of the city's approximately forty thousand residents, with about 37 percent of blacks living in poverty. This poverty rate is more than four times greater than the poverty rate of whites. For decades, most of the city's blacks have lived in a segregated neighborhood just south of the downtown area and west of the railroad tracks. A news article described Titusville's black area as one of "chain-link fences with barbed wire, vacant lots with overgrown weeds, industrial complexes, homes with bars on the windows, junk piles and broken down cars" (Manolatos 2001). A longtime black leader echoed this view: "Our minority community looks like a third-world country." Although Titusville's small black population has left whites feeling relatively unthreatened and thus less resistant to racial change, pressing poverty has made it mostly impossible for most blacks to achieve economic gain.

Even with a progressive city manager and well-implemented affirmative action plan, city employment of African Americans has remained low. In 1994, blacks made up 14 percent of the municipal workforce but held only eight of the fifty-nine upper-level positions. In the seventy-eight-member police department, there were four blacks (5 percent), and the fire department had no African Americans. Some blacks criticized city officials for "unfair hiring practices that discriminate against blacks" (Evans 1994, 1B). Others condemned black leaders for not doing enough to rectify the situation. At the time, there were no African Americans serving on the city council, and the local NAACP was in disarray and inactive on issues regarding black employment (Evans 1995). White officials claimed the low number of black city employees was due to a lack of qualified minority applicants and to low rates of employee retention. Police officials in particular stated that trained black recruits were hard to find, and when they were recruited and hired, they were often lured away to larger departments that offered bigger salaries and better job opportunities (Decker 1996).

Racial inequality in the schools was also a barrier that confronted many black youths. In a special investigation in 1994 of student suspensions from school, *Florida Today* reported that in Titusville schools black students were two to three times more likely to be suspended than white students. Suspended students were not allowed to make up missed schoolwork, and if suspended ten days or more, students were typically expelled or ultimately dropped out of school. Some critics of these suspension policies and the resulting racial disparities in the treatment of students claimed that principals and teachers, almost all of whom were white, harbored negative beliefs about minority students. Others believed the problem had to do with social class rather than race. The well-respected black principal of a middle school in Titusville stated that teachers are ill equipped to deal with "undersocialized kids." He said, "Many of the inherited middle school problems are ones that were not corrected during the first six years. Parents are at fault for not establishing that first-line discipline, and teachers, in most cases, are not keeping pace. Now, through suspensions and expulsions, we are trying to demolish that monster—and in doing so, are becoming monsters ourselves" (Donnelly 1994, 1). Whatever the reasons for the racial differences in suspensions, the schools' disciplinary codes resulted in increasing the number of black youths who were either turned off by the schools or dropped out altogether. As a result, only 68 percent of blacks twenty-five years old or older had graduated from high school in 2000, while the comparable figure for whites was 86 percent.

Although blatant racism has been relatively uncommon in Titusville, both whites and blacks agree that subtle forms of prejudice linger. In 2000, a high-level white city official exclaimed, "Racism still exists here. A minority friend of mine was recently pulled over unnecessarily by the police and harassed. I talk to people everyday who have racist beliefs. We grew up in the South. . . . It's impossible not to be racist." A black employee at the Kennedy Space Center concurred: "We don't have to dwell on past [racial] problems . . . we still have enough current ones. We still do not have equal representation in the system and now we have a Congress eliminating affirmative action programs. We are becoming more, not less, polarized" (McAleean 1995, 4A). Black citizens feel particularly disenfranchised in the new millennium since they have no black representation on the city council, county commission, or school board. In 2000, only 8 percent of city registered voters were African American, and black voter turnout rates tended to be relatively low. White voters in the area, however, were known to be somewhat conservative, mostly Republican, and had never elected a minority member to county office, to the school board, or to a seat in the state legislature (*Florida Today* 2000).

In 2000, a controversy occurred that created a serious racial divide. In nearby Melbourne, a white councilwoman, faced with a proposal to rename a street after Martin Luther King Jr., made several racially sensitive remarks. The councilwoman said she opposed renaming the street after King because she doubted whether "he really accomplished things" or just "caused a lot of riots." She also claimed the late civil rights leader was a communist and a womanizer who did not deserve having a holiday named after him. The council member went on to state that the city should not give blacks "everything they ask for" and expressed opposition to affirmative action because "we're not responsible for what happened to them" (Glisch 2000). The councilwoman's comments triggered local outrage and gained national media attention. Hundreds of local citizens, both black and white, reacted as some were deeply offended by her statements while others defended her right to express her views.

Although exacerbating normally suppressed tensions regarding race, the controversy also brought about serious discussions of and actions toward dealing with local racial issues. The largest and most progressive newspaper in the area, *Florida Today,* published a series of articles entitled "Bridging the Gap," which analyzed racial problems and suggested ways to improve black-white relations. Among the important topics explored was the role of affirmative action in the workplace and the status of minority hiring and promotions (*Florida Today* 2000). In Titusville, the mayor appointed a special Racial Justice Task Force to "provide our community with a systematic approach for identifying and dealing with specific manifestations of racism" (White 2001, 1A). The task force, chaired by a former black school principal, issued its report in July 2001. The report described "hidden racism" that was manifested most often by other races continuing to "attach all things that are negative to the black community" (White 2001, 1A). Included in the strategies issued by the task force were recommendations to encourage the elimination of discrimination in both public and private sector employment, "to promote cultural diversity training for city employees and citizens of the city" (White 2001, 1A), and to encourage diversity in recruitment for the police and fire academies. Upon receiving the report, the city council vowed to take action after ranking the strategies by order of importance.

Even before the racial controversy of 2000, Titusville had taken progressive steps to improve race relations. In 1987, the city council voted to appoint a black man, a school principal, to fill a vacant seat on the council. He was the first black person to serve on the city body. This individual moved away from the city for professional reasons in 1990, and two other blacks were elected to the council in 1996. This election, in a city where 88 percent of the registered voters are white, was considered a watershed in local race relations (*Florida Today* 2000). Later that year, the city adopted a policy of "zero tolerance" on racism, and by the late 1990s, the city manager had implemented a program for city supervisors in which understanding cultural diversity was a primary goal. By this time, moreover, complaints of police brutality in black neighborhoods and reports of racial conflicts in local schools had become relatively rare.

Despite improvements in public institutions, the city's black population continues to lag behind whites in private sector jobs. According to 1998 EEOC data, most minority employees in the county are found in lower-tier and service industry jobs instead of management and professional positions (*Florida Today* 2000). Even with special recruitment and training programs, high-tech space industries still were not able to find many qualified local minorities for highly skilled jobs. The sprawling metropolitan area of nearby Orlando provides job opportunities for some blacks with transportation, but, in turn, whites with professional training commuted from Orlando to compete for high-level positions in Titusville. In addition, racial issues continued to present barriers to black workers. According to a black businesswoman and former public official, "Business managers feel they can work with and understand white women, but this is not true for blacks. . . . They [managers] feel there are major cultural differences, unless blacks are middle class and have social contacts." But most African Americans in Titusville have a low socioeconomic status with few contacts and gaining decent jobs and economic mobility are still beyond the grasp of space coast black residents.

Daytona Beach

Popular as a major tourist city, Daytona attracts about 8 million visitors annually to its famous twenty-three-mile-long beach and its renowned International Speedway for auto-racing fans. In addition, hundreds of thousands of college students visit the city during their spring breaks. More recently, Daytona Beach has developed additional events, such as Bike Week, that encourage more tourists. Furthermore, the Ladies Professional Golf Association headquarters, along with several golf courses and major housing developments, was established just west of Daytona in the early 1990s. In an attempt to diversify the local economy in the past few years, a small number of moderately sized industries, primarily technology companies, have been attracted to Daytona. Yet the growth of middle-class suburban communities just north and south of the city has provided a better-educated labor force that competes for better-paying, high-skilled local jobs. Nonetheless, Daytona Beach's labor market is largely service oriented, and this economic sector has experienced the most growth in the past decade.

African Americans constitute one-third of the city's population, a size that represents a potential threat to white power. Nevertheless, race relations in Daytona have historically advanced in a relatively progressive atmosphere, with blacks achieving a level of political activism and power that was both earlier and greater than in most Florida cities. Factors that have accounted for this remarkable progress include the presence of a significant black middle class, a number of fair-minded and helpful white allies, and the existence of a respected historically black college (Bethune-Cookman) that has helped provide black political leaders in the vanguard of social change (Button 1989).

Despite the city's progressive record on race relations and significant political gains in black voting and representation, there were still several black-white issues plaguing Daytona in the late 1980s and 1990s. In a special series of articles in 1991, the local *News Journal* highlighted not only the progress of local blacks but also the problems they continued to confront (Hawthorne 1991). Among the barriers facing blacks, according to the newspaper series, was the lack of economic progress. Blacks in Daytona still earned much less than whites; the median family income for blacks in 1989 was $16,335 compared with $27,520 for white families. Blacks also had higher rates of joblessness and were more likely to rely on government benefits and other forms of social aid. While integration enabled blacks to shop wherever they wanted, it also crippled many black-owned businesses that had once catered to a black neighborhood clientele. Moreover, problems of joblessness and poverty were exacerbated by drug distribution and use, and high crime rates pervaded many black neighborhoods. In 1990, for example, blacks composed a third of the city's population but represented 43 percent of drug arrests (Deger 1991). Finally, it was reported that African Americans and whites in Daytona still lived in mostly segregated communities but that this racial residential separation was due more to blacks' lack of income than to whites' racial intolerance (Hawthorne 1991).

As an indication of racial and economic problems, in 1990 approximately 250 African Americans protested at city hall over the lack of public employment and the unfair treatment of black employees. The protesters also complained of the lack of economic development in the black community (Wisniewski 1990). Later that year, about one hundred blacks demonstrated in front of the police department over alleged police brutality in arresting black drug suspects (Hill 1990). In 1994, the county sheriff was the focus of a NAACP protest for targeting blacks and Hispanics for traffic stops and cash seizures as part of his drug interdiction policy. This alleged "racial profiling" activity was soon challenged in court in the form of a civil rights lawsuit. The sheriff's department was also criticized for the low number of black and Hispanic employees, especially in the top-level positions (Holland 1994).

City officials responded positively to complaints by African Americans leveled at the city. The mayor claimed that since 1980, 31 percent of all police officer vacancies, 33 percent of firefighter job openings, and 22 percent of all administrative vacancies had been filled by minorities (including women). He added that the city's voluntarily adopted affirmative action plan had been implemented successfully over this time and would continue to provide preferences for minorities. The mayor also noted that a number of minority hires had left the city for better-paying jobs in other cities, a problem Daytona was unable to rectify due to financial constraints (Wisniewski 1990).

In terms of ensuring adequate black representation on the city commission, the city approved single-member districts through a voter referendum (Carter 1992). In response to police brutality charges, the police chief suspended a white officer for use of excessive force during a drug arrest and announced that police and black ministers would conduct "sensitivity" workshops at public housing projects to help reassure blacks regarding police tactics (Hawthorne 1990). Furthermore, police promoted the Police Athletic League, an after-school program developed in 1989 for inner-city youths to help students improve academic and athletic skills, as well as to cultivate positive relations between the police and minority youths. The program, located at a recreation center in a major black neighborhood, involved about 250 youths a day by 1992 (Whitney 1992b).

In terms of economic development in the black community, city officials initiated a $1 million project to renovate the primary black business district. The funds were diverted from another downtown project in hopes of increasing business in the decaying black area. In addition, the local black chamber of commerce, established in the mid-1980s, received small grants from both the city and county to promote African American businesses (*Daytona Beach Evening News* 1983). City officials, civic leaders, and the chamber of commerce also raised $80,000 to erect a monument to black baseball legend Jackie Robinson and to rename the local ballpark for Robinson. The first racially integrated major league baseball game, involving Robinson, was played in the Daytona stadium in 1946. Officials hoped the project, completed in 1990, would improve racial harmony in the city (Moore 1990).

In addition, the city and county vowed to emphasize their minority business "set-aside" programs, which had been initiated in the 1980s. Both governments set goals of steering at least 10 percent of their business contracts to minority- and women-owned companies. The city also attempted to maintain a level of 10 percent participation rate of minorities and women in the workforces of its contractors and subcontractors (Davidson 1989). During most years of the late 1980s and 1990s, the county was able to achieve the 10 percent goal. Daytona Beach proved somewhat less successful, but city officials claimed that lack of insurance, bonding, and experience on major projects precluded many minority businesses from qualifying for sizable jobs and contracts (Whitney 2000)

Like other cities, Daytona Beach faced several racial issues in its public schools. In the late 1980s, the NAACP, the most politically active black organization in the city, leveled a number of complaints at the school board. The main criticisms included a decline in black teachers, the failure to promote blacks to administrative posts, the lack of black head coaches at the high school level, the high suspension and dropout rate among black students, inadequate instruction in black history, and the failure to protect black students and teachers from racial discrimination and harassment (*Daytona Beach News-Journal* 1987).

The leadership of the NAACP, however, was reputed to be overly strident and prone to exaggeration, and the superintendent's responses to the charges indicated that some of the complaints were less valid than others. For example, data showed that 16 percent of the teachers were black, as were 21 percent of principals and 30 percent of assistant principals. Countywide 17 percent of students were African American (Button 1989). The superintendent promised to establish a special task force on black teacher recruitment and stated that a school dropout prevention plan was being implemented. He also appointed the first black head coach since integration at a Daytona high school. Furthermore, he claimed that black history is integrated throughout the year in social studies courses and that textbooks are checked to ensure that they depict blacks as part of American culture. Moreover, school administrators were concerned about remaining racial disparities. School student suspension rates were 4.8 percent for whites but 13.2 percent for blacks. African American youth were also more likely than whites to receive corporal punishment and to be expelled from school. Finally, whites composed 94 percent of students assigned to gifted programs, while black students made up 53 percent of those in educable mentally handicapped programs (O'Toole 1991).

Clearly, the most divisive racial issue of the 1990s, however, was Black College Reunion (BCR). Beginning in the mid-1980s, black college students from many states began coming to the beach area in Daytona to celebrate spring break. BCR occurred later in the spring than did other predominantly white student vacations and therefore was a separate event. Historically, African Americans had been banned from the city's public beaches. Only blacks who were service workers at beachside motels and restaurants and had identifying passes were allowed to cross the bridge over the Halifax River to get to the beach. After desegregation of public accommodations in the mid-1960s, small numbers of blacks frequented the beach area, which was dominated by whites and considered to be "unfriendly" to blacks.

Nonetheless by 1991, and yearly thereafter, BCR attracted fifty thousand or more black college students to the beach for as long as a week's stay. Almost immediately, beachside merchants complained that black students were often unruly and disregarded the law, while black college youth claimed they were treated poorly in hotels and restaurants. Specifically, black students cited higher motel prices, excessive minimum stay requirements, and threats by merchants to close their doors during BCR (Whitney 1992a).

The city responded to complaints surrounding BCR by establishing a task force to investigate claims and make recommendations, reinforcing the city's police force of 250 officers with an additional 320 personnel from the Florida Highway Patrol, and forming a group of forty police chaplains and volunteer ministers to accompany police officers in attempts to calm the large crowds (Smith 1996). City officials were concerned not only with the claims of merchants and students, plus the rising costs of additional police forces, but most importantly with the growing image of the city as a place that did not want African Americans but would welcome white spring-breakers.

By 1998, however, BCR had expanded to more than one hundred thousand African Americans, many of them nonstudents, and incidents of violence and traffic gridlock had become common. As a result, the city's task force issued recommendations calling for a code of conduct for BCR participants, strict enforcement by police of the code and city laws in general, a traffic plan to ease road congestion, and greater support from the African American community in enforcing the code (Bozzo 1998). Despite the city's adoption of the task force proposals, the next year's event did not go smoothly. Violence continued to mar the celebration, with one man dying from a gunshot wound (the previous year four police officers were wounded and another man died in a shootout). Black students complained to NAACP officials who helped monitor BCR that some restaurants were closed or would not let students in, and that hotels increased room rates, chained off parking lots to prevent access, and often removed hotel furniture (Frederick 1999).

Critics of the task force plan to restrict access to the bridges leading to the beaches as a form of traffic and crowd control argued that the proposal was racist. The city had never carried out such restrictions for white students' spring break or Bike Week, events that attracted approximately 1 million visitors. "Some [Daytona residents] are still living in the 1960s. There's an innate fear of this many black people coming into town (particularly beachside)," stated the black director of the BCR Redevelopment Committee. "Just because it's black faces out there, everything that happens gets special attention" (Wilks 1999, 2B). Indeed, a NAACP lawsuit over the beach access plan resulted in a federal court ruling that blocked the plan because it unfairly singled out the event (Justice 1999b).

To support the claim of racism, in 1999 black BCR hotel guests and the NAACP filed a class-action racial discrimination lawsuit against the Adam's Mark Hotel, one of the largest establishments on the beach. Later that year the U.S. Department of Justice also filed a discrimination claim against the hotel. Both suits charged the Adam's Mark specifically with setting higher rates for blacks than whites, offering blacks less desirable rooms, and demanding more security from African Americans, including the requirement that they wear orange wristbands for identification purposes (Justice 1999a, 1999c). A hotel manager claimed special security measures were necessary during BCR because of the excessive damage caused by guests. A year later, however, the hotel chain settled the suits by agreeing to pay $8 million, revising its policies regarding black customers, and seeking more minority guests. The chain, although it admitted no wrongdoing, also agreed to bring in a national equal opportunity firm to train its employees in nondiscrimination and monitor compliance. The settlement was one of the largest and most comprehensive agreements of a racial discrimination claim involving hotels (Zuckerman 2001). Although a federal judge later threw out the settlement, Adam's Mark ultimately agreed to a consent decree to pay $1 million to former guests and four of Florida's historically black colleges. In addition, the hotel chain pledged to treat black guests fairly and to commit to employment diversity by hiring large numbers of minorities (Brownfield 2002).

The lawsuits against the Adam's Mark sent a message to other hotels, merchants, and city officials that blacks suffered from discrimination during BCR and that such mistreatment would not be tolerated. Subsequent Black College Reunions were orderly, as the NAACP and other human rights organizations monitored possible discrimination, businesses kept their doors open and were generally more sensitive to black concerns, and the city agreed not to treat BCR differently from other special events (Grimison 2002). In addition, the city commission established an independent Human Relations Commission to help improve community relations generally in the city (Bozzo 2000). Nonetheless, BCR conflicts left a deep scar on the city's progressive image. In the words of a high-level Daytona official, "Black College Reunion has raised lots of racial issues, most notably the race and cultural differences between whites on the beach area and blacks on the mainland. Whites just aren't used to having blacks in their backyard."

Riviera Beach

This south Florida city is a study in contrasts, two cities in one, with little in common. Singer Island—its self-appointed identification—to the east is a barrier island with "pristine beaches, modern high-rises and affluent, almost all-white and retired inhabitants" (Pounds 1986, 1A). To the west, across the intracoastal waterway bridge, are the predominantly low-income blacks on the mainland, where many areas are blighted by poverty and crime. While blacks make up a majority of the population (70 percent in 1990), the well-organized island residents have often successfully battled blacks politically. Confrontations between the two groups in city politics have been frequent and bitter, with racial overtones.

Economically, Riviera Beach has long been considered a backward community in a growing and prosperous metropolitan area, made up of Palm Beach and Broward and Dade counties. Since the early 1980s, however, city officials have discussed new economic development that would bring in industry and revitalize the city's downtown and large lakefront area. Waterfront development in particular was believed to have great potential for major commercial and residential harbor growth (Ocker 1986). These ambitious ventures, according to city leaders, would promote significant economic revitalization and provide greater long-term employment opportunities for blacks. Nevertheless, ongoing political instability, along with the city's reputation as an "all-black, crime-ridden town," have seriously hampered efforts for economic redevelopment (Button 1989, 110).

Political turmoil in the late 1980s and much of the 1990s has had a tremendously negative effect, as Riviera Beach struggled to achieve greater stability and a positive community image. In 1986, a controversial black police chief was fired, and community groups targeted several council members responsible for the dismissal for removal from office. At the same time, after a 1982 investigation ended with the imprisonment of the previous black police chief for bribery, the FBI returned to city hall to explore charges of corruption. Amid this, the black city manager resigned (Ocker and Pounds 1986). A year later, as part of a "reform" campaign, four new members were elected to the city commission even though none of the new representatives had held political office previously. The reformed commission ousted six top-level city officials, including the new police chief, leaving city departments "divided and demoralized" (Sullivan 1987, 1B).

While race was a factor in this political instability, it became more clearly an issue in 1989 when three black city council incumbents were voted out of office and replaced by three whites, creating a 3–2 white council majority in a city that was almost three-quarters African American (Holloway 1989a). Flyers distributed during the campaign urged citizens to "vote black" (or "white") and depicted whites on the council as "wearing devilish horns and tails" (Holloway 1989b, 2B). The newly elected whites on the council soon dismissed several department heads, typically replacing blacks with whites. Between 1985 and 1990, the city employed four police chiefs, three city managers, and three city attorneys, and made several other leadership changes. During the late 1980s, the city also faced budget problems and lawsuits, some of which alleged race discrimination, from disgruntled city workers. Because of the racial conflict and political chaos, the city's image reached an all-time low.

Trouble continued to brew in Riviera Beach through the 1990s. In 1993, Singer Island residents attempted to secede from the predominantly black mainland, arguing that they paid more than their fair share of city taxes and received relatively little in municipal services. Blacks argued the request by white islanders was motivated by racism and was a serious threat to the city's economic stability. By a narrow vote, state legislators rejected the secession, but the issue further exacerbated already tense race relations (Douthat and Fuchs 1993; Fuchs 1994).

The conflict-ridden police department developed additional problems as well. In 1993, white officers sued the city, alleging the unfair promotion of black officers who were less qualified. In turn, black police blamed subtle discrimination for blocking their ability to advance, citing that blacks filled a mere 25 percent of management positions in the department (Fuchs 1993). Four years later, three white police lieutenants conspired to have the police chief fired and to take over a department they charged was badly mismanaged, filled with corruption, and favored blacks over whites for promotions. The chief fired the lieutenants before the plan was executed (Trontz 1997). Nonetheless, the three police officers won an appeal in court, were reinstated, and successfully sued the city (*Palm Beach Post* 2001). The police chief—the city's sixth chief in eleven years—resigned. Other suits filed by both white and black police officers, as well as by other city employees, alleging various kinds of race discrimination, ultimately cost the city more than $2 million (Clifton 1999b) and increased Riviera's liability insurance to more than $1.6 million by 2001. The city, according to high-level officials, teetered on bankruptcy.

At the same time, the police department was embroiled in serious turmoil, as the city's already high crime rate, focused almost totally on the mainland, increased precipitously. Riviera's predominantly black main thoroughfare, which until the late 1980s had been a relatively safe working-class neighborhood with thriving businesses, changed dramatically by the early 1990s.

The center of the city experienced increases in crime, drug dealing, drive-by shootings, and prostitution, transforming the area into closed businesses, storefronts with metal bars protecting the windows, and a virtual barren wasteland at night. Few customers shopped or traveled downtown, and many businesses moved out, leaving the area fighting for its economic survival. While the residents of the neighborhood sought increased police protection to deal with the rise in crime, the police department has reduced its force because of budget cuts (Aoki 1991). However, following several citizen marches and rallies protesting against drugs and crime, the police department developed a special force called the Violent Crimes Unit to help provide greater protection, and the city began a late-night recreation program to provide an alternative for youths on the streets (Pallesen 1992a, 1992b).

As economic opportunities in Riviera Beach dwindled, blacks were forced to compete for jobs with whites who typically had more formal education and greater skills. According to the 1990 U.S. Census, among adults aged twenty-five and over, only 59 percent of Riviera's African American adults had graduated from high school, while the comparable rate for whites in the city was 81 percent. Part of the problem of lack of education for blacks was the persistent and overwhelming racial segregation and poor condition of local schools. Despite attempts by the school board to desegregate all schools in the county through busing and greater integration of neighborhoods, school enrollment in Riviera Beach was more than 80 percent black in 1990 (Holloway 1992).

Continuing white flight from the city had left the schools with fewer white students, and many blacks opposed the large-scale busing of black students to schools outside of Riviera. According to an editorial in the area's major newspaper, the *Palm Beach Post:* "In the past, politicized school boards have ignored Riviera parents' concerns about the excessive busing of their children to achieve a racial balance in the county... their children were used as pawns in the desegregation wars, [and] the district neglected their schools" (*Palm Beach Post* 1991, 14A). Black residents complained to the federal OCR that the city's schools provided an inferior education because they were predominantly black and therefore neglected, and OCR officials agreed. In addition, in 1990, ministers and students from Riviera Beach protested outside school board offices, complaining that black students and employees were treated unfairly. The protesters, along with the county NAACP, requested the renovation of a Riviera elementary school in poor condition, the reduction in suspensions and expulsions of black schoolchildren, and an increase in hiring and promoting African American teachers and administrators (Gienger 1990b; Holloway 1990).

Prompted by pressure from protesters and the OCR, the school board moved ahead with plans to establish four magnet programs at the main high school in Riviera Beach. Previous attempts to bus white students from outside the city to the school had met with strong objections from white parents. Once the magnet programs were developed, however, white students were quickly attracted to the school. Within two years, the proportion of black students dropped from 90 percent to 62 percent. Yet the magnet programs resulted in racial segregation within the school. There proved to be little mixing of races in advanced classes, where only one in ten black students were enrolled compared with three in four white students. Thus, many African American youths were not receiving the benefits of increased educational opportunities at their school (Gienger 1990a). School district officials responded to this problem by developing "feeder" school programs in elementary and middle schools in Riviera to better prepare black students for admission into the high school magnet programs (*Palm Beach Post* 1990). A few years later, these feeder programs became magnet programs themselves with the intent to attract more white students, thereby integrating all public schools in the city (Gienger 1994).

By the end of the 1990s, the magnet school approach was a success at Riviera's high school. The school was well integrated, with black enrollment at the target goal of 38 percent in 1998. More important, black students were performing better academically than at any other high school in the county. With its International Baccalaureate and math, science, and technology magnet programs, the high school was now considered one of the best in the county, with 82 percent of its graduates going on to college (Desmon 1998b). At the city's elementary and middle schools, however, physical renovations and magnet programs brought no change in the schools' racial makeup as black enrollments remained at approximately 90 percent at both schools (Desmon 1998a). Clearly, both white and black parents have continued to support the neighborhood school concept at lower-school levels.

By the end of the decade, city politics had become less conflict ridden. Affluent Singer Island residents turned out in large numbers in attempts to elect whites, or carefully selected moderate blacks, in city elections. Yet the black mainland, with a united coalition of African American voters, was able to maintain its majority on the council as well as the mayor's seat, despite relatively low voter turnout (Clifton 1999a). With more capable professional city administrators and department heads, and a popular, energetic mayor, conflicts in city hall diminished. The earlier suit against the city by the three white police officers who attempted to take over the department was dropped on appeal. The mayor unveiled new plans for a $700 million waterfront redevelopment project to attract businesses and consumers, and the major proposal was gaining support (Clifton 2000; Cooper 2000).

Yet racial tensions continued to afflict local politics at the turn of the century. Singer Island and other residents complained of the high costs for taxpayers, while many in the downtown area objected to the planned relocation of individuals and businesses along the waterway (Clifton 2000). Furthermore, the city's negative image as a crime-ridden black community filled with racial animosity and bickering city officials prevailed, driving away federal grants and new business ventures. According to a high-level black city administrator, "Blacks here are disproportionately poor and struggling for economic survival. Our community and schools are racially segregated, so blacks and whites are separated and don't trust one another." In contrast, a Singer Island political leader claimed, "Those on Singer Island very much dislike blacks on the mainland, often fearing to drive through the city they consider too dangerous and crime-filled, and where city officials are perceived as incompetent." In the end, these racial conflicts are fundamental barriers to attempts at political stability and economic revitalization.

These six cities—three in the Old South and three in the New South, ranging in size from the relatively small African American population in Crestview to the much larger one in Riviera Beach—offer rich laboratories for an in-depth exploration into the ongoing quest for equality by African Americans in the South. The portrait that emerges is one of impressive gains coupled with stubborn challenges. The chapters that follow draw on a wealth of qualitative and quantitative data to elucidate the nature of racial inequality in these six cities and to evaluate strategies for overcoming it.

3

Blacks and Business Sector Employment

THE MOST IMPORTANT INSTITUTIONAL FORCE affecting the economic well-being of African Americans is private sector employment. One's job largely defines one's status in society and contributes to feelings of self-esteem and self-worth. In addition, we know that employment often provides an effective deterrent to crime, youth delinquency, welfare dependency, and other social ills (Cherry and Rodgers 2000).

Nationally, the prosperity of the latter 1990s improved the economic condition of most black Americans. Between 1993 and 2000, 22 million new jobs were created, and with inflation under control, productivity gains resulted in increases in earnings for all income groups. During this period of economic growth, the black unemployment rate declined from 11 percent to below 8 percent, median black family income rose to $29,000, and the black family poverty rate fell to 26 percent. Many black workers benefited from this lengthy period of fiscal growth (National Urban League 2002).

Nonetheless, African Americans have continued to face several labor-market barriers. Exclusionary practices and discrimination because of race still plague many blacks. Racial queuing in the form of the glass-ceiling effect keeps blacks from attaining higher-level positions. Moreover, with higher-paying jobs requiring greater skills and education, blacks are often at a disadvantage and are excluded from such jobs (Spriggs and Williams 2000). Furthermore, many employers harbor negative stereotypes of black workers, and even a tight labor market does not seem to alter these attitudes (Moss and Tilly 2000). Finally, the continuing concentration of blacks in depressed areas of major cities or in isolated rural areas in the South, far removed from the locations of most industries and better-paying jobs, maintains the "spatial mismatch" that also makes it difficult for blacks to compete in the workforce (Holzer 1996).

The purpose of this chapter is to explore the factors that enhance or inhibit African American private sector employment in these six cities of the South. This investigation has several components. First, we present the empirical results and analysis of our survey of businesses in the cities. Second, we summarize the views of employers, community respondents, and job training supervisors regarding issues affecting black employment. Finally, we summarize the experiences of African American workers, collected through focus groups.

Businesses and Minority Workers

Since the focus of the survey is on employers, their hiring and promotion practices, and characteristics of the businesses, it is important to look at a variety of factors that may affect employment. Previous studies suggest that several characteristics of firms affect the employment of African Americans. Larger businesses, as measured by number of employees, are more likely to hire minorities than small establishments (Brown, Hamilton, and Medoff 1990; Holzer 1996). Large firms pay higher wages and benefits and therefore attract more applicants; they also use more formalized hiring procedures that reduce the likelihood of racial bias.

National- and regional-affiliated businesses draw on and employ more minorities than do locally owned firms. National or regional firms express a greater visibility and concern for the importance of diversity, as well as a fear of lawsuits and negative press coverage if blacks are refused employment (Button 1989; Button and Corrigan 1997). In addition, the nature or kind of business may affect the employment of African Americans. Industries, retail stores, and restaurants are relatively open to the public and more committed to a diverse workforce than traditionally segregated businesses such as financial institutions (banks, real estate, insurance) and private recreational establishments (bowling alleys and country clubs; Button 1989; Wirt 1997). Moreover, black workers make up a small percentage in professional and managerial positions regardless of the business because of a racial "glass ceiling" (Cherry and Rodgers 2000; Schiller 2001). The location of businesses, in terms of proximity to black neighborhoods, may make a difference as well

(Moss and Tilly 2001). Distance and commuting costs create barriers to black employment. Finally, businesses with many African American customers are also more likely to hire and to promote blacks. To minimize racial tension and boost minority business, employers tend to hire blacks to act as "cultural brokers" with their black clientele (Lee 1998, 930).

In addition, hiring and promotion procedures, including recruitment, screening, and skill requirements, may influence African American employment. In terms of recruitment, employer reliance on informal networks, such as word of mouth, employee referrals, and walk-ins, tends to disadvantage minorities who come from socially isolated neighborhoods with few working adults (Holzer 1996; Wilson 1996). More formal methods of recruitment, including newspaper ads and employment services, are used more frequently for higher-skilled and professional/managerial positions. Such formal methods may favor blacks because they reduce potential employer prejudices and afford greater equality of opportunity for job applicants.

Increasing numbers of jobs demand some cognitive skills (reading, writing, math, computer aptitude), and thus many employers require high school degrees and general work experience. In terms of screening applicants, the greater the emphasis on such "hard" skill requirements and various hiring screens (such as drug tests and the criminal records), the less likely African American candidates will be hired (Holzer 1996; Moss and Tilly 2001). Yet, with a service-oriented economy, there has also been a growing emphasis on "soft" or interpersonal skills such as teamwork, customer service, personality, work ethic, and anger management as hiring criteria (Moss and Tilly 1996; Reskin 1998).

White employers typically evaluate black applicants, especially black men, as lacking social skills, as lazy, and as hostile and therefore as unqualified for employment (Moss and Tilly 1996; Neckerman and Kirschenman 1991). Thus, the race and sex of employers are potentially important influences affecting the hiring process, with white males being the least likely to hire and promote African Americans.

There are indications that affirmative action remains a vital policy in terms of black employment. Major U.S. businesses have supported affirmative action since the mid-1980s, with recent studies indicating that almost half of all firms engage in affirmative action, many voluntarily (Reskin 1998). Affirmative action has recently been reinforced by a growing corporate emphasis on "diversity" in hiring to mirror the changing customer base (Kelly and Dobbin 2001). We shall explore this variable in much detail in a later chapter, but we introduce it here as a potentially significant predictor. Affirmative action is measured in terms of the degree of employer support for this policy in the hiring and promotion of blacks and females.

Several community contextual variables are also likely to influence the employment of African Americans. The proportion of blacks in the city's population is usually related to black employment by supplying African American job applicants and customers (Button 1989). Political culture may be a factor in that Deep South (or Old South) communities are more traditional and conservative and therefore are expected to resist black employment and promotions more so than Border South (or New South) communities (Black and Black 1987). Table 3.1 lists all of the independent variables and their indicators.

Methods and Results

In each community, we randomly selected a variety (in terms of size and function) of businesses from a combination of Chamber of Commerce and Yellow Page telephone book listings. The kinds and numbers of private establishments chosen were restaurants (39), industrial or manufacturing firms (23), financial businesses (banks, insurance, real estate, car dealers, 20), motels and apartment complexes (30), retail stores (43), and recreational establishments (bowling alleys and country clubs, 12). The total sample size is 167, with city size determining the apportionment of businesses by community. However, we weighted equally the differing number of businesses in each city so that larger cities with a greater share of establishments did not overdetermine the results and vice versa for smaller communities. The median size of the businesses was 17 employees, with a range of 3 to 3,043 workers. For each business, we personally interviewed the primary person charged with hiring and promotion decisions, typically the owner, manager, or human resources director. Interviews were carried out between June 2000 and August 2001, and the race of the interviewer and respondent were matched in 92 percent of the interviews. A letter of support from the local mayor encouraged participation in this study, and business refusal rates averaged a relatively low three per city, with a high 88 percent overall response rate.

Despite significant interest in the relation of race and employment, few studies have been carried out at the level of the firm, or queried employers directly about their hiring and promotion practices regarding black and

TABLE 3.1 List of Independent Variables

I. Characteristics of Business
  • SIZE of firm (total number of employees—log estimate)
  • TYPE of business (0 = local affiliation; 1 = national or regional affiliation)
  • KIND of business (0 = financial, private recreation, motels/apartments; 1 = retail stores, industry, restaurants)
  • LOCATION near (within 7 blocks or less) black neighborhoods (0 = No; 1 = Yes)
  • METHODS of recruitment (0 = informal; 1 = formal)
  • TRAITS of employees (0 = interpersonal, "soft"; 1 = credentials, "hard"

II. Employer or Hiring Manager Characteristics
  • Race and Sex of MANAGER (0 = white male; 1 = minority and/or female)
  • Perception that many black applicants are UNQUALIFIED (0 = No; 1 = Yes)
  • Employer personally SUPPORTS Affirmative Action (0 = No; 1 = Yes, somewhat; 2 = Yes, a lot)

III. Contextual Factors
  • % BLACK in city population (2000)
  • Political CULTURE (0 = Old South; 1 = New South)
  • Percent BLACK APPlicants of all job applicants in last year
  • Percent black CUSTOMERS of all business customers in last year

other minority workers (Neckerman and Kirschenman 1991). In this sense, this survey is unique.

Table 3.2 presents the mean proportion of African American employees for various groups of cities, including the Old and New South, and the percentages of blacks in the population. Table 3.2 also summarizes findings for three major job skill levels (professional/managerial, skilled/semiskilled, menial/unskilled) and for the differing kinds of businesses.

The results show that the average black employment for businesses surveyed in all six cities is 26 percent. In comparison, the black population in these communities averages 39 percent and blacks aged sixteen and over composed 37 percent of the labor force in these cities in 2000. By occupational level, African Americans fill a mean of 14 percent of professional and managerial positions, 28 percent of skilled and semiskilled jobs, and 41 percent of unskilled employment. However, only sixty, or 36 percent, of these firms have unskilled labor positions, reflecting the loss of menial jobs due to macro-level changes in the U.S. economy (Farley and Allen 1989).

Data by kind of business indicate that restaurants, industries, and retail stores employ the highest proportions of blacks (45, 26, and 24 percent, respectively), while financial and recreational firms have the lowest (13 and 12 percent, respectively). Professional opportunities for African Americans

TABLE 3.2 Reported Mean Percentages of Black Employees by Community Group

Kind of Business	All Cities (N = 167)	Old South (N = 63)	New South (N = 104)	Low % Black (N = 50)	Medium % Black (N = 66)	Majority Black (N = 51)
All businesses	26 (14, 28, 41)	30 (18, 31, 49)	23 (10, 25, 35)	12 (6, 13, 29)	20 (7, 21, 31)	47 (30, 50, 63)
Restaurants	45 (29, 48, 57)	48 (37, 50, –)	43 (19, 47, 51)	26 (10, 29, 28)	29 (7, 34, 39)	82 (70, 82, 95)
Industry	26 (8, 27, 40)	35 (14, 38, 47)	17 (3, 18, 27)	9 (8, 9, 27)	11 (5, 10, 21)	37 (9, 41, 64)
Financial	13 (5, 15, 26)	9 (4, 10, –)	16 (10, 19, –)	1 (0, 2, –)	9 (7, 10, –)	24 (12, 27 –)
Retail stores	24 (15, 25, 44)	28 (17, 27, 48)	19 (11, 21, 18)	9 (7, 11, 14)	18 (9, 19, 32)	50 (31, 53, 62)
Motels, apartments	18 (6, 19, 28)	16 (2, 17, 29)	19 (8, 20, 28)	12 (2, 11, 20)	22 (8, 22, 27)	22 (10, 22, 44)
Recreation	12 (3, 10, 56)	13 (5, 14, –)	10 (0, 4, 37)	7 (0, 4, 75)	9 (0, 7, 62)	26 (15, 29, –)

NOTE: Community samples were weighted equally to control for variations in number of businesses surveyed from one community to another. Regarding the data, the first number = the mean percentage of all employees who are African American. In parentheses, the first number = the mean percentage of professional or managerial employees who are African American; the second number = the mean percentage of skilled or semiskilled employees who are African American; the third number = the mean percentage of unskilled or menial employees who are African American. The dash (–) indicates that the figure was less than one but not zero.

are best in the fast-growing business sectors of restaurants and retail stores. Skilled black workers are most likely to be found in restaurants, in industry, and in retail stores, while unskilled blacks number more than 40 percent in almost all businesses.

Looking at employment by community groupings reveals that opportunities for blacks are somewhat better in the Old South than in the New South (30 percent to 23 percent, respectively). This finding runs counter to our expectations. Indeed, businesses in the Old South cities show higher black employment figures for every kind of firm, except financial institutions and motels where the tourist-oriented economies of the New South provide an advantage. The Deep South communities are physically isolated in rural areas, whereas cities in the Border South are part of or close to major metropolitan centers. Thus, blacks in the Old South face little competition for available work, while New South blacks must contend with many other job seekers from nearby cities. Nonetheless, when other factors are controlled for, demographic differences between Old and New South cities have no effect on black employment.

There is a clear linear relationship between the proportion of blacks in the population and in employment. In majority black cities, African Americans make up 47 percent of employees. This is more than twice the employment rate in medium-percentage black cities and four times the proportion in cities with small black populations. Majority-black communities depict better black employment for all kinds of businesses and at all skill levels. Only motels and apartments offer a partial exception, with medium-black cities showing similar employment figures to those in communities that are predominantly black. Cities with low percentages of African Americans have relatively little black employment (12 percent), with only restaurants showing much higher job rates.

What Factors Make a Difference?

Correlations show the level of relationship between the independent variables or factors that may influence employment and the proportion of African Americans filling jobs in the businesses we surveyed. Table 3.3 presents the simple bivariate correlations between independent variables and black employment, both total and by skill level. The table indicates that several characteristics of these firms are associated with black employment. Type and kind of business are both statistically significant, suggesting that national or regional firms and industries, retail stores, and restaurants are more likely to employ blacks. Such businesses tend to be larger than local businesses, more likely to recruit widely, and more committed to diversity. Location of firms near black residential areas is also significant, indicating the importance of a spatial match that encourages black applicants. Surprisingly methods of recruitment and traits of employees are not highly associated with any level of black employment.

Among employer characteristics, two factors are significantly related to jobs for African Americans. Having a black, Hispanic, or female manager responsible for hiring is significantly associated with black employees. Minority managers are more likely to give some advantage to hiring from their own group members, and larger numbers of minority workers often result in greater chances of minority promotions into managerial positions (Huffman 1999). Employer support for affirmative action is also positively related to the level of black workers, suggesting that affirmative action in the form of minority hiring preferences tends to boost black employment.

TABLE 3.3 Correlations of Independent Variables with Black Employment

	Percent Black Employment			
	Total Employment	Professional/ Managerial	Skilled/ Semi-skilled	Unskilled/ Menial
Business Characteristics				
SIZE of business	.08	−.05	.02	.13
TYPE	.26***	.24***	.19*	.19
KIND of firm	.31***	.26***	.31***	.24
LOCATION	.32***	.33***	.30***	.29*
METHODS of recruitment	−.05	−.03	−.11	−.19
TRAITS of employees	.08	.01	.04	−.01
Employer Characteristics				
MANAGER, race and sex	.28***	.27***	.27***	.10
SUPPORTS AA	.22**	.32**	.21**	.05
UNQUALIFIED black applicants	−.13	−.10	−.15*	−.03
Contextual Factors				
% BLACK of city population	.52***	.39***	.51***	.45***
Political CULTURE	−.12	−.15*	−.11	−.22
% BLACK APPlicants	.77***	.60***	.76***	.52***
% black CUSTOMERS	.36***	.26***	.35***	.16

* p < .05; *** p < .001.

Contextual factors show the highest correlations with black workers. Demographic variables such as size of the black population and proportion of job applicants that are African American indicate the importance of having a readily available source of black workers. Moreover, larger proportions of black customers relates moderately to employment, suggesting that employers hire more blacks to boost minority business.

Multivariate Analysis

To explore the relationship between the various independent variables and the proportion of blacks among employees, we used ordinary least squares regression procedures and path analysis. Path analysis is useful in this case because the level of black applicants is the primary predictor of black employment, as expected. Thus, it becomes important to look at indirect, as well as direct, effects of factors related to African American workers. The hypothesized path model, based on the literature review, is found in Appendix A (fig. A.1).

Analyses are performed for total black employment for all businesses as well as for the proportion of blacks at each major occupational level (professional/ managerial, skilled/semiskilled, and menial/unskilled). The four path models are presented in figures 3.1–3.4. The first three models are robust, explaining more than 60 percent of the variation in black employment. The last model, unskilled black workers, is less successful but is based on only sixty cases since menial labor is increasingly rare in the restructured U.S. economy.

As we suggested, the results indicate that the percentage of job applicants who are African American is the variable most highly and directly related to the level of black employment. This is the case for every occupational level, except professional/managerial, where the proportion of blacks already em- ployed at the skilled level is the best predictor. Since most firms promote from within, this finding is not surprising. Nor are the results showing that the greater the application efforts by blacks to secure jobs, the more likely they are to be hired. Of course, some blacks may be attracted to firms that already employ a number of blacks.

Variables related directly and positively to black applicants and therefore indirectly to black employment include the proportion of the city's popu- lation that is African American, the percentage of customers that is black, employer support for affirmative action, businesses that are nationally or regionally based, and business hiring managers that are female or minority. Several of these factors are also associated directly with the level of black em- ployment. Although this varies somewhat by occupational level, size of the black population, employer endorsement of affirmative action, and female/ minority employment managers all are related directly to black workers in two or more of the four path models. Clearly, contextual and black resource variables are extremely important to black employment. Larger numbers of black residents, customers, and minority employers, as well as business support for affirmative action, are all helpful in creating a "black-friendly" environment that attracts sizable numbers of black job applicants and, ulti- mately, increases black employment.

White women, black, and Hispanic managers who are charged with em- ployment decisions are consistently, directly, and positively related to black jobholding. Forty-nine percent of these managers were women or minorities: 32 percent were white female, and 8 percent were African American. They are most likely to be found in restaurants, in retail stores, in industries, and in the Deep South cities. With female and minority managers, mean black employment amounts to 33 percent, while in businesses with white male

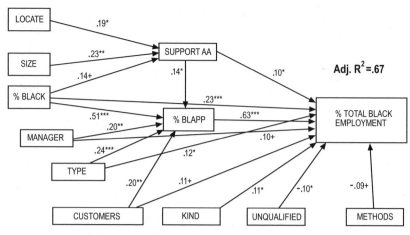

FIGURE 3.1 Path Models of Black Employment

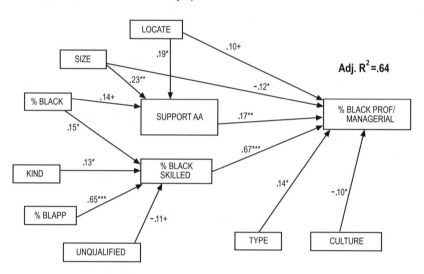

FIGURE 3.2

employers, the average black job rate was only 19 percent. In addition, having diversity among managers most likely helps to overcome race and gender stereotypes since minorities in high-level positions have a role in establishing the norms of the firm.

Other factors are often directly associated with black job success in general and at various levels of work. The kind of business, specifically restaurants, retail stores, and industries rather than other firms, increases the likelihood of hiring African Americans. These service-oriented businesses were more common in the U.S. economy of the 1990s. Moreover, such firms tended

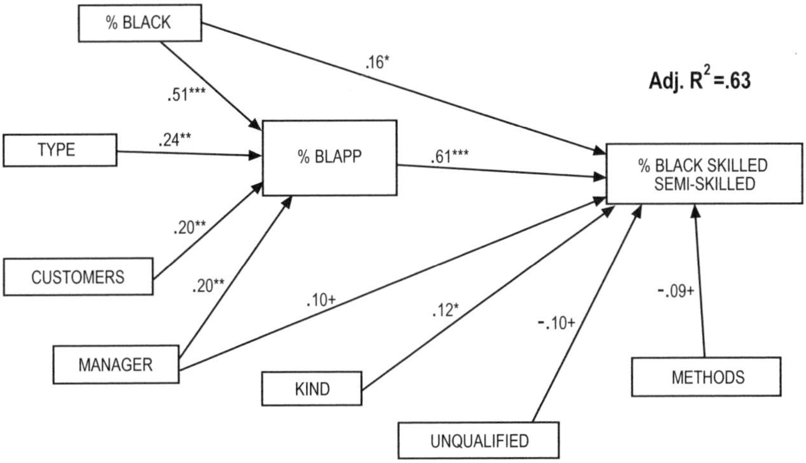

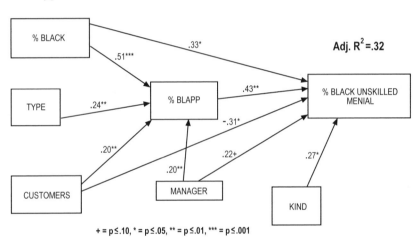

FIGURE 3.3

FIGURE 3.4

to be larger, to be national or regional affiliated, and to have minority or female managers. These are all characteristics that indicate a greater potential for black job seekers. Indeed, all of these variables, except firm size, are also separately and directly or indirectly related to black employment.

Whether a firm is national or regional based rather than locally owned and operated is a factor consistently and positively related to black workers. National- and regional-affiliated establishments, which make up 64 percent of our sample, tend to emphasize a diverse workforce as well as harbor a fear of potential lawsuits and negative publicity due to claims of race and sex discrimination. These businesses not only attract greater numbers of African

American applicants but also hire and promote blacks at higher rates than local firms. For example, national or regional businesses average 31 percent black workers and 18 percent blacks in professional or managerial positions, while the comparable figures for local businesses are 18 percent and 7 percent, respectively.

Surprisingly, neither methods of recruitment nor traits of applicants have much influence on the selection of black workers. In two of the four path models, "methods" are negatively related to employment, indicating that informal approaches such as word of mouth, walk-ins, and previous applications on file are more useful than formal methods. It may be that in a full-employment market, employers are less demanding in the hiring process. Indeed, in our survey, most employers stated that their most serious problem was finding employees who were willing to work and who had the ability to do so.

Nonetheless, even in a tight market, unqualified black workers are perceived to be a problem. As depicted in three of the four path models, employer claims that there is a lack of qualified black applicants is negatively and directly or indirectly related to black employment. Only at the unskilled job level, where few qualifications are required, is this perception not a significant factor. In all, 43 percent of employers claim that unqualified black job seekers is a problem. These employers tended to belong to firms that demanded greater requirements for applicants, such as work experience, good previous work record, formal education (usually a high school degree or more), passed an exam or were licensed to work, no drug use, or no previous criminal record. Later in this chapter, we will elaborate on this finding by presenting the views of business managers about African American workers.

The results concerning black customers are somewhat different than we anticipated. Black clientele is moderately and positively related to black applicants, but it is negatively associated with minority employment in two of the path models. It seems that black customers may indicate "black-friendly" firms, usually located near minority neighborhoods, and thus encourage African Americans to apply for jobs in these businesses. In terms of black employment, however, African Americans are increasingly holding jobs in businesses that service racially diverse clients or customers. Traditionally, in the South, blacks were hired to serve as "cultural brokers" with black customers, but that appears to be less true today. Larger retail businesses, restaurants, and industries, often with largely white customers, employ sizable numbers of African Americans.

As for the role of affirmative action, the path models indicate that employers' support for affirmative action is positively and directly related to total black employment and to black professional or managerial positions. The latter is the most statistically significant relationship and suggests the importance of support for affirmative action in helping African Americans gain higher levels of employment. Fifty-four employers (32 percent) advocated giving preferences to blacks and women in hiring and promotions. While only thirty-one of these fifty-four employers claimed to have a formal affirmative action policy, personally supporting such an approach had a major effect on African American employment and promotion. For firms in which employers advocated affirmative action, black employment averaged 32 percent. This compared with a mean of 24 percent for businesses in which employers expressed no support for preferential black hiring. At the professional/managerial level, the differences were even greater. African American employment averaged 25 percent in businesses that supported affirmative action, and only 10 percent in firms that did not favor such a policy. We will explore affirmative action policies and their effects more fully in a later chapter.

The quantitative results of our business survey indicate that African American workers are found primarily in skilled/semiskilled and menial jobs in service-oriented businesses, such as restaurants, retail stores, and small industries. Relatively few blacks have gained high-level professional or managerial positions. In terms of explanatory factors, black applicants and black population size are resource and contextual variables that are highly related to the employment of African Americans. Similarly, the presence of female or minority employers, whether firms are national or regional based, informal recruitment methods, and employer support for affirmative action are all factors that favor black workers. A barrier to African American employment, however, is the belief by employers that there is a lack of qualified black applicants.

What Employers Think

Racial discrimination is a complex phenomenon. In the past several decades, social scientists have claimed racial prejudice has shifted from "old-fashioned," blatant racism to modern, symbolic, and subtle patterns (McConahay 1986; Sears 1988; Bobo, Kluegel, and Smith 1997). Instead of "openly stated aversion" and "assertions of biological inferiority," newer versions of racism focus on the "perceived 'excessive' demands and privileges" as well as on the assumed cultural or social inferiority of African Americans (Moss and Tilly 2001, 88).

Employers often fit the mold of modern racism by stating prejudicial views of black workers while couching these claims in terms of skills or qualifications. Interviews with employers in Chicago, for example, indicated that they believed African American workers "have a bad work ethic," "create tensions in the workplace," "are lazy and unreliable," and "have bad attitudes" (Kirschenman and Neckerman 1991, 13). Although it is difficult to differentiate between racist attitudes and accurate views of work skills, employer assessments of black employees are most likely shaped by both factors.

Our personal interviews with employers provide a useful method for learning about their views of African American workers. Questions pertaining to employee turnover rates by race, perceived lack of qualified black job applicants, African American employment at various job levels, and the effects (both positive and negative) of having black workers elicited a range of comments from business owners or hiring managers.

The most common view voiced by employers is criticism of black workers, in particular their lack of motivation on the job. More than four in ten employers claimed a lack of qualified African American workers. Moreover, as we have shown, this perception reduces significantly the likelihood of hiring blacks. What are the most serious shortcomings of black workers according to employers? One of the chief criticisms has to do with the unwillingness to work or lack of a proper "work ethic." According to a white restaurant manager in Daytona Beach, "Blacks have a different work ethic. . . . They lack discipline—don't show up on time, or quit, or don't come in at all." Similarly, a white Titusville businessman claimed that "black people are not motivated and they are lazy. Blacks only work because they need the job. Blacks think that whites are still one level above them, even though they have the same opportunities. It's what you make of those opportunities."

The reasons given for blacks' lack of motivation at work tend to vary. For some employers, it is a basic cultural deficiency, or cultural gap, that divides lower-class blacks from more middle-class workers. Whether due to environmental, neighborhood, or family influences, blacks are viewed as having cultural characteristics that negatively affect their work performance. Such an explanation is most prevalent in the Old South, where the black-white cultural divide is most apparent:

From the cradle on they [blacks] are not taught to be responsible. They have
higher rates of absenteeism and turnover than other workers. Most do not
have a high school education and language is a problem for some, as is lack of
transportation. But mainly blacks are simply not taking responsibility.
—WHITE HUMAN RESOURCES DIRECTOR, INDUSTRIAL FIRM, QUINCY

There's a lack of black employees here. It's a cultural thing. Blacks see banks
with pillars and dressed up white men . . . it's like plantations. So they
stay away. But they also have poor skill levels.
—WHITE MANAGER, BANK, LAKE CITY

Black culture in the South does a disservice to black workers. When you
foster the mentality that you are owed something, then you are
not inclined to go out and make your own destiny. The
victim mentality hurts blacks more than it helps.
—WHITE MANAGER, RETAIL STORE, QUINCY

Employers also expressed the belief that many blacks are on public assistance and that welfare and other public programs undermine the work habits
of blacks. Such government programs are strongly condemned for creating
a sense of dependency, thereby reducing the work incentive among African
Americans, particularly black females:

Many blacks are on welfare or don't want to work. That's why most blacks
work in kitchens and housecleaning. I don't want to eat, sleep or live
with them . . . they can trash a community. That's what they did in
this city . . . it's a dump on the mainland where most blacks live.
—WHITE BUSINESS OWNER, RIVIERA BEACH

Many blacks want to be on welfare rather than work. They have it figured out . . .
they know the system. Why work if government will pay you. Our
black housekeeper supervisor says this too.
—WHITE OWNER, MOTEL, RIVIERA BEACH

There is very high turnover among blacks in housekeeping. They are
low paid ($5.50 per hour), into drugs, want to claim
unemployment, and don't want to work.
—MIDDLE EASTERN MANAGER, MOTEL, TITUSVILLE

In addition to welfare, the other public institution that is widely criticized
by employers is public education. Business owners or managers frequently
cite poor-quality schools as the primary cause of low-quality black workers.

Increasingly, jobs require "hard" skills, such as reading, writing, and math. The demand for educated workers has increased rapidly, especially in industry and special skill jobs. Thus, employers report the need for educated minority employees:

> There are just not many qualified black workers. They need a high school diploma minimally. Some blacks can't even read and write well. We have to help them fill out a job application. And most of our jobs are skilled-level.
> —WHITE PERSONNEL MANAGER, INDUSTRY, TITUSVILLE

> Blacks lack education here, especially in vocational training. Without it, many young blacks are left with stealing and drugs. They need an alternative.
> —WHITE MANAGER, INDUSTRY, RIVIERA BEACH

> Blacks do not hold as many good jobs as I would expect they would because of poor education. Those [blacks] who are qualified do not stay here because of greater opportunities elsewhere. If we could improve the school system, we would be able to retain a number of qualified minorities and their families.
> —WHITE, INDUSTRY EXECUTIVE, QUINCY

> Blacks haven't been introduced to this business or don't have the necessary education. They have not been trained to think in terms of finance or insurance . . . many have only recently arrived from farm and domestic work. . . . Few are qualified for this.
> —WHITE OWNER, INSURANCE AGENCY, CRESTVIEW

> Not a large number of blacks go to college here and then stay here. . . . So they're not a lot of qualified blacks in this small rural community
> —WHITE PERSONNEL DIRECTOR, INDUSTRY, LAKE CITY

In a service-oriented economy, interaction, or interpersonal, skills in the workplace are emphasized. These skills include personality, attitudes, and behavior rather than formal or technical knowledge (Moss and Tilly 2001). Among the businesses we surveyed, retail stores, restaurants, motels, and financial institutions place great emphasis on interactive skills for most positions. Judging these skills in job applicants is necessarily subjective to some degree, and standard stereotypes of blacks are frequently found in the comments by employers. In fact, business owners or managers often mentioned specific examples of what they characterized as "black behavior" in their business or community to support their judgments:

Decency and cleanliness is a problem with blacks. . . . They're not "pleasant" or "graceful," like whites. Blacks talk too loud as well—it sounds like they're fighting.
—ASIAN MANAGER, MOTEL, TITUSVILLE

Black attitudes are a barrier to jobs. Some blacks feel whites owe them something because of slavery. But I'd like to tell blacks, "You're not a slave and your father wasn't a slave . . . nor am I a slaveholder or was my father. Therefore I don't owe you a thing!"
—WHITE BUSINESSMAN, QUINCY

Blacks are the same as they always have been, no respect for us [whites]. They are not dependable and don't want to work for things. . . . Blacks get away with a lot of things in Daytona, especially during Black College Reunion, like drinking and driving. There are some good blacks, but you can count them on your hands.
—WHITE OWNER, MOTEL, DAYTONA BEACH

Another set of comments by employers emphasizes the continuing significance of racial discrimination in the job market. While few whites today will admit to the presence of old-fashioned blatant racism, a surprising number of employers confessed that it was a factor and sometimes even a major influence. However, these employers were also quick to point out that racial discrimination was the practice of others, not themselves:

It's tough to get jobs here as a black. They're not enough jobs and many whites won't hire blacks—discrimination. I've seen it and my black help talk about it. Whites are uncomfortable and scared around blacks. With a number of black workers and customers here, it's difficult to get whites to come here to landscape or paint this place.
—WHITE OWNER, RESTAURANT, RIVIERA BEACH

Things are not too good for blacks here. Lots of prejudice . . . jokes about black people—their hair, interracial dating, and marriage. People here have not seen blacks in affluent professional positions. There are no black role models. Most blacks are kept down and are menial laborers, and that's all people see.
—WHITE MANAGER, INDUSTRIAL FIRM, LAKE CITY

There's too much prejudice here . . . it really limits blacks. Some still see the company as a white male place. This used to be a prevalent attitude, but it's slowly changing.
—WHITE PERSONNEL DIRECTOR, INDUSTRIAL FIRM, LAKE CITY

Some people here don't like our having black workers. Some customers object to
our black cook. We have "rednecks" who come in here and just don't like blacks.
—WHITE MANAGER, RESTAURANT, TITUSVILLE

To be honest, we had some black waitresses. They were good workers, but white
customers did not feel comfortable with them. A lot of men were very rude
to them. Blacks quit . . . we have no black waitresses now.
—WHITE MANAGER, RESTAURANT, LAKE CITY

Racial friction between white and black employees was also reported by
some 10 percent of business owners or managers. The animosity between
racial groups is most apparent in Old South communities, where traditions
of racism run deep. In addition, restaurants, with lots of interactions in close
proximity and often under duress, create conditions of probable conflict:

Some white workers act out of prejudice toward black employees.
They used the word "nigger." I stopped it.
—WHITE SUPERVISOR, RESTAURANT, LAKE CITY

Plenty of racist people work here, but not the majority. There is some name-calling
both ways [black and white]; "N" word by whites and "white bitch" by blacks
—WHITE MANAGER, RESTAURANT, CRESTVIEW

We get black jokes and a few racial comments here, both from white customers
and workers. . . . Even some of our white managers have made racial
slurs, and these bothered black employees.
—BLACK MANAGER, RESTAURANT, CRESTVIEW

Although Latino workers are a small proportion of employees in these
businesses (4 percent on average), the worst racial conflicts are often between
blacks and Latinos. Differences in language and culture, along with perceived
competition for jobs, create conditions that alienate both groups according
to employers:

Sometimes blacks and Latinos get into fights and conflicts. They just don't get
along well. We've even considered separating them on the job.
—WHITE PERSONNEL DIRECTOR, INDUSTRY, RIVIERA BEACH

There are some problems between black and Hispanic workers. This work
[harvesting crops] used to be done by blacks and then Hispanics came
in. Hispanics claim that blacks pick on them.
—WHITE HUMAN RESOURCE DIRECTOR, INDUSTRY, QUINCY

Some employers did not state their perceptions of African Americans in the workforce or denied racial differences among employees. No doubt a number of these businesspeople were sincere, while others appeared to be offering a socially desirable response. Nonetheless, in communities with relatively few blacks (Crestview and Titusville) and thus a small proportion of the workforce, they are seen as less of a problem or threat to white employers and workers:

> We still have some "rednecks" here, but not most whites today... they're better educated and have learned to accept blacks. The South has a special culture of caring and warmth, and we've always been kind to most blacks here.
> —WHITE OWNER, INSURANCE AGENCY, CRESTVIEW

> Race is not discussed much or thought about... it's not an issue. There are not many blacks here and a relatively low crime rate... they're just not noticed.
> —WHITE PERSONNEL DIRECTOR, RETAIL STORE, TITUSVILLE

> There have been few racial problems, not even in the 1960s... no riots or threats by blacks. We have good relations in this business and the community.
> —WHITE OWNER, RETAIL STORE, TITUSVILLE

Finally, employers offered relatively few positive views of black workers. When queried about the effects of having black employees, most business owners or supervisors (56 percent) claimed that it made no difference. African American workers were praised, however, for improving business by attracting or by offering better service to black customers (27 percent) and for creating diversity that enriches the workforce (16 percent). Employer comments here included the following:

> It helps to have black and Hispanic employees. With diversity comes a better outlook on the community among workers, and it's helpful with clients who may have different buying habits or language.
> —BANK MANAGER, RIVIERA BEACH

> Diversity adds to our business. We can't be just "country club types" here, the market is more diverse. We are hiring to reflect the entire community. We do what's good for business.
> —MANAGER, CAR DEALERSHIP, TITUSVILLE

We do some targeting of minorities to promote diversity in the workplace.
We want to be seen as an "upstanding place in the community" . . .
not as biased, or dealing with lawsuits.
—WHITE MANAGER, RESTAURANT, DAYTONA BEACH

Perceptions of Community Respondents and Employment Agency Personnel

While employers offer an "on-site" view of African American workers, others in the community are also aware of issues of black employment and were able to contribute valuable insights. In Lake City, Daytona Beach, Titusville, and Quincy, job training or employment agencies are actively engaged in assisting primarily black workers, and we interviewed the directors of these programs. In all cities, we also identified and interviewed both white and black respondents considered most knowledgeable about race relations and minority employment. While their perceptions sometimes reinforced the views of employers, they discussed many other problems confronting blacks on the job. In general, these individuals and the directors of employment programs were less likely than employers to focus on the deficiencies of black employees and more likely to emphasize structural barriers and white racism as impediments to African American jobholders.

Lack of formal education is a major obstacle to decent jobs for many blacks. Every employment agency supervisor, as well as many community interviewees, stressed this factor. "Lack of education means a lack of training in the early years. Black kids need basic skills, like reading and math, and they're not learning them . . . neither at school nor at home," claimed a black director of a job training program in Daytona. These basic skills are necessary for decent-paying jobs as skill requirements have increased. Yet many poor black youth drop out of school to get a job, to have a child, or because they perceive that even with an education there are few opportunities for good jobs. Moreover, blacks are often treated poorly in school. "Blacks have been shot down in every effort to gain an education, and if they've dropped out, they fear going back. They often are labeled as 'special ed' or 'stupid,'" stated the head of a Lake City employment agency.

School suspension rates support these claims of racial differences in treatment. In Titusville middle and high schools, black student suspension rates are typically twice those of white students. Reasons given for this vary. "There are no black role models [in school]," claimed a middle school guidance counselor. "Not at the district level, not at the principal level, and not at the teaching level" (Donnelly 1994). As of the mid-1990s, only 16 percent of principals and 6 percent of teachers in the school district that includes Titusville were nonwhite, and all school board members and top-level administrators were white. According to a county NAACP official, black students are "not getting educated. It's easier for the school just to get rid of them" (Donnelly 1994, 1). A black principal in Titusville agreed, claiming that teachers are ill equipped to deal with what he terms "undersocialized kids." While broken homes and low socioeconomic status often explain students' behavioral issues, the principal stated that "the school system needs to adapt to students with economic problems" (Donnelly 1994, 1).

African American males in particular are seen by school officials as prone to violence and in need of discipline, and are often suspended for offenses that get whites only a scolding. Because of this and other forms of discrimination in school, black students, especially black males, drop out in high numbers. "Only seven of thirty-two black boys in my son's class graduated from high school," stated a Titusville African American school official. "Only athletes, who are socially promoted so they can play sports, and black students from families of the top ten percent in socioeconomic status, graduate . . . and most of the athletes don't go beyond high school."

In Quincy, both blacks and whites admitted that the segregated (90 percent black) public schools are a dismal failure. According to a white businessman, "whites won't move here because of the schools. If they do, they pay to put their kids in private schools or transport them to Tallahassee [twenty-five miles away] to public schools. Businesses won't locate here either due to the poor schools and unskilled workforce." Even when the schools are desegregated, as they are in most of the communities we studied, black and white students are often separated internally. "Look at the cafeterias in the schools—blacks sit at one table and whites at another. This is true at social times and other occasions as well," claims an African American Lake City public official. "Though we're integrated, we're still segregated, and this breeds lack of trust and respect." Schools are the one major institution controlled by the state that can bring about race mixing at early ages. Integrated schools are where children learn respect for other groups, all of which is necessary for a truly multiracial workforce and society.

Sometimes racial animosity flares into fights between white and black students. Although such conflicts are less frequent than during the early days of desegregation in the 1960s and 1970s, a number of high schools and middle schools still experience racial rage. Titusville High School, for example, closed down for a day in February 2000 when white and black students began to fight and exchange racial slurs (Meyer 2000). Previously, there had been some racial incidents after high school football games. Similarly, in the early 1990s, Crestview High was the site of a violent altercation between black and white students. According to a school administrator, the conflict was triggered by racial animosity over interracial dating and white students wearing Confederate flag shirts (to which blacks responded by donning Malcolm X shirts; Furry 1992). While such outright conflicts in schools are less frequent in the new millennium, racial tensions among youth have not disappeared and are often exacerbated by school settings that are internally segregated.

Race discrimination in employment, as already mentioned, is a continuing factor that plays out in old as well as new ways. While more overt forms of racism are less common, even in the Deep South, aversive forms of racism, entailing managerial discomfort or anxiety about contact with minority employees (Brown 1995), has become increasingly evident. "There is still discrimination in getting jobs," claims a black Daytona job-training specialist. "Blacks can get work but only entry-level; higher-level jobs are reserved for others. Black workers are 'steered' this way. As a result most blacks are housekeepers, maids, dishwashers, and cooks." A Titusville employment agency director echoed this sentiment: "Employers stay with people they're comfortable with, so whites hire whites. Also employers are looking for particular mind-sets, and color may not be an obvious factor but it does result in discrimination."

Only recently have white businesspeople become more sensitive to subtle forms of racism, according to employment officials, and much of this transformation is due to an increased awareness of customer diversity. "Employers now know it's important to have black workers to make black customers feel comfortable," stated a Daytona jobs program director. "They're becoming more aware and are beginning to put a few blacks up front in stores, restaurants, and motels. But they still have to be careful because some white customers are not comfortable with this."

There is also discrimination in the treatment of blacks on the job. An African American city commissioner and longtime businessman in Daytona Beach observed blacks at work and concluded that "they're often given different jobs than whites, the worst jobs, and supervisors often talk down to blacks. It's degrading. And blacks sometimes get fired for no good reason." White managers were described as holding stereotypical views of blacks, especially black men, as combative and unwilling to work. "Whites think black workers complain too much and are lazy . . . that young blacks, particularly men, don't want to do much but listen to music," stated a Lake City NAACP leader. "They're always suspicious of us and don't think we work hard enough."

Some community respondents also perceive that whites still hold deepseated prejudices that influence the way they respond to blacks in employment as well as in other facets of life. In the words of a black female leader in Daytona, "Whites do not see African Americans as people of value . . . they're not seen as equals. Our new human relations board will have minimal effect because black complaints will not be listened to the way whites [complaints] are." Others spoke of the cultural gaps between whites and blacks that created major obstacles in the workplace and elsewhere. According to a white Lake City businessman and city official, "Cultural and race differences run deep here. Many blacks only know fear, hunger and poverty, and want someone to blame for this. This may sound racist, but these people are just different by God's will or whatever." These prejudices are most apparent in communities with a relatively sizable black population (35 percent or more), where African Americans represent a threat and racial conflicts are more numerous.

Perceptions of African Americans as criminals are most evident in the way some businesses treat black customers. Several black community respondents talked about the way they are treated in various stores and restaurants. A black health agency director in Titusville stated, "I am watched closely in stores when I'm dressed in jeans. They think all blacks are going to steal something. In other places, I get a slow response in service or am ignored altogether." A black school administrator in Lake City commented similarly: "It offends me to walk into a store and have them watch me and other blacks all the time, even following me up and down aisles and showing me only cheap things, like that's all I can buy. White employers really fear us as criminals." These remarks are especially salient since they come from middle-class blacks, who are often, but erroneously, assumed to be beyond the bounds of discrimination.

Other structural barriers are also important in affecting the job opportunities of blacks. Lack of public transportation, particularly in the rural areas of north Florida, has proved to be a major obstacle to poorer blacks who cannot afford a car. In Quincy, many blacks need to commute to jobs in Tallahassee twenty-five miles away, and there is no public transit. Even in New

South communities, black neighborhoods are often far from places of work; yet only Daytona Beach has a city bus system. This phenomenon supports the "spatial mismatch" theory, whereby distance and commuting costs contribute to black labor market disadvantage (Jencks and Mayer 1990; Holzer 1996). Whether businesses intentionally locate away from black neighborhoods—as a way to limit black employment—is not clear. But this is the effect, according to employment agency officials, as some businesses want more skilled (usually white) labor and also want to avoid proximity to high-crime black areas. In Riviera Beach, several business owners in the mostly black downtown area were trying to relocate because of the crime rates. "It's really dangerous around here after five o'clock . . . hookers, drug dealers, and stores getting burglarized," stated a manager of a restaurant. He claimed he was able to buy the business for very little money because of its location in a high-risk area.

Black females in transition from welfare to work face additional barriers. Employers are critical of government welfare programs, believing that they undermine the incentive to work. Even with welfare reform and the significant reduction in welfare rolls, many businesspeople still perceive former welfare recipients negatively. "There's strong prejudice among business owners against black women who have been on welfare," stated a white Lake City job-training supervisor. "The belief is they don't want to work or they have too many kids and can't work. And this attitude is passed on to their children . . . it becomes a generational norm." This employment supervisor claimed that some businesses target these welfare-to-work women for low-paying, start-up jobs in fast-food restaurants and low-end retail stores such as Dollar General. Such jobs do not pay well enough to enable former welfare recipients to escape poverty, and most transitional education and job training is not sufficient. Moreover, many women lose their health care insurance (Medicaid) in the transition and need affordable childcare to work full time.

Women in general face a certain amount of sex discrimination in the job market. "Employers do not like to hire single women with children—they think such women are less dependable due to childcare responsibilities," claimed the white director of a Titusville employment agency. Poor single mothers, especially black mothers, often do not receive child support from absent fathers to help provide childcare. According to a black director of a Daytona job-training program, welfare mothers, many of whom are African American, are entrapped in a vicious cycle from which it is nearly impossible to escape: "Managers don't want to hire them, there's not enough training or education, and most end up in low-paying, dead-end jobs. None of this changes their low self-esteem and lack of communication skills. Many black women turn to drug dealing and prostitution as a result."

Workplace drug testing has increased significantly in the past decade, supposedly to reduce absenteeism, accidents, and turnover rates. While these potential effects have not been substantiated (Ehrenreich 2001), drug screening presents another obstacle for many blacks. It deters blacks from applying for jobs that require such a test for fear of failing; it has the same effect on a number of whites. While only larger firms can afford drug testing for all applicants, these businesses offer better-paying jobs and greater chances of promotion.

Another barrier for blacks is employers that require criminal background checks. It is very difficult to grow up in a black neighborhood without being arrested and often convicted. Nationwide, about 22 percent of all black men and 30 percent of those black men under age forty have been incarcerated (Holzer and Offner 2004). However, most of the criminal charges are minor, such as domestic disputes or possession of drugs. Police are known to patrol black areas frequently. "Many blacks are arrested but not convicted," stated a black Daytona employment agency director. "Yet business managers will often ask if you have ever been arrested. Other blacks simply don't have the money to hire a lawyer and often plead guilty to lesser charges." Whether simply arrested or convicted, such a requirement disqualifies a number of blacks, mainly black men (Holzer 1996).

Although structural issues are perceived to be the most serious impediments to black employment, individual and family characteristics are often mentioned as well. Community interviewees and employment agency officials cited "family values" as another contributor to the poor quality of black workers. Some blacks are often raised in single-parent families, with little educational achievement and with typically intermittent, low-skilled, or unstable employment. Many live in low-income housing surrounded by similarly situated neighbors. Fathers may be absent from the family, and violence and encounters with the law may be common (MacLeod 1995).

"This family environment provides no positive role models in terms of a work ethic for young blacks," according to a white Lake City job-training director. A black employment supervisor in Daytona Beach concurred: "Their [blacks'] parents don't have job skills and don't stress the need for such skills even when job training is available." The supervisor continued:

"There's a high teen pregnancy rate among blacks. Many blacks have trouble finishing high school and few aspire to college and others can't afford it. Parents are important in this . . . it all starts at home. Even the mind-set of black youth, they're 'living for today.' They wear expensive clothes and jewelry, for example, and don't save money. They go to cash advance firms, not credit unions."

The family breakdown has meant that there is little support in general for many young blacks, and other institutions, such as black churches, have not successfully filled the void. "There's lots of black churches, but they're not of much help to youth," claimed a longtime black leader in Titusville. "Young blacks are disillusioned with the church, and most black churches have little money and give little attention to young people."

The Views of Black Workers

It is necessary to explore how workers themselves respond to the job market and opportunities for promotion. Listening to employers, community respondents, and supervisors of employment agencies offers views of reality from primarily decision makers and persons in positions of power. In addition, many respondents are white. Although some may be empathetic and understanding of the job-market experiences of African Americans, they are no substitute for the perceptions of black workers. Using focus groups in Daytona Beach and Lake City, we elicited the views of black workers drawn from the businesses we surveyed or similar establishments. This approach seriously limited the number of black employees to whom we talked. However, focus groups of eight to ten workers provided a richness of data that goes well beyond most surveys to address the complexities of issues involved in the workplace (Krueger 1994).

The first issue we explored was the difficulties black workers confronted in getting and keeping their jobs. Their personal experiences in the labor market, along with the experiences of their friends and relatives, made them conscious of many class and race-based barriers to economic achievement. In their words, here are some of the typical obstacles they face:

> Blacks can get entry-level, low-paying jobs. . . . These are accessible. But it's difficult to even get applications for higher-level positions.
> —RESTAURANT EMPLOYEE, DAYTONA BEACH

I can get a job, but I know I'm not paid what I'm worth.
—AIR CONDITIONING REPAIR WORKER, DAYTONA BEACH

This is one of the lowest-paying areas in the state. There are people here
with money, but they don't pay people well for their work.
You have to move to another place.
—MAINTENANCE WORKER, MEDICAL CENTER, DAYTONA BEACH

You need to have a valid driver's license, and eventually a truck driver's license.
There are special qualifications for some jobs.
—TRUCK DRIVER, LAKE CITY

Applicants need inside information. Personnel staff hire their friends and don't
advertise jobs. The only way to know about it is to have a friend
who works there. It's not equal opportunity.
—RETAIL SALESPERSON, LAKE CITY

Lake City has not allowed larger companies to come in here. We don't have a
chance to get factory jobs that pay 10–15 dollars an hour. It's stunting
the growth of the city and keeping wages low.
—OWNER, CAR-WASHING BUSINESS, LAKE CITY

Not having an education or certain skills for a job I wanted . . .
skills like computer literacy and typing speed.
—SECRETARY, DAYTONA BEACH

These black workers have no illusions about the openness of the job opportunity structure, particularly for the working class. These respondents are
all employed, but mostly in low-paying, dead-end jobs. They believe that
they are blocked from better-paying positions by the nature of the hiring
process, the lack of good jobs in the area, or the special job requirements
that they do not possess. To gain promotion or higher-level jobs is perceived
as being much more difficult, not only because of the greater skill requirements but also because of the informality of the process. Most businesses
promote from within, and friendship and nepotism often determine the winners. Here are representative comments by focus group members about barriers to promotion:

Promotion demands experience, hard work, and dedication. But it's also
a matter of who you know and who knows you.
—UNIVERSITY SECURITY WORKER, DAYTONA BEACH

Promotions are given to friends, despite how hard you work.
—MEDICAL CENTER EMPLOYEE, DAYTONA BEACH

I needed more training and mentoring to learn various skills, but my manager
wouldn't help me. . . . They think you'll want to take their place.
—RETAIL STORE EMPLOYEE, LAKE CITY

It's who you know, hanging with the in-crowd, staying around after
business hours . . . despite what you know. You need to be with
them [bosses] on that personal level.
—REAL ESTATE EMPLOYEE, DAYTONA BEACH

According to employees, racial discrimination remains one of the most
formidable barriers facing African Americans in the labor force. Discrimination is more likely to be found in smaller firms than in larger ones and
in jobs that involve significant contact with white customers (Holzer 1998).
The greater amount of informality and subjectivity in the hiring process of
smaller businesses helps to explain their more discriminatory actions. In addition, evidence indicates that employers have greater fear of black men than
of black women and thus tend to discriminate in hiring against black males
(Kirschenman and Neckerman 1991). In many employers' minds, black men
are linked with crime and violence, while black women are perceived as more
motivated, better educated, and easier to work with (Moss and Tilly 2001).

Virtually all of our black workers stated they have faced some kind of
racial discrimination, either in seeking or holding a job or in both circumstances. The forms of discrimination they mentioned, particularly black men,
are unusually blatant and persistent. Here are some common examples, initially from the experiences of African American men.

If you're black you have to work ten times as hard, know twice as much,
and be twice as professional as whites in the same job. If you don't,
you're called unmotivated, lazy, and they'll question your intelligence.
There are days I've worked till my back ached, yet my white
colleagues were having a beer and relaxing. . . . They put twice as
much work on me, and I have to be twice the worker to make it.
—RESTAURANT EMPLOYEE, DAYTONA BEACH

If I'm late for work, they [whites] think it's because I was out late last night
partying or dealing with crack. As black men, we not only have to
deal with the general stereotypes of being men, but the stereotypes
of being black men. It's extra baggage for us.
—MEDICAL CENTER WORKER, DAYTONA BEACH

I've been in work situations with racial slurs and comments. They [whites] think blacks are stupid people . . . and they're scared of us—see black men as dangerous. I think they see it in the media—black-on-black crime.
—SECURITY EMPLOYEE, DAYTONA BEACH

I was arrested once but the charges were dropped, yet it still comes up on my record. Employers don't look into the circumstances. . . . I've lost a lot of jobs due to that reason. I wasn't convicted, but it made no difference. For a white man, they would check the circumstances.
—AUTO DEALER, LAKE CITY

Black females expressed some of the racial situations they face in the workplace:

A doctor called me all sorts of things besides my name, including "big mama." I called him on it. But it's mental abuse . . . people putting me down, suggesting you're not going to be nothing. It feeds into your spirit.
—HOSPITAL WORKER, DAYTONA BEACH

In the hotel where I work, they split blacks and whites in terms of positions. Most blacks are put in housekeeping jobs while whites get the better jobs.
—HOTEL WORKER, DAYTONA BEACH

I went to a business and they hired me part time. There was a customer that refused services because they had a black (me) working there. The manager came up and removed me from the front counter. A couple days later, he told me he couldn't use me. I paid my fees and took the training classes for the job, and I was let go.
—TAX BUSINESS EMPLOYEE, LAKE CITY

A white guy at work liked to tell black jokes with racial slurs . . . words like "swamp monkey" and "coon." I went to my supervisor, who is black, but his supervisor is white. We had a meeting to talk about race group jokes, but nothing serious was done. It was all a joke to them.
—RETAIL STORE EMPLOYEE, LAKE CITY

While these experiences are examples of blatant racism, there was a consensus among black workers that such overt forms of prejudice and discrimination are becoming less common. It is also apparent that working-class blacks are more likely to confront forms of old-fashioned racism than are blacks in managerial or supervisory positions. In addition, several African Americans pointed out that whites' negative assessments of black workers are shaped not only by feelings of racial aversion but also by blacks' lack of skills, education, motivation, knowledge of their basic rights, or poor job performance. Some examples of such claims by black workers include:

> Many blacks seem stuck in their jobs. . . . It's part of the black mind-set. They're comfortable in traditional jobs, like it's part of our culture. Somewhere between kindergarten and high school graduation, we lose hope.
> —MOTEL WORKER, DAYTONA BEACH

> Blacks don't deal directly with racial insults. I don't take any guff on the job. . . . I cut them off and tell them it's unacceptable. I'm also aware of my rights, what the antidiscrimination policies are, and where to get a civil rights lawyer. Most blacks are unaware of the judicial system and how it works.
> —RESTAURANT EMPLOYEE, LAKE CITY

> Blacks have to get an education to get good jobs. And black men have to stay and help their families and neighborhoods. Young blacks need male role models to care about them and keep them in school.
> —RETAIL STORE EMPLOYEE, LAKE CITY

> I needed to overcome barriers for the job I wanted. I had to get more education, gain computer literacy, increase typing speed, and get to work on time. Blacks need to push themselves, show initiative and drive . . . that gets you where you want to go.
> —REAL ESTATE EMPLOYEE, DAYTONA BEACH

Even black managers were sometimes critical of black workers. This was surprising since most managers of color are less likely than white supervisors to find fault with their own race. Yet an African American medical center employee in Daytona claimed that "if blacks are promoted, they have an 'overseer mentality' . . . they try harder to weed out blacks. It's a bias toward other black people." Another black worker in the same community concurred: "It's a 'hatchet-man mentality.' . . . Black people get promotions if they play by the rules and keep others of their own background out. If a black hires or promotes another black, people think they're showing favoritism toward their own race—it creates animosity." Black managers are influenced by dominant white attitudes toward people of color, and often such managers want to distance themselves psychologically from others of their race (Moss and Tilly 2001). In addition, black supervisors want to be perceived as not too "pro-black" and fair to all, and this sometimes results in deliberately ignoring qualified blacks in promotion and hiring decisions.

Conclusion

One of the most important goals of African Americans is to achieve a decent-paying job that has a degree of economic security and affords an opportunity for advancement. For blacks in the South, however, the fulfillment of this goal has been difficult. Indeed, our survey of businesses indicates that black jobholders are still disproportionately found in lower-skilled, service-oriented employment with relatively few blacks having achieved high-level professional or managerial positions. Feelings of hopelessness and helplessness overwhelm many blacks who for years have toiled in low-level, dead-end jobs.

A number of barriers have impeded blacks' success in the labor market. First, race (and to a lesser extent sex and class) discrimination is a major factor in recruitment, hiring, and promotion. Old-fashioned, blatant forms of racism are less common, but subtle, aversive race discrimination is pervasive. Employers often hold negative stereotypes of blacks, including assessments that African Americans lack the motivation to work, have poor attitudes, and are prone to hostility. Informality and subjectivity in the hiring and promotion process explain why such employer attitudes are harmful to blacks. White racism is most prevalent in the Deep South and in communities where African Americans make up more than 35 percent of the population and thus are perceived as a threat to white privilege.

Deficiencies among black workers are also important impediments. Lack of education and basic academic skills such as reading and math is an obstacle to gaining decent jobs and promotions for many blacks. Almost half of surveyed employers believe that black job seekers are not qualified for employment, and interviews with business owners and workers emphasized this shortcoming. Other behavioral characteristics that are perceived as undermining black workers include an overdependency on public assistance, lack of two-parent child rearing, and high crime rates.

Beyond racial discrimination, a variety of structural barriers seriously limits black employment opportunities. Systemic constraints mentioned most frequently by interviewees are lack of transportation, limited job opportunities, inadequate schools, lack of job training, the need for affordable childcare, and unnecessary and often unfair drug screening and crime checks. While blacks do not have to be passive recipients of structural forces, these barriers create a hostile environment from which there is no easy escape.

Despite these obstacles to black employment, our survey showed that several factors help to boost the hiring and promotion of African Americans. Larger numbers of black residents and customers translate into greater proportions of job applicants and, ultimately, African American workers. In addition, white females and minorities constitute half of all employers and are more likely to attract and hire blacks than are white male employers. Similarly, national- or regional-based firms (rather than locally owned establishments) emphasize a diverse workforce and thus employ and promote African Americans at relatively high rates. Finally, employer support for affirmative action, found in one-third of establishments, increases black jobholders, particularly at higher levels of employment. All of these factors provide incentives to black employment, but it is doubtful that they are sufficient to overcome race discrimination and other significant barriers confronting black workers. The next chapter turns to the public sector, where blacks have made greater inroads but still face challenges.

4

African Americans in the
Municipal Workforces

THE EMPLOYMENT OF BLACKS IN MUNICIPAL SERVICE JOBS is a good indicator of racial equity at the local level. Public employment not only provides a valuable source of income, but it also confers a degree of status or prestige not found in low-paying, service-oriented jobs held by many blacks in the private sector. Within city employment, police and fire forces are among the largest and best-funded departments. Moreover, as these human-safety services have become increasingly technical and professionalized, police and firefighters have attained higher pay, benefits, and social status. This has been true for many other city personnel as well. Southern cities, however, have traditionally employed blacks in low-level positions with little opportunity for promotion to higher-status, better-paying levels of employment (Button 1989; Rodgers and Bullock 1972; Wirt 1970). Thus, it is not surprising that recent data depict serious underrepresentation of racial minorities in upper-level management and supervisory positions in most cities (McCabe and Stream 2000).

Beyond increases in individual status and salary, city employment of blacks has also brought other important resources for southern minority populations. Poverty-stricken black neighborhoods suffer disproportionately from high rates of crime, dilapidated housing that is susceptible to fires, poor streets and drainage, and limited or inferior parks and recreation facilities. Moreover, blacks have long been the victims of police brutality (Myrdal 1944; Keech 1968; Wirt 1997). With the hiring of increased numbers of blacks in police, fire, recreation, and other city departments, the treatment of black residents often improved and more services were provided (Button 1989;

Karnig and Welch 1980). In addition, black police and firefighters in particular serve as role models for many blacks who rarely see African Americans in public positions of authority.

Insights from Previous Studies

Previous research has demonstrated that minorities do better overall in public sector employment than in the private sector (Reskin 1998), but blacks, Hispanics, and women disproportionally hold lower-level jobs, while white males are disproportionally in upper-level management jobs (Hall and Saltzstein 1975, 1977; Cayer and Sigelman 1980). Given that blacks, Hispanics, and women all disproportionally occupy the lower rungs of employment, it is reasonable that competition might exist among these groups since they are competing for the same jobs (Alozie and Ramirez 1999; McClain 1993; McClain and Karnig 1990).

Most studies have included a host of explanatory variables about the success of blacks in garnering public employment. These variables include the presence of minorities in city government, the proportion of minorities in the community, region, minority growth rate, affirmative action policy, residency requirements, economic variables, and institutional variables (election type, government type, city manager system, etc.; Mladenka 1989).

Several of these studies have suggested that the presence of black elected officials greatly affects the minority share of city jobs. Dye and Renick (1981) found that black representation on the city council is the most significant determinant of black employment in administrative, professional, and protective service (police and fire) positions. Eisinger (1982) demonstrated that the size of the black population has the greatest effect on total black employment but that the presence of a black mayor, not other African American elected officials, had a significant effect on blacks holding high-level professional positions.

Stein (1986) offers perhaps the most complete model of minority public sector employment. The model includes measures of government type, minority representation, the presence of an enforcement agency, residency requirements, unemployment rate, region, city size, the size of the minority population, the change in workforce demographics over time, and the presence of an outreach agency. The model predicts a significant positive relationship between minority employment and the size of the minority population, the change in workforce demographics, residency requirements, region, and the presence of a minority chief executive. Although black population size was the most important factor, the presence of a black mayor and a mayor-council form of government were also important variables.

In a longitudinal study (1960–79) of ten California cities, Browning, Marshall, and Tabb (1984) reported that black and Hispanic city employment gains were generated by minority protests and minority representation within liberal coalitions on city councils. Neither size of the black and Hispanic populations nor bureaucratic factors were adequate explanatory factors. In a similar study of black municipal employment in six Florida cities from 1960 to 1985, Button (1989) found that the proportion of blacks on the city council was by far the most significant variable, controlling for other seemingly important factors.

Saltzstein (1989) also identifies a positive relationship between cities with a black mayor and black city council representation and African American employment. The control variables include population, reformism, legal pressure, department size, expenditures, insulation, legal requirements, and professionalism. This model does a good job of isolating the effects of having a black mayor but does not offer many of the previously mentioned explanatory factors. However, Kerr and Mladenka (1994) examine the effects of having a black mayor, as well as that of having a Hispanic mayor, on minority public sector employment. They find no significant effects, contending that previous findings were a result of the limitations of cross-sectional data, as they use pooled time-series data. Their differing results may also be a product of including the number of black council members as an explanatory variable. According to Saltzstein (1989), this model may be misleading because cities with a black mayor may also have many black council members. In other words, the influence is a result of a collective presence rather than a singular one.

The literature offers tests of all the aforementioned explanatory factors of minority public sector employment, but no one study offers a complete (or at least comprehensive) model that accounts for all of these factors while also assessing the possible competition between racial minorities and white women. In addition, few studies have empirically investigated the effects of affirmative action on black municipal workers (Reskin 1998). The assumption is that affirmative action, as a government-oriented policy, has had a greater effect on minority public employment than on private sector minority workers. Certainly, the black share of state and local government jobs increased during the 1970s and 1980s when affirmative action was in effect. In local police departments, the percentage of officers who were black grew from 6.5 percent in 1975 to 10.5 percent in 1990 (Walker, Spohn, and DeLone 1996). Moreover, both court-ordered and voluntary affirmative action plans resulted in increased minority police hiring, with court orders forcing 40 percent of police departments to engage in affirmative action because they had systematically discriminated against minorities (Martin 1991). Yet, in a more methodical study of 281 police departments across the country, Zhao and Lovrich (1998) reported that when controlling for other theoretically important variables, affirmative action is not a statistically significant factor in explaining black employment. In this study, the size of the black population was the predominant contributor to the representation of black police officers.

This examination of previous research has sought to identify explanatory factors that determine the level of black representation in the public sector as well as potential sources of competition. These factors range from minority population to the presence of minorities in city government, from the structure of local government to the presence of affirmative action programs, from residency requirements to economic variables. Because most of these studies are based on secondary data, they cannot measure other variables of potential importance in minority hiring, such as affirmative action goals and requirements, and the hiring attitudes of high-level administrators, elected officials, and department heads. Using in-depth interview data to help compile a quantitative data set allows us to ascertain better measures of affirmative action and city officials' views. Further, looking at blacks that have been promoted to supervisory positions provides a more complete view of black progress in municipal departments. Focusing on black municipal workers in the South, traditionally the region of greatest resistance to black hiring, is also a unique aspect of this study. Finally, it is important to explore these data over time, not to rely simply on cross-sectional data but to be able to make inferences as to causality.

Variables and Methods

The literature indicates that black political representation and black resources are often the most important predictors of black municipal employment. We found that the black proportion of city council members, the presence of a black mayor, the presence of a black department head, and the size of the African American population were all significantly intercorrelated and loaded highly on the same factor in a factor analysis routine. Thus, we used the factor scores for these four variables, naming the combined indicators "black political power." Black socioeconomic resources, an indicator of the quality of potential black job applicants, are measured by black median family income. Minority intergroup competition is also expected to influence African American city workers. Since white females have been entering the labor force in large numbers in the past decade or two, we explore the proportion of this group among municipal employees and the possible effect on black employment. Hispanic employees, also potential competitors with blacks, are too few in number in these departments to be considered a viable factor.

In addition, affirmative action policies and informal equal opportunity actions may affect minority employment. While federal affirmative action requirements did not begin until the mid-1970s for municipalities, not all cities actually implemented a formal plan, while others informally sought to hire or promote more blacks for political or other reasons. Thus, we developed three indicators of affirmative action: (1) presence of a formal city affirmative action plan, (2) the city's degree of implementation of affirmative action, and (3) department head's degree of emphasis on hiring blacks. The city's implementation of affirmative action was measured by the number of affirmative action components, such as special recruiting efforts, training programs, and mentoring programs. The indicator of departmental affirmative action support was the number of departmental programs or special efforts to increase black hiring and promotion. These data were obtained from city records and personal interviews with municipal officials, including department chiefs, every fifth year from 1975 to 2000, the period of implementation of affirmative action in these municipalities. These affirmative action indicators were highly intercorrelated and loaded on one factor in a factor analysis routine, allowing us to develop affirmative action factor scores for each department.

Several contextual factors may affect African American employment as well. We have already mentioned, and included, the relative size of the black population. Another major contextual variable is political culture. The Deep South–Border South (or Old South–New South) dichotomy is one standard for depicting the unique cultural characteristics of diverse regions within the South (Key 1949; Scher 1997). Another indicator represents more precisely the degree of conservatism in the community, and this is the percentage of city votes cast for Republican candidates in presidential elections (Colby 1985). Without public opinion data for these communities, voting results provide the best available evidence of local political ideology. Moreover, this indicator is relatively highly correlated ($r = .52$) with the more conservative Old South, as opposed to the more progressive New South cities, and is thus considered a valid measure of political culture (Button 1989).

Local political structure, or institutional variables, is also potentially important. These factors include form of government (mayor-council or manager-council) and election system (at-large or district). The literature claims that mayor-council cities are more responsive to racial minorities than are non-elected professional city managers (Lineberry and Fowler 1967; Stein 1986). In terms of election type, district systems tend to elect more residentially segregated blacks to office and to better represent minority interests than at-large elections or some combination of the two systems (Engstrom and McDonald 1981; Mladenka 1989). Partisan or nonpartisan elections also may make a difference, but all of the cities in our sample have nonpartisan elections, so this factor could not be tested.

As for dependent variables, we collected data on the public employment of African Americans, both total and those in supervisory positions, in four city departments: police, fire, recreation, and public works. These departments represent a range of city services and are among the largest municipal departments, thus offering plentiful employment opportunities. We took a time-series approach, using measures gathered every fifth year over a forty-year period (1960–2000). Over six cities, this provided an N of 54 for each department. This approach enabled us to undertake a long-term view of these phenomena and to better infer causality. Data were collected from public records, newspapers, and personal interviews with department heads, city managers, mayors, personnel officers, council members, and other knowledgeable city officials.

Results

Table 4.1 summarizes the number and rate of black total employment and supervisors in the police, fire, recreation, and public works departments of the six cities for every tenth year from 1960 to 2000. The total percentage of black city workers increased in every department except public works, where African Americans have held low-level jobs since 1960. As supervisors,

TABLE 4.1 Black Municipal Employment in Six Florida Cities (1960–2000)

Years	Police N (%)	Fire N (%)	Recreation N (%)	Public Works N (%)
	Black Employment by Department			
1960	14 (9.5)	0	9 (23.1)	84 (38.2)
1970	20 (9.0)	6 (3.5)	29 (29.0)	149 (48.9)
1980	62 (17.3)	22 (9.4)	63 (37.1)	215 (47.6)
1990	95 (19.9)	29 (10.8)	63 (35.6)	168 (36.8)
2000	108 (20.0)	42 (13.7)	77 (37.2)	194 (35.3)
	Black Supervisors by Department			
1960	0	0	2 (16.7)	0
1970	4 (7.6)	0	6 (28.6)	3 (8.8)
1980	9 (11.4)	2 (3.5)	15 (44.1)	12 (28.6)
1990	22 (19.6)	6 (7.2)	12 (34.3)	19 (27.5)
2000	35 (31.3)	11 (14.1)	13 (26.0)	26 (29.2)

by 2000, blacks increased their proportions steadily, reaching 25 percent or more in every department except the fire department.

In terms of specific departments, the protective services of police and fire are similar in their patterns of relatively slow growth in hiring blacks. Historically, southern police departments, a powerful symbol of white authority, were more likely to harass or to even brutalize blacks than to hire them. Fire departments were also a traditional bastion of white male supremacy that often refused employment to blacks principally because of the intimacy of work relations (eating and sharing sleeping quarters together; Myrdal 1944; Keech 1968). The civil rights movement was instrumental in politically mobilizing blacks to pressure city departments, especially the police, to employ and promote blacks and to provide better services (Button 1989). Even then, racial changes in these traditional white male–dominant departments occurred slowly but have been greater in police than in fire departments.

Recreation and public works departments are much more pluralistic in their racial makeup. As early as 1960, blacks constituted 23 percent of recreation employees, rising to 37 percent by 1980 and then leveling off. City officials typically believed that African Americans should be hired to work with black youth and in black neighborhood parks (Myrdal 1944). This segregationist orientation declined with time, and recreation departments have become increasingly multicultural. By 1990, white females headed these departments in two cities, and black males directed recreation in two other communities.

Public works has historically been the department most likely to hire blacks. Jobs in this department, such as street, water, and sewage development and maintenance, required heavy labor for little pay. Not only did this kind of work fit whites' stereotypes of black men ("strong back, weak mind"), but blacks were common among the low-skill potential employees who were willing to perform this menial labor (Myrdal 1944; Rodgers and Bullock 1972). By the 1990s, the proportion of blacks in public works declined somewhat, and the proportion of white males increased accordingly, as the work required greater skills and training to operate new, more technical equipment. While blacks did not gain many supervisory positions in a department that viewed them as strictly menial laborers until 1980, their proportions have remained approximately the same since then.

Multivariate Analysis Results and Discussion

Although descriptive statistics illuminate the patterns of minority employment over time, they do not explain the factors that have influenced black hiring and promotion. To explore the potentially causal relationships, we employed a series of ordinary least squares regression models to ascertain the effects of the previously discussed explanatory factors. The outcome variables on the public employment of African Americans in the police, fire, recreation, and public works departments were converted to percentages by dividing the number of black employees, respectively, by the total number of employees in each department. This procedure was replicated for blacks in supervisory positions. This controls for the size of each department.

It is not reasonable to assume that the errors in this time-series regression are independent; therefore, we tested for correlation within each vector of the explanatory variables and outcome variables by using correlograms to determine visually whether there is autocorrelation (Hibbs 1974; Fox 1997). Assuming a first-order autocorrelation process, the correlograms indicated no discernible pattern of decay exponentially toward 0. The values of these variables at time (t) are not dependent on the values at time $(t-1)$, and thus it is not necessary to lag any of these variables, making a pooled time-series ordinary least squares regression suitable.

All of the outcomes were modeled as a function of median black family income, black political power, presence of a city manager, presence of

TABLE 4.2 List of Independent Variables

I. Characteristics of City Government and Departments
  • Black political power (combined factor scores of percentage of blacks in population, on city council, presence of a black mayor, and presence of black department heads)
  • Presence of city manager as chief executive (0 = no city manager; 1 = city manager)
  • Presence of district elections for city council (0 = at-large or mixed election system; 1 = district elections)
  • Percentage of white female employees or supervisors in department
  • Affirmative action (combined factor scores of presence of formal AA plan, city implementation of specific AA policy components, department head's support for hiring blacks)

II. Contextual Factors
  • Political conservatism (percentage in city voting for Republican candidate in U.S. presidential general election)
  • Black median family income

---

district elections, degree of political conservatism, and the affirmative action measure. Table 4.2 lists these independent variables and their coding. To ascertain levels of competition with blacks, a measure of either percent white female employment or white female supervisors was included in each model. Hispanics, however, have not yet achieved more than a token presence in these departments (Hispanics averaged only 2.1 percent of city employment in 2000), and thus we omitted them from these models.

We first explored the simple correlation coefficients between these independent variables and the percentage of black employees and black supervisors in each department (tables 4.3 and 4.4). As expected, black political power is most highly and consistently correlated with all measures of African American employment. In addition, black median income is very significantly related to black employees and supervisors, suggesting the importance of resources in the black community. The presence of city managers and district elections, two institutional measures, is also moderately and positively correlated with most measures of black city workers. Furthermore, political culture, measured by the vote for Republican presidential candidates, is significantly but negatively related to black employment and supervisors, suggesting that the conservative politics of the Deep South depresses municipal black hiring and promotions. Surprisingly, white female employees are not strongly correlated with blacks, suggesting little, if any, interminority job competition. Affirmative action, too, shows only a modest (but positive) relationship to very few measures of black jobholders.

TABLE 4.3 Correlation Coefficients of Independent Variables and Percentage of Black Employment

Independent Variables	Police	Fire	Recreation	Public Works
Black median income	.43***	.54***	.54***	.12
% white female employment	−.12	.23*	−.17	−.32**
Black political power	.89***	.67***	.82***	.60***
Presence of city manager	.20	.31**	.41**	.30**
Presence of district elections	.20	.33**	.32**	.22
Political conservatism	−.45***	−.29**	−.47***	−.42**
Affirmative action	.02	.29**	.11	−.20

* p < .10; ** p < .05; *** p < .01.

TABLE 4.4 Correlation Coefficients of Independent Variables and Percentage of Black Supervisors

Independent Variables	Police	Fire	Recreation	Public Works
Black median income	.61***	.40***	.41***	.59***
% white female supervisors	−.07	−.11	−.05	−.12
Black political power	.79***	.51***	.71***	.75***
Presence of city manager	.40**	.31**	.51***	.43***
Presence of district elections	.39***	.42***	.27**	.14
Political conservatism	−.38***	−.21	−.54***	−.44***
Affirmative action	.18	.07	.24*	.23*

* p < .10; ** p < .05; *** p < .01.

Next, we used regression analysis to look at the independent effects of these various factors on black total employment and supervisors in each of the departments (tables 4.5 and 4.6). Of all the regression models, those explaining the percentage black employment and black supervisors in the police department performed the best. Yet all of the equations explained 44 percent of the variance or more, except for the fire department, where there was relatively little variation in black supervisors.

Black political power is the strongest and most consistent predictor of black employment and supervisors. The relationship is positive and highly significant across all models. As previously stated, black political power is measured as a factor score of the black proportion of city council members, the presence of a black mayor, the size of the African American population, and the presence of a black department head. Our results reinforce previous findings that contend these are the most important factors in determining black employment (Stein 1986; Dye and Renick 1981; Eisinger 1982; Button 1989).

In terms of job competition, a moderate degree of competition exists between white females and blacks for employment in the police departments.

TABLE 4.5 Regression Analysis Results for Black Employment by City Departments

Independent Variables	Police	Fire	Recreation	Public Works
Median black family income	.000	.000	.000	.000
	(.000)	(.000)	(.000)	(.000)
% White females	−.401*	−.470	.296**	.640
	(.250)	(.443)	(.145)	(2.16)
Black political power	.108***	.005***	.173***	.220***
	(.013)	(.012)	(.024)	(.053)
Presence of city manager	.015	.026	.149***	.213**
	(.026)	(.026)	(.050)	(.092)
Presence of district elections	.003	.030	−.009	.020
	(.021)	(.022)	(.044)	(.081)
Political conservatism	.001	.001	.000	.002
	(.001)	(.001)	(.002)	(.003)
Affirmative action	−.017	.008	−.003	−.076*
	(.013)	(.013)	(.026)	(.042)
Constant	.080	−.014	.133	.366**
	(.051)	(.051)	(.098)	(.179)
Adj R2	.788	.500	.746	.443

* $p < .10$; ** $p < .05$; *** $p < .01$.

In both the total employment model and the supervisory models, an increase in white females is significantly and negatively related to black employment. However, this competition with white females is not indicated in other departments.

Black median income has a significant and positive relationship with black supervisors in the police departments. Black income is an indicator of black resources and socioeconomic status, suggesting that greater resources result in better-qualified black candidates for high-level positions. Police departments, for example, are typically the most demanding in terms of the training, experience, skill, and education levels required for promotion.

Perhaps the most surprising finding is that affirmative action policies have little effect on black employment. Only in recreation, a department recognized for its diversity, is affirmative action positively related to black supervisors. However, in public works employment and police supervisors, affirmative action is significantly associated but in a negative direction. The percentage of black public works employees was declining during the 1980s and 1990s, the period in which most of these cities implemented an affirmative action program. In the police department, affirmative action is positively related to white female supervisors, whose numbers lag well below blacks, thus making them the "disadvantaged minority." As a result, affirmative action is much less supportive (negatively associated) of black police supervisors.

TABLE 4.6 Regression Analysis Results for Black Supervisors by City Departments

Independent Variables	Police	Fire	Recreation	Public Works
Median black family income	.000***	.000	.000	.000
	(.000)	(.000)	(.000)	(.000)
% white female supervisors	−.160***	−.227	−.261	−.977
	(.385)	(.310)	(.229)	(.586)
Black political power	.092***	.053***	.141***	.168***
	(.016)	(.020)	(.031)	(.037)
Presence of city manager	.065*	.067*	.132**	.197***
	(.034)	(.041)	(.059)	(.068)
Presence of district elections	.042	.052	.047	−.121**
	(.027)	(.034)	(.053)	(.060)
Political conservatism	.003**	.002	−.001	.002
	(.001)	(.001)	(.002)	(.003)
Affirmative action	−.041**	−.027	.083**	−.017
	(.017)	(.020)	(.036)	(.032)
Constant	−.174**	−.118	.321***	−.098
	(.066)	(.080)	(.119)	(.133)
Adj R2	.803	.347	.643	.662

$* p < .10; ** p < .05; *** p < .01.$

One of the institutional measures also offers an intriguing finding. The literature suggests that the presence of a city manager system deters black employment in the public sector and a mayoral system encourages black employment (Lineberry and Fowler 1967; Stein 1986). However, the findings for total black employment in the recreation and public works departments, and for black supervisors in all departments, indicate that having a city manager strongly encourages black employment. Greater professionalism seems to reduce racial discrimination in employment. We will elaborate on this important finding later in this chapter.

No other independent variables are significantly and consistently related to black municipal workers or supervisors. Largely, this is because black political power overwhelms most other variables by explaining such a high proportion of the variation in black employment.

The Views of City Officials and Employees:
Black Political Power and Resources

Black political power, measured as a combination of black population, black elected council members, black department heads, and black mayors, is the strongest predictor of African American municipal employment. As a further

TABLE 4.7 Mean Percentage Black Employment by Black Population Size (1960–2000)

Departments	Communities		
	Low % Black	Medium % Black	Majority Black
Police	6.8	3.4	28.4
Fire	2.6	10.2	11.7
Recreation	19.0	31.8	49.4
Public Works	27.9	42.9	79.2

indication of the influence of black population size, table 4.7 summarizes average black employment over the forty years for each department by the proportion of blacks in these communities. Large increases in black municipal employment occur as the population of the black citizenry grows. This is particularly the case when blacks achieve a numerical majority of the population and ultimately gain political control. For example, in the low percent, medium percent, and majority black population cities, the average proportion of elected black council members was 10, 16, and 39 percent, respectively. Moreover, in Riviera Beach and Quincy, where blacks numbered 60–70 percent of the population, by the 1990s African American mayors were elected to power and black department heads were the norm.

Thus, black population size provides the resources or numbers that, once mobilized politically, produce African American municipal decision makers in the form of city council members, mayors, and department chiefs. Table 4.8 shows the growth of black political power, which parallels the increases in black city employment over time. While the average black population size of the six cities remained relatively stable from 1960 to 2000, the number and proportion of black power holders increased greatly. During this forty-year period, black elected council members rose from zero to thirteen, which is 41 percent of all city council members; black mayors were elected in one-third of the cities; and African American department heads grew from zero to five, which amounts to more than 20 percent of department chiefs. These sizable increases in blacks holding key positions in city government provide the political power that is necessary to expand black municipal employment.

Comments by city officials and employees also emphasize the importance of black political power, particularly that of black city council members. In Daytona Beach, a black councilman stated, "We [city council members] try to get blacks to stay in school and become better qualified for jobs, although we don't do enough. We also encourage businesses and the city to break barriers to hire blacks. We're the messengers who state the city has not met its

TABLE 4.8 Indicators of Black Political Power

	Number and % Black Elected Officials	Number of Black Mayors	Number and % of Black Dept. Heads	Mean % Black Population
1960	0	0	0	32.4
1970	4 (12.5%)	0	0	32.8
1980	6 (18.8%)	2	3 (12.5%)	37.4
1990	10 (31.3%)	1	3 (12.5%)	38.4
2000	13 (40.6%)	2	5 (20.8%)	39.1

goals in minority hiring . . . we continually bring the issue to the fore." A black former city official in Titusville echoed this sentiment: "Just being on the council means a voice is heard [for blacks], and management wants to meet the desires of their bosses. It's helped to open doors for blacks. There is an extreme difference now that no women or blacks are on the city council . . . no 'eyes and ears' for blacks and black employees feel this."

In other communities, black officials were instrumental in providing public job information and actively encouraging blacks to seek city jobs. "She [black council member] does announce city job openings in church and she lets blacks know—usually these jobs are only posted in city hall," claimed a black officeholder in Lake City. "We feel strongly about letting people know about job openings and promotions. But I also raise questions at city council meetings, like 'Is our affirmative action program on target?'"

Nonetheless, some black elected officials are more effective than others, and simply having black council members or a black mayor is not always an antidote for low numbers of African American jobholders. "We traded a lion for a lamb in the last city elections," contended a black leader in one Deep South city that had grown weary of a black official who was often out of town on work but had been a strong black advocate. "Our new black councilman does little to help the black community . . . he made his first motion after nearly two years on the city council."

In another case in a Border South community, a white department head maintained that one of the city's black council members was "not very productive because he is too adversarial. He once encouraged black rioting . . . he's too bitter and angry. He came out to this department once and looked at our hiring plan, saying he was only interested in black hiring. His tone and mood were negative, and he irritated me." Other officials in this city, both white and black, concurred with this view and thus perceived this black elected official as ineffective and, at times, harmful to black employment interests.

Despite occasional reports of unproductive black officials, most municipal employees believed that key elected council members are helpful in encouraging black employment. "Our black commissioners, from time to time, urge black hiring. They believe it's important for city employees to represent the racial makeup of the community, which is 60 percent black," stated an African American recreation department worker in Quincy. The idea that the racial composition of city employees should reflect that of the community was a popular and often-expressed view. In some cases, black council members worked closely with department heads and city managers who were supportive of increases in black jobholders. According to a white fire chief in the New South, "I urged our black councilman to recruit a black who we thought was interested in our department. He did it, and we were able to hire this person."

In other instances, particularly in cities where blacks are a majority of the council, outright political force is used sometimes to achieve more black hires and promotions. "When black city commissioners are in control, they pressure the city manager, who then pressures the department heads, not just to hire qualified blacks but their friends and relatives too," asserted a Quincy white male employee. "There's great focus on the police department, which has been run by whites for so long," claimed a black policeman in this same city. "Some whites are leaving and others are getting fired in order to get more African Americans on the force." A similar dynamic was occurring in majority-black Riviera Beach as well.

In our multivariate analyses, the median income of blacks is significantly associated with black supervisors in police departments. The level of economic resources is typically linked to education and suggests that cities with greater proportions of blacks with high incomes and more education provide better-qualified candidates for municipal jobs. Well-educated and skilled job seekers are particularly preferred by police (and fire) departments, where professional training, formal education, and job certification are required. This is also the case for supervisory positions in almost every department. Indeed, the primary criticism of black job applicants for protective service departments and other more highly skilled positions is the lack of qualified African Americans. "I will not hire someone just because someone is black (or white). . . . I want good workers and that's best for the city," stated a white department head in Lake City. "I get a number of black applicants, but they need a driver's license and a high school degree and many don't have these qualifications. I won't look at applicants without these [credentials]."

Many heads of departments made similar claims about African American job applicants. Even the black director of personnel in one New South community admitted that "in general, blacks score lower than whites on the civil service exam that must be passed for job consideration, and thus this exam excludes many blacks. Blacks need to study the materials more . . . they're given the same materials as whites." The increase in black income and education over the past several decades has helped many black applicants to improve their general qualifications, ultimately resulting in gains in black employment and promotions.

City Managers

In terms of institutional factors, our analyses indicated that the presence of a city manager translates into greater numbers of black employees in two of the four departments (recreation and public works), as well as black supervisors in all departments. Thus, mean black employment for all four departments in communities with a city manager was 31 percent compared with 21 percent in municipalities with mayors as chief executives. In recreation and public works departments, the average black employment figures for cities with a professional manager were 40 percent and 52 percent, respectively, while with mayors as chief executives, these departments averaged only 21 percent and 38 percent black workers, respectively. Even controlling for other variables, the differences are apparent.

These findings contradict the results of other studies where unreformed political structures, including a mayor rather than a city manager as chief executive, are more sensitive to the demands of minorities. The rationale for mayors generally being more responsive to the needs of blacks is that mayors are elected to office, whereas city managers are appointed by the mayor-council. Mayors show greater responsiveness to constituents, including minorities, because of the direct electoral connection that managers do not have (Ross and Levine 2001).

In our relatively small southern cities, however, municipal employment was historically carried out through informal, white male–dominant networks in city hall, particularly in departments such as recreation and public works that had few formal education and job certification requirements. Chief executives were typically mayors, particularly in the Deep South, and with the disenfranchisement of most blacks, their constituents were almost all white. Mayors were supportive of and often in collusion with the good old boy network that controlled city politics, including municipal employment. Jobs were dispensed to loyal supporters as part of a patronage system that enabled mayors and other city leaders to consolidate their power and control.

As part of the reform movement in American cities, a trained professional, such as a city manager, performed the daily tasks of administering municipal affairs. As the technical problems of running a city became more numerous and complex, larger cities (typically more than twenty-five thousand residents) began hiring city managers to perform major administrative functions (Kweit and Kweit 1999). In the six cities studied, each of the Border South communities, being somewhat larger than Deep South cities, had city managers by the 1960s. In municipalities in the Old South, where the traditional practices of white, good old boy politics were entrenched, reform politics and city managers came later. By the early 1980s, Quincy and Lake City had hired city managers, but Crestview resisted, even voting down such a change in local referendums, and thus has maintained its mayor-council system.

City managers brought professional norms that reduced the influence of parochial and traditional concerns. In terms of employment, city managers tended to institute more formal hiring and promotion procedures and emphasized equity goals, including affirmative action plans and requirements. These actions served to reduce racial bias and thus boost the employment of minorities, especially blacks (Frederickson 1990; Nalbandian 1991).

In one New South city, for example, the hiring of a progressive city manager in the 1980s brought major changes in minority employment policies. Perceiving that there "was a limited sense of community or social obligation to affirmative action and black employment at higher levels," he appointed the first black department head and carried out a national search to find and employ a black lieutenant in the police department. This city manager also instituted the controversial bureaucratic "rule of three," whereby the top three candidates for any promotion must include at least one minority, typically the highest-scoring black applicant regardless of the minority member's rank in performance on promotion exams and other requirements. This rule did not always result in the promotion of a minority, but it did ensure that blacks in particular were provided greater opportunities. Because of these equity actions, the city manager was strongly criticized by those who opposed affirmative action, especially white men in the police and fire departments. Yet, because of his political savvy in building political support and the presence of significant black political power in the community, the city manager was able to increase black promotions and stay in power for more than a decade.

In the Deep South, city managers have found it more difficult to alter entrenched bureaucratic practices and racial attitudes that restrict black municipal employment. Nevertheless, managers in these cities have often pushed to expand minority recruitment, promote blacks into higher-level positions, carry out diversity and sexual harassment training for supervisors, and create a greater awareness of the legal ramifications (primarily discrimination lawsuits) of not treating minorities fairly. "My goal is to have proportional representation of blacks in city jobs, but we aren't quite there, especially at higher-level positions," stated a city manager in one Old South community. "I have stressed this goal in staff meetings and have expanded recruitment strategies. I've also talked with white supervisors about the need to accept and be able to work with all races, and that minorities are a major part of our society. We have discussed this issue in [city] council meetings as well, and they are supportive."

Although this city manager faced resistance, particularly to black promotions, from some white employees and department heads, he was able in 2002 to appoint the first black department chief (fire department). Yet racial progress in employment has been difficult, with several discrimination lawsuits filed by black and female workers during the 1990s. Moreover, partly because of racial turmoil in city hall and the community, the turnover rate of city managers in this municipality has been high.

Limitations on Black Employment

In the city departments we examined, African American employment increased at a significant rate during the 1960s and 1970s (see table 4.1), the period when black political power developed. After 1980, however, the number of black municipal workers rose more slowly, if at all. Overall, the police and fire departments showed small amounts of growth in black employees between 1980 and 2000 (2.7 percent and 4.3 percent, respectively). During this same period, the proportion of blacks in recreation remained the same (37 percent), while that in public works actually declined about 12 percent. By the new millennium, there are still relatively few African Americans in most police and fire departments, where white males maintain control, and in other departments black workers are typically found in low-skill, poorly paid positions.

So why have the great initial gains by black city workers not continued over the past two decades? Our in-depth interviews with departmental employees, both black and white, male and female, provided several consistent answers to this question. Most explanations fit what sociologists term "social closure" theory or processes (Tomaskovic-Devey 1993), whereby superordinate groups attempt to preserve their advantages by restricting access to resources and opportunities. In this case, white males continue to uphold or create new formal and informal rules to exclude blacks, women, and other nonpreferred groups from government jobs. Social closure theory emphasizes that racial exclusion involves not only discrimination or economic job market mechanisms but also white male privilege. Moreover, historical and social processes have created the advantages that white men possess and defend.

In accordance with this theory, a number of formal job requirements deter many African Americans from applying for certain city jobs and exclude others from obtaining employment when they do apply. Formal education requirements, civil service exams, mandatory training courses, drug screenings, special licenses to operate certain equipment, and clean criminal records are the most commonly mentioned job requirements that disproportionately exclude blacks from municipal employment. According to a black firefighter in one Deep South city:

> When I was offered the position of assistant fire chief, a city official said that I would have to go to Florida State University to study and then pass a municipal inspector's exam. This was suddenly a new requisite for this position, one which had not been asked of previous white applicants. The test is very challenging, and only 10 percent or so of those who take it pass. I thought the official's motivation for having me take the exam was based in part on the fact I am black and the first of my race to be seriously considered for this high-level position.

Qualifying and promotion exams and requirements are often a barrier for blacks, who generally have had less formal education than whites. "Blacks are afraid to take promotion exams," claimed a high-ranking black police officer in Riviera Beach. "They're afraid to fail, and blacks do fail the exam disproportionately." Having grown up in poor neighborhoods with high rates of crime, black applicants are more likely than whites to be disqualified by background checks. In Titusville, which in 2001 had no African American firefighters, a former fireman who is black explained, "In the application process the requirement that eliminates blacks is the question, 'Have you ever been arrested?'—not 'convicted,' but 'arrested'—and it doesn't matter how long ago." This barrier to black employment was mentioned by workers in other departments and cities as well. In Quincy, a high-ranking black police officer stated that "even a poor credit rating is worse for black than white applicants . . . it's an unfair process for blacks." Drug testing is another formal requirement that disqualifies a number of blacks. According to the white male director of public works in a Deep South community, "Fifty percent of our applicants are black, but they have problems with our drug screening . . . a lot fail."

In several departments, new technology has created a greater demand for computer and heavy equipment operator skills. This "digital divide" has often been the source of a division based on race because blacks are less likely to possess these special skills (Moss and Tilly 2001). A good example of the results of "hard skill" screening and demands is described by a longtime black employee in public works in the Deep South: "When I first started working for this department it was predominantly black . . . about 90 percent. The work then was more manual and lower paid. When the budget increased and the equipment got better, there was a shift in race. Now public works is almost 90 percent white due to greater education and special licensing requirements."

Police and fire departments in particular demand specialized training and certification by exam. Yet even recreation departments, relatively undemanding in terms of hard skills, have denied jobs to blacks due to their failure on swimming and life-saving tests. "Black parents don't pay for swimming lessons—and historically city pools and beaches were segregated," claimed one black recreation worker in Lake City. "So many blacks cannot swim, or we would otherwise hire them." Yet some blacks see this as an unnecessary and arbitrarily applied requirement for recreation employees since few actually work at swimming pools, and therefore it is perceived as a screening device to keep many blacks out of the department.

While municipal departments are demanding more formal education and greater skills, job applicants face relatively low salaries in virtually every department. Table 4.9 summarizes entry-level annual pay by department for Old and New South cities. The greater the proportion of blacks in a department, the lower the pay. Recreation and public works departments, for example,

TABLE 4.9 Average Annual Beginning Wages by Department (2001)

	Region	
Department	Deep South	Border South
Police	$23,200	$28,900
Fire	21,200	24,000
Recreation	14,300	18,000
Public Works	12,600	17,900

SOURCE: Municipal records.

employ a much larger percentage of blacks (average of 37 percent and 35 percent, respectively, in 2000) than police and fire departments (20 percent and 14 percent, respectively). Moreover, as shown in table 4.9, recreation and public works pay the lowest initial annual salaries by far, averaging approximately $7,000–$11,000 less than police and fire departments in both the Deep and Border South cities. Traditionally, black workers have been viewed by southern employers in both the private and public sectors as low skilled and therefore of low economic value. This perception has changed very little. "Low wages are a big problem," claimed a black public works employee in Quincy. "I think it's because we are black, our department is all black except for the director. We get $6 an hour, and they won't give us a raise; yet, we're busting our butts."

As blacks gain greater amounts of formal education, their job and salary expectations increase accordingly. As a result, it has become increasingly difficult to attract well-qualified blacks to low-paying public employment. Even police and fire departments, while offering higher salaries than other departments, are often unable to compete with similar skill-level jobs in the private sector. "There are multiple hurdles for applicants," stated a fire chief in the New South. "They need to be certified as a firefighter or a paramedic, and few minorities gain certification. Then they apply to the city for employment and must take the city's screening exams, and then pass departmental tests for physical and other skills. Few blacks are interested in a job with all these requirements and a low salary of $20,000 to start."

Virtually every city faced the problem of low public wages for relatively high-skilled jobs, a situation that attracts few minorities and results in high turnover rates. Black police and firefighters in New South cities were well aware of other nearby cities that recruited them with the promise of higher pay. In the more isolated Old South communities, prisons and county sheriff departments provided competition for qualified minority police and firefighters.

White city employees also confronted the issue of low wages, but whites perceive that if they perform well and stay at the job, there is a reasonably good opportunity for promotion and increased pay—a view not shared by blacks. For African Americans, promotions are less likely for several reasons. Most importantly, promotion decisions, particularly at higher levels, are largely subjective decisions made by the department head alone or in consultation with other high-ranking employees and city officials. Almost all heads of departments and other ranking supervisors are white men, with the exception of those in majority black cities. In terms of objective requirements for promotion, city departments typically require a certain number of years of service and the passing of a written exam dealing with technical aspects of the job. For some highly skilled positions, additional schooling or training may also be mandatory.

Beyond these basic demands, however, other criteria for promotion are largely subjective and are typically judged by high-ranking white men. Interviews and job performance evaluations are the primary processes used to judge promotion applicants, and they are often the determining factors for higher-level positions. According to a police chief of an Old South city, "Lieutenants and the assistant chief are appointed by the chief. Personality clearly enters into this. All supervisors vote on promotion applicants. We're trying to make this process more objective, *but we want people you can work with and who can command police*" (italics added). This department has only one ranking black officer out of eleven supervising police in a city that is 37 percent African American.

Old South cities in particular lack objective, professional processes for promotion, and sometimes even for hiring in nontechnical jobs. A common perception voiced by a black city official in Crestview is that most city employees are "still hired and promoted by who you know, and whites tend to favor whites. They go to the same churches and country clubs and know each other well. It's still a good ol' boy system." A black female police officer in Lake City concurred: "There's a big problem with minorities being overlooked for promotion despite being qualified. Nepotism is the problem—it's hard for blacks to get hired or promoted because they are not close friends or buddies of the people in charge." In the larger New South cities, professionalism in hiring and promotion is more the norm.

Informal networks and mentors or sponsors are also valuable as sources of new skills and important information that often guides one toward career advancement. Yet, informal networks tend to be segregated by race (and sex), and minority workers are less likely than whites to have mentors (Reskin 1998). According to a black police lieutenant in Daytona, "We need to prepare blacks more for promotion. . . . They tend to get low scores on the tests. But blacks socialize with blacks primarily—they feel more trust amongst themselves—and whites with whites." In the Deep South communities, there are relatively few blacks in high-level positions who could serve as potential mentors for workers of color, and there is little social mixing. "We socialize separately [by race], even at dinners of city employees," stated a black female in Quincy's recreation department. "It's because of past history and continuing racial tension in this town."

City manager–type government has long been present in each of the New South cities, and most of these communities also have had personnel or human resources departments since the 1970s. This system of governance has emphasized rational, objective decision making as opposed to the more subjective, "who knows who" method of hiring and promoting in the Deep South. For instance, in recreation departments that have few skill or exam requirements, the method of promotion involves performance evaluations, experience, and skills tests. Previously, seniority or longevity in the department was the sole criterion. In Daytona's police department, perhaps the most professionalized of all departments, promotion involves written tests, objective and essay; performance evaluations; and oral interviews. This process is carried out by independent evaluators from outside the county and coordinated by the city's human resources department. The police chief is given a short list of finalists and, with input from high-ranking commanders, makes the final decision. The only arbitrary part of the process is a preference given to a minority finalist if that group is underrepresented among ranking officers. This is the subjective element that is criticized by many white police officers.

Nonetheless, smaller cities and majority-black municipalities in the New South proved less professionalized than Daytona in promotion procedures. In Titusville, where city departments are approximately half the size of Daytona Beach, criteria for upgrading one's rank are fewer and more subjective. The fire department chief, for example, claimed that "informal assessment and an oral exam" are all that is required and that the chief alone makes the final decision. No blacks are in supervisory positions, and a black member of the department with six years of experience contended that "training opportunities for promotion are denied. I presented an idea for advancement in different areas within this department—jobs that I am qualified to do and was trained to do previously in a [northeastern city] fire department—but I was denied. They claimed economics was the reason, yet money has been found for others for similar training."

Beyond job-market requirements and institutional barriers, some black workers are perceived as simply "not measuring up" in terms of work ethic and proving themselves to be competent employees. Most of these perceptions were voiced by white men, but not all. "I have a problem with women and blacks who don't work hard and prove themselves," claimed a white female police officer in Lake City. "They feel they should be given the job just because of their gender or race." In Titusville a white male police officer stated, "Some blacks have not done a good job . . . they're late for work, and do poor reports. Yet they're able to remain on the force—this would not be allowed for white officers."

A number of whites complained that standards were lowered, particularly in police and fire departments, to hire and promote more blacks. "It goes back to if you are qualified or not," claimed a white Daytona policeman. "I think the department has lowered requirements for minorities, and as a result black officers are looked at differently. Other officers question why a black officer got the job or was promoted. Was it because of affirmative action? Blacks will never get full respect because of this question." Even a black fire chief in the New South was aware of this issue: "Some black supervisors complain that whites do not respect them or follow orders as well because they are black. Blacks in the department feel whites think they can't do as good a job as whites . . . that they're seen as not competent."

Finally, and most importantly, blacks face a great deal of both blatant and subtle racial discrimination. According to sociologists Feagin and Feagin (2003), blatant discrimination is overt, "in your face" racial treatment, while subtle discrimination is unequal and harmful treatment that is apparent to the victim but not to others. Both forms of racism are most prevalent in the Deep South, in majority-black communities, and in police and fire departments where racial tensions are greatest.

Although many observers believe that blatant racial discrimination is a thing of the past, a number of our respondents presented current examples. "One employee who left the department recently used to publicly call the one black firefighter here our 'token nigger,'" claimed a white female firefighter in Titusville. In public works in rural Quincy, a black employee complained, "White men in our department get to go out to eat breakfast and have radios in their trucks when we [blacks] don't. Sometimes we're overlooked. We have a thirty-minute lunch and have to park in the back, while whites take an hour lunch and don't have to park in the back." In addition, a white female in the Lake City fire department stated that "white men give women and blacks a hard time. One black fireman switched shifts because of the racial tension, and another black is suing the department for racial discrimination in the promotion process." A similar criticism was made by a white female firefighter in Daytona: "The chief is facing a lawsuit for making jokes about blacks and offending blacks. Blacks still get a lot of heat from racist white males who don't like blacks. . . . Blacks stick together and speak mostly in Ebonics so whites can't understand them."

Even within each community, African Americans, especially police officers, face racial hostility, often from other blacks. Some white residents, for example, still prefer city employees who are white. "A citizen recently complained about having a 'nigger' firefighter come into his house to put out a fire," claimed the fire chief in Lake City. Black police in Lake City encountered similar responses. "The public here has trouble with black officers in authority—they do not like to be stopped and questioned by a black officer. As a result, black police usually patrol the black area of the city," stated an African American policeman.

Perhaps the most hurtful animosity encountered by black police is from their peers, especially younger blacks who resent the police drug sweeps of minority neighborhoods. In the words of a black officer in the Deep South: "Blacks give us a bad time in the community—we're called 'Uncle Toms' a lot and other names, lots of names. Blacks think we are crooked and traitors. Blacks treat black police worse than whites, much worse. Some teach their kids not to even talk to you." Similarly, a black policeman in Titusville commented, "Blacks on the street think I'm a traitor, and whites think I can't arrest them. It's getting better [but] I'm still called bad names by some blacks, like 'Cracker Nigger Mother Fucker.' "

Perceived Benefits of Black Employees

While black city workers confront a great deal of race discrimination, at the same time there is a consensus among some employees and city officials that African Americans are advantageous to these city departments in many ways.

The most commonly mentioned benefit is that black police, firefighters, recreation workers, and others who work directly with the public are better able than whites to provide services to the black community. "We need to understand all citizens and can't understand blacks without having blacks on the force," claimed a police chief in the New South. "It helps us deal with a culture we [whites] don't understand. Blacks can be loud, boisterous, and in your face—most white officers don't understand this."

Moreover, when serious trouble erupts in black neighborhoods, black police have a calming effect. "When it gets 'hot' in black areas, they [blacks] want and need black officers," stated a black policeman in Quincy. "Blacks frown on white police . . . they're a symbol of white control and power. Black police are trusted more and have an attachment to blacks." This benefit is also apparent in recreation departments. According to a white female recreation director in the Border South, "Blacks provide better services to African American youths. There is more of a cultural understanding—like during Kwanzaa celebrations. And they can control black kids better . . . whites sometimes have a difficult time with black youth."

Successful black workers are likely to ameliorate racial attitudes as well. "Black employees serve to help counteract the prejudices and stereotypes of whites, both inside and outside of city hall," claimed a white official in Daytona. "This gives comfort to whites, who then open more doors of opportunity to blacks." For black citizens, having African Americans in city jobs is often a source of pride and an indication that the black community is fairly represented in public employment. As a white fireman in Lake City put it, "The black community looks upon blacks in the department as role models, especially for black kids. It shows them blacks with rewarding, secure jobs." The youth fire cadet and police explorer programs also promote a positive image of black firefighters and police as these programs attempt to attract more young people into these departments.

Conclusion

Between 1960 and 2000, blacks achieved major gains in municipal employment. In police and fire departments, traditionally dominated by white males, black progress occurred slowly. African Americans found greater opportunities (but lower wages) in recreation and public works, departments that required fewer skills and were open to hiring minorities. Over time, blacks were also able to win promotions to supervisory positions, making up 25 percent or more in every department, except fire by 2000.

Black political power had the greatest and most consistent effect on African American employment and supervisors. Since the civil rights movement of the 1960s, city employment, especially in police departments, has been one of the primary goals of black politics. Moreover, the civil rights movement served to politically mobilize blacks, a force that in turn pressured local governments to hire and promote African Americans. Evidence that the political process works for blacks in the South, the region where resistance to black demands has been most implacable, is an important finding of this study.

The presence of city managers as chief executives also helps to boost black municipal employment, particularly at the supervisory level. This, too, is an important finding of this study and suggests that the implications of reform government for black municipal employment depend on the context. In these relatively small southern communities, hiring and promotion decisions have typically been carried out through informal, white male–dominant networks. Professional city managers act to formalize employment procedures, thus reducing racial bias and increasing employment opportunities for minorities. It is also important to acknowledge that although our regression analysis attempts to control for intercorrelation between the independent variables, the positive influence of the city manager on black municipal employment is likely to be related in complex ways to components of black political power, specifically the number of black city council members. Between 1960 and 2000, black council membership in these cities increased by 41 percent. Under the city manager–council form of government, the manager is hired by and reports to the council. Our qualitative data support the notion that presence of a city manager acts to professionalize hiring and promotion in city government but also that these managers are responding to pressures from increasingly diverse city councils to act affirmatively in hiring blacks.

While blacks have increased their numbers and proportions in each city department, several barriers have reduced the rate of growth among black city workers. Numerous formal job requirements, particularly in police and fire departments, limit the employment and promotion opportunities for many blacks. Formal education requirements, mandatory training courses, and civil service exams pose barriers to African Americans who have less education and skilled-job experience than most whites. At the same time municipal departments are demanding greater skills and more formal education, annual salaries remain too low to attract and keep qualified minorities.

Finally, as we found in the private sector, racial discrimination in various blatant and institutionalized forms continues to be an obstacle for many African Americans. From white good old boy networks that exclude blacks in Deep South communities to open racial hostility on the job, blacks confront prejudice and institutional discrimination that seriously constrict public employment opportunities. As the next chapter explains, blacks are also now, and in the future, likely to confront competition from other minority groups.

5

Race, Gender, and Ethnicity: Competition for Employment Opportunities

THE INCREASING PRESENCE OF RACE/ETHNIC MINORITIES in urban areas has provided the potential for intergroup competition for scarce community resources, especially jobs. Such competition is an issue when two or more groups strive for the same goals, so that the success of one group may result in lesser achievements by others (McClain 1993). The rivalry for jobs is thought to be greatest between blacks and Hispanics because of their large numbers in many cities and their similar socioeconomic profiles. In addition, the influx of non-Latino immigrants, particularly Asians, may be leading to the displacement of black and other low-skilled native workers (Waldinger 1997). Moreover, while often neglected in studies of intergroup competition for jobs, white women are likely to be hired over other groups in a labor market where demands for job skills have risen (Moss and Tilly 2001). Whatever the dynamic among these groups in the labor market, there is relatively little empirical research that explores this phenomenon. Our study investigates the extent to which blacks, Hispanics, and white females compete for private and public sector jobs in the six Florida cities.

What Other Studies Suggest

Some research indicates that in many communities, blacks and Hispanics have competed for employment since at least the early 1980s (Falcon 1988; McClain and Karnig 1990). More specifically, as the black population increases to the point that blacks are a plurality or majority of the population, Hispanics tend to fare less well socioeconomically (McClain and Karnig 1990;

McClain and Tauber 1998). Studies of municipal employment have reported much the same pattern (Alozie and Ramirez 1999; McClain 1993). Even when Hispanics were a majority or plurality of the populace, which was relatively rare, the Latino share of municipal jobs increased but with little effect on black employment. Furthermore, in police employment, white females also competed with Hispanics (Alozie and Ramirez 1999). Some evidence shows that blacks have benefited more than Hispanics in securing public and private sector jobs because of affirmative action policies that favored African Americans (Falcon 1988). These findings suggest that affirmative action has exacerbated the rivalry among minority groups in the labor market.

Other research contends that job competition among race/ethnic groups, particularly Latinos and blacks, is much overstated (Moss and Tilly 2001; Waldinger 1997). When no minority group has a large plurality or majority, the employment prosperity of one group does not come at the expense of other groups, but instead they do better together (Muth 1971). This has been particularly the case for Hispanics and blacks (McClain and Karnig 1990). Further, the job-displacement theory that claims that black and other low-skilled native workers have lost their jobs to immigrants has not been supported by econometric research (Borjas 1990; Simon 1999). In a study of the effect of the Mariel boatlift on the Miami, Florida, labor market, economist David Card (1990) concluded that this rapid and sizable influx of Cuban immigrants had no negative effect on the wages or unemployment rates of less-skilled workers, including blacks.

Determining with any degree of precision that one group has directly displaced another in any labor market is arguably a daunting task and made even more daunting in a market as large and complex as United States (U.S. Department of Labor 1989). In some cases, immigrants move into sectors of the job market that a native group has vacated, and in other cases, immigrants create new market niches such as the ethnic enclave economy established by Cubans in south Florida (Portes 1987). One study of Miami found, for example, that while blacks had not benefited from the city's economic progress, a changing occupational distribution, not displacement by immigrants, was to blame (Cruz 1991). Another concluded that: "There was no one-to-one substitution of blacks by Cubans in the labor market. . . . There was, however, a new urban economy in which the immigrants raced past other groups, leaving the native minority behind" (Portes and Stepick 1993).

Globalization has intensified the fluidity and complexity of labor markets and further confounded the identification of clear winners and losers and the nature of the relationship between them. As such, some studies have modified their analysis to capture aspects of interminority competition that extended beyond direct one-to-one job displacement. Surveys of employers in Chicago (Kirschenman and Neckerman 1991) and Los Angeles (Waldinger 1997) found that employers operate with a hierarchy of race/ethnic preferences, with native whites at the top, followed by immigrant whites, Hispanics, and blacks. In particular, employers favor the immigrant and Latino work ethic, which many employers find lacking among African Americans. White city leaders and businesspeople have also been shown to contribute to the perpetuation of the claim that immigrants displace black workers as a way to deflect blame away from an established Anglo elite (Croucher 1997). With the increase in skill demands, white women have had an advantage over other, less-skilled groups in the job market. However, blacks with limited skills and negative employer assessments have increasingly dropped out of the traditional job market (Moss and Tilly 2001).

Thus, the relatively few empirical assessments of interminority competition have produced mixed results. At the least, it seems that studies of this phenomenon should explore the conditions under which competition appears. Relative size of the black population is one such variable mentioned in the literature. With our focus on the South, it is also expected that Border South cities may differ from Deep South communities in employment patterns. In addition, as emphasis on upward mobility in employment has increased, it is important as well to look at possible competition at higher job levels. Finally, we analyze intergroup rivalries, not in isolation but with partial correlation analysis that controls for white male jobholders.

Interminority Employment Findings: Private Sector

We shall first explore intergroup competition in the private business sector. On the basis of our survey of businesses, we present (table 5.1) the average employment figures for white males, blacks, white females, and Hispanics broken down by occupational level (professional/managerial, skilled/semiskilled, and unskilled/menial) and various community groupings discussed above (Old and New South, low, medium, and majority black). Several notable minority employment patterns emerge from these data. First, white females are the most heavily employed group, especially at higher occupational levels. Only white males, considered a nonminority group, hold a

TABLE 5.1 Reported Mean Percentages of White Male and Minority Employees in Private Sector by Community Groups

Levels of Employment	All Cities	Old South	New South	Low % Black	Medium % Black	Majority Black
Total employment						
White male	33	32	34	36	36	29
Black	26	30	23	12	20	47
White female	37	35	38	49	42	18
Hispanic	4	3	5	3	2	6
Professional/managerial						
White male	49	46	53	45	56	46
Black	14	18	10	6	7	30
White female	35	35	34	47	36	21
Hispanic	2	1	3	2	1	3
Skilled/semi-skilled						
White male	32	32	34	37	34	27
Black	28	31	25	13	21	50
White female	36	35	36	46	43	17
Hispanic	4	2	5	4	2	6
Unskilled/menial						
White male	27	26	30	32	37	12
Black	41	49	35	29	31	63
White female	25	19	27	35	26	13
Hispanic	7	6	8	4	6	12
Number of businesses	$N = 167$	$N = 63$	$N = 104$	$N = 50$	$N = 66$	$N = 51$

NOTE: Community samples were weighted equally to control for variations in number of businesses surveyed from one city to another.

higher proportion of top-level jobs, as expected. In professional/managerial positions, white women hold 35 percent of jobs overall, compared with 14 percent for blacks and 2 percent for Hispanics. This proportion is two and a half times that of African Americans in top-level positions. In skilled/semi-skilled jobs, white females also have the advantage (even over white males), although their margin over blacks is smaller (36 percent to 28 percent, respectively). In the businesses surveyed, professional/managerial positions composed 17 percent of jobs while skilled/semiskilled workers made up 52 percent of laborers, a combined total of almost 70 percent of all workers.

Second, blacks dominate the labor market at the lowest-level, unskilled, or menial employment. Menial labor is increasingly rare in the restructured U.S. economy (Holzer 1996), and in our sample of 167 firms, only 60 employed unskilled workers. Blacks fill 41 percent of these positions overall, with white females holding 25 percent and Hispanics with 7 percent. Along with blacks, Latinos, who compose 4 percent of total employees, are over-represented at the menial job level.

Finally, contextual characteristics of the communities make a difference. In terms of the Old and New South distinction, black employment is, as we have seen, somewhat higher in the Old South. The employment of white females (and white males) is slightly better in the New than in the Old South and continues to outpace blacks even in the Old South with the exception of the lowest skill level. Hispanics, as expected, hold a greater proportion of jobs in the New South cities where their numbers are larger.

The relative size of the black population has a major effect on minority employment. As the black populace increases, so does black employment, as we would predict. At the same time, however, black employment is associated with decreases in jobs held by white women, an indication of workplace competition. When blacks achieve a majority of the population, their share of the labor market increases dramatically at every skill level, even outnumbering white females (and white males) by sizable margins. White males, however, continue to dominate the upper echelon of employment, even in majority-black cities. Hispanic workers also do relatively well in these mostly African American communities where Latinos seem to compete successfully but mainly for lower-skilled jobs.

Simple correlation coefficients tend to confirm these findings, as seen in table 5.2. Blacks and white women covary negatively in the labor market at every level of employment, meaning that one group does well at the expense of the other. The high negative correlations between black and white female employment suggest a great degree of competition. Similarly, white males are also contending with these two groups for jobs, especially with blacks, as evidenced by the high negative correlations between white men and blacks and between white males and females at almost every level. As for Hispanics, their low employment figures in general suggest little or no competition with any other group.

Controlling for white male jobholders, a major factor particularly at higher employment levels, allows us to test more rigorously for the black-white female negative covariation relationship. Using partial correlation analysis (results in column 2) introduces these statistical controls. The results are clear and unambiguous at every level of employment. Indeed, controlling for white males, the negative correlations between blacks and white females actually *increase* at every job level. These results provide strong support for the black-white female job competition model.

TABLE 5.2 Correlations Between Black, White Female, White Male, and Hispanic Employment in Private Sector

	Simple Correlations	Partial Correlations (Controlling White Males)
	Total Employment	
Black–white female	−.51***	−.95***
Black–white male	−.54***	—
Black–Hispanic	.00	−.11
White female–white male	−.41***	—
White female–Hispanic	−.10	−.19*
White male–Hispanic	−.17*	—
	Professional/Managerial Employment	
Black–white female	−.36***	−.55***
Black–white male	−.44***	—
Black–Hispanic	−.01	.02
White female–white male	−.27**	—
White female–Hispanic	−.07	−.10
White male–Hispanic	.04	—
	Skilled/Semi-skilled Employment	
Black–white female	−.38***	−.75***
Black–white male	−.54***	—
Black–Hispanic	−.06	−.15
White female–white male	−.38***	—
White female–Hispanic	−.03	−.10
White male–Hispanic	−.17*	—
	Unskilled/Menial Employment	
Black–white female	−.51***	−.60***
Black–white male	−.28*	—
Black–Hispanic	.02	−.04
White female–white male	−.21	—
White female–Hispanic	−.04	−.09
White male–Hispanic	−.20	—

* p < .05; **p < .01; *** p < .001.

Views of Employers

As mentioned in the previous chapter, we conducted face-to-face in-depth interviews with employers because we wanted to understand how they viewed the world of work. Beyond obtaining employment data, we were especially interested in how employers perceived workers of varying backgrounds. In terms of exploring interminority competition, we asked why particular minority groups had gained (or lost) in the hiring and promotion process, any on-the-job conflicts among workers, and qualities they liked and disliked about various minority group employees. In the attempt to validate employers' views, we also interviewed employment and job-training agency supervisors, heads of local Chambers of Commerce, and community and minority respondents who were knowledgeable about local employment.

Employers expressed an awareness of an increasing variety of job applicants in terms of race, gender, and ethnicity. Moreover, employers of firms of even modest size asserted their desire for a more diverse workforce. In the words of a car dealership manager in Daytona Beach, "Black employees help with black customers. We learn more about race and ethnic buying habits. This is true for Hispanics too. People who speak Spanish are more comfortable with a Hispanic salesman. It's a trust factor. . . . And women have brought a more friendly, family-like atmosphere to the business . . . and women sell better to women." Similarly, a bank-hiring supervisor in Riviera Beach stated, "We've hired blacks, Hispanics, and Asians. With diversity comes a better outlook on the community, and it's helpful with the growing variety of clients. . . . Language ability, especially Spanish-speaking, is helpful." Labor and consumer markets have changed, and employers, particularly in the multiethnic New South, have responded with a greater dedication to enhancing employee diversity.

Yet business owners or managers must make choices among applicants, and some groups are favored over others. As suggested in the employment data, white females are generally viewed as superior to other minorities and are thus more likely to be hired and promoted in a service-oriented economy. Some of the characteristics commonly attributed by employers to white females (and often to females in general) are "women have better organizational skills, are good at detail work, and better at human relations"; "women are very nurturing and easy to work with"; and "females are willing to work hard and are dependable." Although most comments about white women were positive, a few businesspeople claimed that they are wary of employing single mothers with young children because of the potential problem of work dependability when the children are sick or do not have care.

In contrast, many employer perceptions of black workers are much more negative in terms of lack of skills and a general unwillingness to work hard. "Blacks have a different work ethic . . . they lack discipline, do not show up on time, or just don't come in at all," stated one restaurant manager in Titusville. Lack of education and job skills plagued many blacks. In the words of a human resources director of a large business in Lake City, "Many blacks do not have a high school education, and language and reading are problems for some . . . and others lack transportation." Employers of low-skilled black employees often expressed the most negative views, with crime, drugs, or welfare being seen as a substitute for work. As a motel owner in Riviera Beach stated, "There's very high turnover among black housekeepers [maids]. They're low paid, into drugs, and want to claim unemployment to get benefits."

While business managers preferred white females, and whites in general, to black workers, they also perceived there are many black workers who are willing to take menial, low-paying jobs that few others would perform. Only low-skilled Hispanics and recent immigrants were also willing to apply for such work, but there are few members of either group in these cities. In addition, employers wanted to have some black employees to attract and provide service to black customers, a growing segment of most firms' clientele.

Beyond negative judgments about the work performance of and possible stereotypes about blacks, employers are more likely to hire and promote white women for other reasons as well. A black Daytona Beach businesswoman and job-training supervisor, who had helped to employ many women and minorities, offered the following insight: "White women are the major source of competition for blacks, partly because there are few Hispanics here. But white women are not really a disadvantaged minority . . . they have larger numbers and more economic advantages than blacks. Beyond this, *hiring them [white women] is white man's way of making sure whites stay on top*" (italics added). Another African American businesswoman in Titusville echoed this theme with only a slightly different interpretation: "White managers feel they can work with and understand white women. This is not true for blacks . . . managers feel there is a cultural gap, unless blacks are middle class and have social contacts, which is rare." These views suggest psychological and cultural explanations that may influence employment decisions.

Relatively few employers commented on Hispanic workers or their possible competition with others. Their low numbers kept Latinos almost invisible in the labor market. "Mexicans and other Hispanics do take some lower-skill jobs that would go to blacks, but there are few Hispanics in this area . . . and many are not legal and are migrant workers," stated a businesswoman in Riviera Beach. Latino farmworkers are most prevalent in the agribusinesses of north Florida where they migrate seasonally to harvest vegetables. "Hispanics have a lock on farm, seasonal work, and there are a few Hispanic-owned businesses. But few Latinos enter job training or welfare transition programs that would improve their skills due to language problems, migrant status, and lack of citizenship," claimed a farm owner in Quincy. This businessman went on to explain that few blacks wanted such "back-breaking," low-paying farm labor, so there was little competition for such work.

Workers' Beliefs About Competition

Increases in immigration, especially among Latinos and Asians, have aroused fear and concern among low-skilled, native-born workers. It has been estimated that about 40 percent of U.S. population growth in the 1990s was due to immigration and that new workers willing to take low-wage jobs have been replacing and reducing wages of working-class Americans (Briggs and Moore 1997; Cherry 2001). Black employees are perhaps the group most threatened by low-skilled immigrant and other workers. Some blacks have been forced to move away from high immigrant areas to avoid the competition. Other blacks may face stagnating salaries, less opportunity for promotion, and reduced government services, such as job training, health, and education, that are absorbed by newly arrived racial and ethnic groups (Cherry 2001; Stoll, Melendez, and Valenzuela 2002). One study found that though immigration raises the per capita income of U.S. natives, it has an adverse effect on the per capita income of black natives (Borjas 1998). Another analysis of immigration and job competition in Los Angeles found that immigration negatively influences both the employment of more skilled native whites and the employment and wages of less-skilled native blacks (Stoll et al. 2002).

Other researchers, however, are more sanguine about the effects of immigration and new workers, contending that the presence of an expanding labor force actually creates more jobs since immigrants are also consumers of homes, services and goods, thus helping to grow the economy (Muller 1993; Piore 1979). One study examined the six U.S. states with the highest immigration, including Florida, and concluded that immigration does not cause unemployment. In fact, these states often boasted unemployment rates below the national average (Erlich 1994). Focusing on how undocumented immigrants affect other U.S. workers, Bean, Lowell, and Taylor (1988) found very little negative effect on wages, and in some cases a positive one. Another study reported that blacks in immigrant-intensive cities such as Los Angeles fared better than blacks nationally (Espenshade and Goodis 1985).

While there are relatively few immigrants and other low-skilled minority laborers in the cities we studied, black workers still expressed some fear of the growing mobility of Hispanics and Asians to these communities. Our focus groups showed black men to be most concerned, and much of the anxiety centered on the work ethic and low-wage expectations of competing groups. "Hispanics are doing more kinds of jobs. They will work until 8 or 9 o'clock at night; blacks won't do that. They're taking people out of jobs, and will work harder and longer," claimed a black construction supervisor from Daytona Beach. Some African Americans blamed the government and businesses for purposely encouraging the immigration of cheap labor to lower production costs, not caring about native-born workers. "The real root of the problem is not Hispanics and others, it's companies and their greed . . . their bottom line. The real culprits are the government and companies . . . to maximize profits they bring in cheap labor and hire them for low wages," stated a black Daytona hospital worker.

Some African Americans blamed themselves for not competing effectively with other minority workers. According to the black owner of a car wash business in Lake City, "We are our own worst enemies. Mexicans, they work hard. It's the same with Chinese . . . and they hire their own kind, as do other ethnic groups. They stick together. But not us . . . we bypass black places of business for white establishments, and we don't hire our own." There was also the perception of the importance of saving capital to develop your own business and create jobs for one's own group. "Other groups make some money and then invest in small businesses . . . hotels, motels, restaurants, and then they make money off other people. The white community, Asian community—somebody makes money and keeps it and passes it on to their own workers and families. Blacks make money and spend it on a Cadillac," stated a black Lake City retail service worker.

Surprisingly, there were few comments by blacks about white women as competitors in the labor market. Yet a black woman in retail sales in Daytona Beach remarked that "competition from whites is always in the back of my mind . . . a feeling of insecurity. It was not instilled in me on purpose, I was just raised to think this . . . that they're going to hire the white 'chick' with the blond hair and blue eyes." Another Daytona Beach black female observed that common prejudicial beliefs about whites and blacks influence hiring decisions: "I feel some companies prefer some groups of people based on stereotypes. For example, it's a stereotype that all whites and Asians are hard-working, smart and dedicated workers, and that blacks are lazy, ignorant, and are only good for entry-level positions. However, it's difficult to crush these stereotypes . . . blacks have to work twice as hard to destroy those negative images." Black workers seemed to understand the informal gradient used by employers in judging job candidates and that, regardless of qualifications, whites are at the top of the scale and African Americans are typically at or near the bottom. They also believed that competition for jobs occurs mainly at lower skill levels and involves blacks, Hispanics, and to a lesser extent, Asians.

Job Competition in Municipal Employment

We expected to find that white females and perhaps Hispanics have been competing with blacks for city employment. Tables 5.3 and 5.4 detail the growing numbers of white women and, to a lesser extent, Hispanics in the four departments. Since 1980, white females have steadily increased their numbers in every department, including at high-level supervisory positions. By 2000, Anglo women averaged 10 percent of these departmental employees and 11 percent of supervisors. Although Hispanics are a small proportion of the population in these cities, they have shown limited but steady increases in municipal employment. In 2000, these departments averaged 2 percent Latino, with three Hispanics having achieved supervisory positions.

Compared with these two minority groups, however, African Americans have gained much greater dominance in city jobs. In the new millennium, blacks make up 23 percent of employees and 25 percent of highest-level supervisory positions. Thus, blacks more than double the proportion of white women in municipal employment as African Americans gained entry early on in these departments and their numbers increased progressively over the forty-year period.

Simple correlations help us to explore the employment interactions among these various groups (table 5.5). As expected, there are high negative correlations between blacks and white males and between white females and white males. There has been intense rivalry for city jobs between these minorities and white men who are losing their dominance of these departments. Beyond this finding, there are no other consistently significant correlations.

Partial correlation analysis enables us to statistically control for white males and thus investigate more closely possible job competition among minorities (table 5.6). Surprisingly, the findings show no consistent covariation between blacks and white females either at the employment or supervisory levels. It appears that African Americans and white women have increased

TABLE 5.3 Public Employment in Six Florida Cities (1960–2000)

Police Department

	Total N	White Male N (%)	Blacks N (%)	White Female N (%)	Hispanic N (%)
1960	146	132 (90.5)	14 (9.5)	0	0
1970	222	201 (90.5)	20 (9.0)	0	1 (0.5)
1980	363	291 (80.2)	62 (17.3)	5 (1.4)	1 (0.3)
1990	477	333 (69.8)	95 (19.9)	29 (6.1)	10 (2.1)
2000	538	338 (62.8)	108 (20.0)	71 (13.2)	13 (2.4)

Fire Department

	Total N	White Male N (%)	Blacks N (%)	White Female N (%)	Hispanic N (%)
1960	141	141 (100)	0	0	0
1970	172	166 (96.5)	6 (3.5)	0	0
1980	234	211 (90.2)	22 (9.4)	1 (0.4)	0
1990	269	221 (82.2)	29 (10.8)	10 (3.7)	7 (2.6)
2000	307	237 (77.2)	42 (13.7)	18 (5.9)	7 (2.3)

Recreation Department

	Total N	White Male N (%)	Blacks N (%)	White Female N (%)	Hispanic N (%)
1960	39	30 (77.0)	9 (23.1)	0	0
1970	100	63 (63.0)	29 (29.0)	5 (5.0)	0
1980	170	82 (48.2)	63 (37.1)	19 (11.2)	0
1990	177	75 (42.3)	63 (35.6)	28 (15.8)	0
2000	207	70 (33.8)	77 (37.2)	41 (19.8)	2 (1.0)

Public Works Department

	Total N	White Male N (%)	Blacks N (%)	White Female N (%)	Hispanic N (%)
1960	220	136 (61.8)	84 (38.2)	0	0
1970	305	156 (51.1)	149 (48.9)	0	0
1980	452	235 (52.0)	215 (47.6)	0	1 (0.2)
1990	457	278 (60.8)	168 (36.8)	6 (1.3)	2 (0.4)
2000	549	321 (58.5)	194 (35.3)	14 (2.6)	14 (2.6)

their employee numbers with little or no effect on the other group. Nevertheless, the analysis depicts strong negative relationships between blacks and Hispanics at each level and in every department, except recreation. The growth of black municipal workers has limited or impeded the development of more Hispanic employees. Finally, the partial correlation results indicate a high positive covariation between white females and Hispanics, particularly in terms of total employment. Both groups entered municipal work at

TABLE 5.4 Public Sector Supervisors in Six Florida Cities (1960–2000)

Police Department

	Total N	White Male N (%)	Blacks N (%)	White Female N (%)	Hispanic N (%)
1960	31	31 (100.0)	0	0	0
1970	53	49 (92.4)	4 (7.6)	0	0
1980	79	70 (88.6)	9 (11.4)	0	0
1990	112	84 (75.0)	22 (19.6)	3 (2.7)	2 (1.8)
2000	112	62 (55.4)	35 (31.3)	9 (8.0)	1 (0.9)

Fire Department

	Total N	White Male N (%)	Blacks N (%)	White Female N (%)	Hispanic N (%)
1960	33	33 (100.0)	0	0	0
1970	45	45 (100.0)	0	0	0
1980	57	55 (96.5)	2 (3.5)	0	0
1990	83	75 (90.4)	6 (7.2)	1 (1.2)	1 (1.2)
2000	78	62 (79.5)	11 (14.1)	5 (6.4)	0

Recreation Department

	Total N	White Male N (%)	Blacks N (%)	White Female N (%)	Hispanic N (%)
1960	12	10 (88.3)	2 (16.7)	0	0
1970	21	13 (61.9)	6 (28.6)	2 (9.5)	0
1980	34	15 (44.1)	15 (44.1)	3 (8.8)	0
1990	35	15 (42.9)	12 (34.3)	7 (20.0)	0
2000	50	16 (32.0)	13 (26.0)	14 (28.0)	2 (4.0)

Public Works Department

	Total N	White Male N (%)	Blacks N (%)	White Female N (%)	Hispanic N (%)
1960	24	24 (100.0)	0	0	0
1970	34	31 (91.2)	3 (8.8)	0	0
1980	42	30 (71.4)	12 (28.6)	0	0
1990	69	46 (66.7)	19 (27.5)	4 (5.8)	0
2000	89	61 (68.5)	26 (29.2)	2 (2.3)	0

about the same time (1970s and early 1980s), and the numbers of both white women and Hispanics have risen steadily since then.

While quantitative analysis indicates that rivalry for city jobs between African Americans and white women is negligible, our interviews with department heads and municipal workers suggest some degree of conflict and competition. At times, white females represent minority contenders with blacks for municipal employment. In general, white women enjoy several

TABLE 5.5 Correlations Between Black, White Female, White Male, and Hispanic Employment in Municipal Sector

	Police	Fire	Recreation	Public Works
	Total Employment			
Black–white female	−.12	.23	−.17	−.32*
Black–white male	−.89**	−.91**	−.79**	−.98**
Black–Hispanic	−.07	.10	.18	−.21
White female–white male	−.33*	−.58**	−.47**	.21
White female–Hispanic	.46**	.63**	.04	.72**
White male–Hispanic	−.24	−.45**	−.21	.10
	Supervisors			
Black–white female	−.07	−.11	−.05	−.12
Black–white male	−.97**	−.90**	−.84**	−.97**
Black–Hispanic	.06	−.02	.06	.03
White female–white male	−.17	−.30*	−.50**	−.07
White female–Hispanic	.14	.14	.09	.14
White male–Hispanic	−.14	−.23	−.18	−.12

* p < .05; ** p < .01.

advantages over most blacks in the public job market. Since the late 1970s, white females have been entering the labor force in ever-increasing numbers, and they bring with them education credentials greater than those of many African Americans. Moreover, studies have shown that employers believe that white women are more dependable and harder working than other minorities, particularly black males (Moss and Tilly 2001; Kirschenman and Neckerman 1991).

As was the case for African Americans, females have historically been rejected for employment in police, fire, public works, and other city jobs. The prevailing wisdom was that only men were able to perform competently in jobs that entailed firearms, physical violence, heavy equipment, difficult manual labor, or life-threatening situations. Only recently have these norms changed, albeit more so in the New than in the Old South. As women (mostly white) have gained employment and proven themselves capable in various departments, traditional male (including black) attitudes have become more accepting of female employees.

Not until the 1990s, however, did women work alongside men in almost every department, including the most recalcitrant departments of police and fire. "Females are good officers," stated a police chief in the New South. "In fact, their interpersonal skills, communications, and report writing are better than most men. So they can't fight—that's no longer important. They

TABLE 5.6 Partial Correlations (Controlling for White Males) Between Blacks, White Females, and Hispanics in Municipal Employment

	Police	Fire	Recreation	Public Works
	Total Employment			
Black–white female	.14	.30*	–.14	.02
Black–Hispanic	–.64**	–.88**	–.11	–.91**
White female–Hispanic	.56**	.46**	.35*	.55**
	Supervisors			
Black–white female	.29*	–.11	.08	–.02
Black–Hispanic	–.36*	–.55**	–.29	–.62**
White female–Hispanic	.47**	.23	.32*	.25

* p < .05; ** p < .01.

are especially good at resolving family disputes and dealing with rape cases." And in a Deep South community, the fire chief noted that "we have no emergency medical services in our department, but women are very helpful in situations where medical care is needed. Women are more sensitive to victims [than men]. They've also cleaned up the language some and created a better atmosphere."

Nonetheless, despite the growth of white female employees, many women continue to confront major problems in their quest for equitable treatment. During the 1990s, sexual harassment lawsuits rivaled race discrimination suits in volume: gender-role stereotypes are still apparent, lack of mentoring and female role models is often an issue, and child care responsibilities are a burden for many, especially single, mothers. Yet white women have gained greater employment, acceptance, and even promotions in almost all city departments. Thus, they have competed successfully with African Americans, including in police departments, even becoming the "preferred" minority in some instances.

Since Hispanics are few in numbers both in the population and in city employment, our queries of municipal workers did not include specific questions related to Latinos. Nevertheless, growing numbers of Hispanics emerged in every community and in every city department within the decade of the 1990s. Police departments in particular began to seek out Hispanics so that its officers reflect the diversity within the community. "We are actively recruiting Hispanics because there are so few in the department," stated the police chief in one Deep South city. "We need someone in the department who speaks Spanish because more Latinos are moving here, and we have to have officers who can talk and relate to them."

Latinos, especially recent immigrants, are sometimes preferred because of their perceived strong work ethic. Blacks in particular voiced concerns about Hispanics as a viable threat to their jobs. According to an African American public works employee, "Our supervisor said that if we don't work hard he's got a list of Mexicans who want our jobs and will work." Several department heads expressed praise of Hispanics for their work habits. "Latinos coming to this country understand the need to work as means to an end," claimed a black fire chief. "These immigrants come in as humble, low-income people and work their way up. They see this country as a land of opportunity. Hispanics understand this better than most blacks."

Now that women and Hispanics have overcome many of the obstacles to their entry into southern male-dominated departments such as police, fire, and public works, we anticipate more nonblack minority applicants in the future. The majority will be white women and they likely will continue to generate competition for blacks. In addition, as the Hispanic population grows in these cities, as predicted, they will also increasingly contest for city jobs.

In most municipal departments, however, black political power has thus far proved to be an omnipotent force, raising significantly the numbers of black employees and supervisors. Potential competition from white women and Hispanics has been overwhelmed by black political power, with African Americans outnumbering white females and Latinos by large margins in every department. Moreover, white men, who have long dominated each of these city departments (other than recreation), continue to make infiltration by minorities difficult. Thus, white women and Hispanics, while making inroads in city departments, continue to be restricted in their job opportunities by both powerful political forces and tradition.

Conclusions

The workforce in the United States has been changing, rapidly growing more diverse. There has been a dramatic increase in the employment rates of white women (and women in general) from 43 percent in 1970 to 59 percent in 1996. During the same period, blacks, Hispanics, and Asian Americans have joined the labor force at high rates. Concurrently, white males are a declining proportion of the workforce because of earlier retirement and poor job prospects in a service-oriented economy. Women and minorities now make up a majority of American workers, with women alone constituting 47 percent of those employed (McGlen and O'Connor 1998).

Our business survey results reflect much of the employment diversity seen nationwide. These employment patterns have created the potential for interminority competition. Our results indicate significant job rivalry in the private sector between white females and African Americans, the two largest minorities in the cities studied. Hispanics numbered too few to be viable contenders in the workplace. White women and black workers also covaried negatively with white male workers, indicating that each minority group competed with white males as well. Only at the highest employment level did white men maintain their dominance. Employers' support for affirmative action boosted black employment opportunities, helping African Americans to gain successfully jobs that would otherwise be filled by other groups. Finally, when blacks increased their share of the population to the point of constituting a majority, they gained a disproportionate share of the labor market at the expense of all other groups.

In the municipal sector, black political power has enabled African Americans to gain employment and promotions at high rates compared with other minorities. Nevertheless, Hispanics and white women are increasing their numbers in every department, thus potentially competing with blacks in the future for valued city jobs. Since the late 1970s, women have been increasingly contending for municipal employment, even in white male–dominant police and fire departments. White females often attained higher levels of formal education than African Americans, thus providing them with an important advantage in professionalized departments. Hispanics, while small in numbers in municipal employment, display a work ethic that many employers believe surpasses that of blacks. In addition, municipal officials are seeking greater numbers of nonblack minorities to reflect the growing diversity of the community as well as meet the needs of minority residents.

The data presented in this chapter point to, in some cases, the existence of interminority job competition and, in other cases, to the potential for such competition. Notably, the nature of the competition is complex and not conducive to drawing foregone conclusions regarding its implications. Our quantitative analysis showed, for example, that in the private sector blacks and white females are competitors for jobs at almost every level of employment. In the public sector, job rivalry between those two groups was negligible. Interviews with employers revealed some preferences for hiring white females based on stereotypes about both women and blacks. Meanwhile, rarely did the black workers we interviewed refer to competition with white women. Hispanics composed a small proportion of the population in these six cities, but black employees nevertheless expressed concerns about potential competition from Latino immigrants, and employers communicated ethnic and racial biases that validate these workers' concerns.

In these six Florida cities, as in cities throughout the United States, global forces are altering the social and political landscape in ways that may advantage some workers and disadvantage others. Macro-level changes in the U.S. economy have resulted in a loss of menial jobs (Farley and Allen 1989). Only 36 percent of the firms we surveyed had unskilled labor positions. Meanwhile, Mexican and Latin American immigration brings workers who are increasingly filling these jobs. Contemporary economic and social transformations are also interacting with traditional biases and cultural stereotypes. Some employers we interviewed believe that Latinos are hardworking and dependable and black workers are not. Some black workers also shared examples of employers who used the availability of immigrant labor as a threat against black employees. This last point is particularly important in that it illustrates the dangers of politics of blame and ethnic division (Croucher 1997). It will be important for scholars and policy makers to monitor the implications of economic competition among minority groups, but it is also important for these actors and others to avoid scapegoating a particular group at the expense of thoughtful analysis of the complex economic, political, and sociocultural circumstances confronting blacks, Latinos, women, and whites.

6

Affirmative Action and Black Employment

AFFIRMATIVE ACTION IN EMPLOYMENT AND EDUCATION has been one of the most controversial social policies of the past forty years. The term ignites culture war debates over equal opportunity, reverse discrimination, unfair competition, quotas, racism, sexism, and diversity (Reskin 1998). A product of the civil rights movement and liberal white elites, affirmative action (AA) has focused a great deal of attention on expanding African American opportunities, particularly in employment. Yet AA has been an extremely politicized policy, maligned by some as an unfair system of reverse discrimination while supported by others as an equitable and effective solution to race (and sex) discrimination (Lynch 1997; Skrentny 1996). As a result, the debate over affirmative action has done "more to exacerbate the tensions of American race relations than it [has done] to solve the problem of overcoming past and present racial [and gender] discrimination" (Hochschild 1998, 351).

One of the major reasons for the controversy over AA is that few citizens and policy makers understand why affirmative action exists, what it actually entails in employment, and what its effects have been. This chapter proposes to help fill in these gaps in knowledge by providing a definition and brief history of AA, a discussion of how affirmative action functions in employment, and what effect AA has had in employment in both the private and public sectors.

Definition and Brief History

Affirmative action in employment refers to "policies and procedures designed to combat on-going job discrimination in the workplace" (Reskin 1998, 5).

Unlike antidiscrimination legislation, which attempts to end discrimination by outlawing it, AA entails going beyond passive nondiscrimination to take proactive measures to promote equal employment opportunities. Specifically, affirmative action requires employers to modify recruitment, hiring and promotion procedures, testing, and other practices to ensure that they use race- (and gender-) neutral employment procedures.

In reality, the definition of AA has been more complex, varying somewhat according to the situation and time frame. For example, firms with federal government contracts are supposed to follow AA regulations along with their own affirmative action programs. Many other businesses have their own voluntary AA policies. These programs are different, moreover, from government-mandated contract set-asides or Small Business Administration help for minorities (Skrentny 2001). Federal, state, and local governments (above a certain size) are required to have some form of affirmative action in employment. At the state and local levels, some plans have been court ordered because of previous blatant discrimination and lack of remedy, while other AA programs are voluntary but in accordance with Equal Employment Opportunity Commission (EEOC) regulations. This great complexity and ambiguity leads to tremendous confusion over what constitutes affirmative action in the workplace.

The history of the development and changes over time in AA adds to the complications surrounding this policy. Affirmative action was one of the consequences of the civil rights movement, and the policy's original intention was to help break the barriers of race discrimination, particularly in the South, against African Americans. However, the earliest uses of the term "affirmative action" lacked clear intentions. The words appeared in President John Kennedy's Executive Orders 10925 and 1114, prohibiting racial and other forms of discrimination and requiring AA to ensure nondiscrimination by government contractors. Affirmative action was also found in Title VII of the Civil Rights Act of 1964 empowering courts to order firms guilty of discrimination in employment to take "affirmative action" to make amend these practices. In 1965, the term was used again in President Lyndon Johnson's Executive Order 11246. Nevertheless, in none of these instances was AA clearly delineated (Skrentny 2001; Lynch 1997). Thus, AA is not a single, well-defined policy but a "set of processes and practices that have evolved over three decades and share [only] the goal of actively preventing discrimination" (Reskin 1998, 2).

To add to the confusion, AA has been a highly politicized policy from its beginning. Political controversy has plagued AA's history from the controversy over the Nixon administration's Philadelphia Plan, mandating the ratio of blacks to whites in the construction industry, which was known for its blatant discrimination, to the Supreme Court's 1978 *Bakke* decision, which approved race as a factor in university admissions. Moreover, the 1980s was a period of many court challenges to affirmative action, most typically in employment (Norton 1996). Thus, the legality of AA has remained unclear.

For many presidential administrations, AA was used as a political football to arouse indignation, get voters to the polls, exacerbate racial divisions, or provide a "wedge issue" dividing the political parties. President Reagan, for example, a staunch opponent of AA as a form of reverse discrimination against white men and bureaucratic overregulation, cut the enforcement of affirmative action by reducing the funding of EEOC. Reagan's position was popular among anti-AA conservatives and political moderates. However, President Clinton openly supported AA and carried out a proactive strategy to save affirmative action by "mending it, not ending it," thus endearing himself to minorities and liberals (Skrentny 2001).

Public opinion on this social policy adds to the controversy and divisiveness. According to polls, most white Americans support outreach programs to find qualified minorities, a form of "soft affirmative action" (Steeh and Krysan 1996). Most other more proactive forms of AA, however, such as quotas and set-asides, garner much less white support. Programs focusing specifically on African Americans are the least popular, while those that benefit women are supported most heavily. The racial gap in attitudes toward AA is substantial. Blacks strongly approve of policies of preferential treatment, whereas whites just as strongly disapprove of most such policies (Schuman et al. 1997). These divergent attitudes about an important social program divide Americans ideologically and racially.

Affirmative Action in the Private Sector

A 1991 *Business Week* survey of about four hundred corporate executives on race and affirmative action in the workplace concluded that by the 1990s companies were aware that their customers were increasingly nonwhite. They were also aware of the rising number of qualified and talented minority workers. For many firms, affirmative action was no longer just the right or legal thing to do but a "business necessity" (Gleckman et al. 1991, 53).

Yet not all corporate managers shared this view, according to *Business Week*. A number of firms hired only enough minorities to satisfy the government and to protect themselves from discrimination lawsuits. Moreover, some black workers claimed that once they were hired, they were often confronted with "indifference or outright hostility" (Gleckman et al. 1991, 53). Blacks also contended that promotions were extremely difficult because of the good old boy network that filled high-level jobs before they were advertised.

In addition to social scientists, high-level members of the business world also debated the meaning and effect of affirmative action thirty or more years after its initiation. The purpose of this section is to explore closely the role of affirmative action in recruitment, in hiring, in promotion, and in training in the 167 businesses surveyed for this study.

Since employers' views on AA may depend on how a question is worded, we decided to ask about this policy in three different ways. First, we asked whether the company "was going out of its way lately to hire and promote blacks." This question leaves out the term "affirmative action" because it triggers such negative responses among many whites, and some minorities (Sniderman and Piazza 1993). Second, we queried whether the business had a formal affirmative action policy. While some firms reported they had such a policy, employers also often mentioned that it was not strictly enforced or that the policy was in place primarily to satisfy federal requirements. Third, we posed a question about employers' personal levels of support for hiring and promotion of minorities. We hypothesized that while formal AA plans may not be in place or enforced, there may still be a personal commitment to equity in employment. Intercorrelations among these three measures, ranging from .36 to .45, are not high enough to combine them into a single factor. Because the third measure is the only AA variable significantly associated with black employment (see table 6.3), it is used in the multivariate analysis.

Table 6.1 presents the wording and results for each question. The third question elicited the greatest amount of support for minority employment, with 32 percent, or fifty-four, of employers responding positively. Interestingly, only twenty-four of these fifty-four advocates of preferences for minority and female workers are employed in firms that have formal AA policies. Question 1 had only 16 percent affirmative responses, and only 18 percent of employers stated that their firm had adopted a formal AA plan with one or more specific components.

TABLE 6.1 Measures of Affirmative Action, Employers' Responses, and Their Relationship to Black Employment

Question and Employers' Responses	% Black Applicants	% Black Employment	% Black Supervisors
1. Some companies have been going out of their way lately to hire and promote more blacks. Is this true or not for this business?			
• No or don't know = 140 (84%)	39	27	14
• Yes, somewhat = 22 (13%)	31	22	15
• Yes, very much = 5 (3%)	49	39	28
2. Do you have a formal affirmative action policy or plan for this business?			
• No or don't know = 136 (82%)	39	26	13
• Yes, somewhat = 22 (13%)	31	26	19
• Yes, a lot (2 or more specific components) = 9 (5%)	46	31	16
3. Do you personally think affirmative action as a policy to give preferences to blacks and females for hiring and promotions should be supported or not?			
• No or don't know = 113 (68%)	27	24	10
• Yes, somewhat = 42 (25%)	32	25	18
• Yes, very much = 12 (7%)	65	55	43

Why businesses opposed or favored affirmative action was an important concern. When queried about their beliefs regarding affirmative action, most employers responded negatively, as we have shown. The reasons for their antipathy are summarized in table 6.2. While we hear much about reverse discrimination and that AA is no longer needed, these accounted for only one-third (32 percent) of the reasons for nonsupport. Instead, the primary justification reported by those who opposed the program was that race was no longer a consideration ("color-blind hiring") and that employers simply hire who they perceive as the best qualified. The majority (52 percent) who mentioned this rationale suggested that if blacks are qualified, they are hired without any assistance from AA. This reason also implies that race discrimination in employment is no longer an issue.

Those employers who support AA most frequently stated that they were committed to equity in the workplace (36 percent). This reinforces our earlier finding that providing preferences to minorities reflects a personal belief, not one typically dictated by company or federal policies (mentioned by only 15 percent). Nor do large numbers refer to AA as increasing black business or improving business relations with minority communities (19 percent of responses). Similar to the concern for greater equity, 29 percent of employers' claims referred to the importance of hiring blacks, but only if they are qualified. Some critics contend that AA encourages businesses to employ unqualified

TABLE 6.2 Main Reasons Reported by Employers for Opposing or Favoring Affirmative Action

Reasons	Number and % of All Responses
For opposing:	
Hire best qualified—race not a consideration	95 (52%)
Affirmative action does not work/no need for it	39 (21%)
Have helped blacks too much already/not fair/reverse discrimination	20 (11%)
Blacks must educate themselves and become qualified	20 (11%)
Blacks not willing to work or don't care	7 (4%)
For favoring:	
Everyone should have an equal opportunity for a job	31 (36%)
Hire blacks if they are qualified	25 (29%)
Promotes more black business	16 (19%)
It's a company/state/federal policy	13 (15%)

NOTE: Respondents could report more than one reason. Total number of responses in opposition to affirmative action was 182; number of reasons in favor was 85. Number of "don't know" responses equaled 9.

minorities (Reskin 1998; Verhovek 1997), but employers in our study tend to refute this.

A relatively large (430 employees) manufacturing firm in Daytona Beach typifies a business that supports AA because of personal employer commitment. According to the white female human resources director, blacks and other minorities are given preference in hiring and promotion "due to historical imbalance and discrimination." As part of the company's AA plan, ads are placed in minority magazines, in local and regional newspapers, on the Internet, and in postings around the city, including in black neighborhoods. While black employees number only 15 percent, the business is located far from the black community and requires relatively high-level skills. The firm also has and publicly posts its "zero tolerance" policy for race and sex discrimination policy. For promotions, the business has formalized its requirements to reduce the opportunity for racial discrimination. "Any group that broadens diversity in the firm is good; minorities enrich the business in many ways, including their perceptions that are different and helpful," stated the hiring director. "Also, we want to help those who need it."

Much more common were businesses that rejected any form of AA. Representative of these firms is a restaurant in Lake City with sixty-five employees. "In this business we need to hire the best qualified, regardless of race, in order to have a good workforce," claimed the manager responsible for employment. "Affirmative action and quotas are not good, they force you to hire unqualified workers." This restaurant does not publicly advertise job openings, but simply accepts walk-in applicants. The business also has no formalized hiring or promotion procedures. Black employees make up only 8 percent of the workforce in a city where blacks are 31 percent of the labor pool and racial discrimination flourishes. In the words of the white manager, "Blacks don't want to wait on tables—many lack patience. Also some white customers object to black waitresses. White employees also act out of prejudice toward black workers, sometimes using the word 'nigger.'"

Does Affirmative Action Make a Difference?

Few businesses have a formal AA plan (less than one in five), and only about one-third of employers have some degree of personal commitment to promote greater equality in the workplace. Does this informal, personal obligation to AA, however, make a difference in black recruitment, employment, and promotion? Table 6.1 summarizes black applicant and employment figures for each AA question response. The results indicate that personal beliefs about affirmative action (question 3) show the highest rates of black applicants and employment, including blacks in high-level professional/managerial positions. Nonetheless, the responses to this question reveal that it is only those twelve respondents (7 percent of all employers) who claimed they were "very much" in support of preferences for minorities that hired the most black workers. In these dozen firms, blacks averaged 65 percent of applicants, 55 percent of employees, and 43 percent of professional/managerial workers. This trend emerges to a much lesser extent in the responses to the other two queries on AA as well. Only employers that report they are extraordinarily supportive of AA create large differences in attracting and rewarding black workers. Modest commitments to AA have only a small effect.

In terms of simple correlations between measures of AA and black employment, only personal support of preferences for minorities is significantly related to black workers (table 6.3). The level of association is highest at the professional/managerial level, while it is lowest (and not statistically significant) for unskilled/menial jobs. When controlling for other variables in multivariate path models (see chapter 3; figs. 3.1–3.4), employers' personal support for AA is statistically significant at certain employment positions.

TABLE 6.3 Correlations Between Measures of Affirmative Action and Black Employment

Question	% Black Employment	% Black Professional/ Managerial	% Black Skilled/ Semi-skilled	% Black Unskilled
Going out of way to hire blacks	.01	.07	.00	−.12
Has formal AA plan	.02	.04	.01	.15
Personally supports job preferences for minorities	.22**	.32***	.21**	.05

** $p < .01$; *** $p < .001$.

In the path models, this variable is positively and directly related to total black employment and to professional/managerial positions. The latter is the largest and most significant relationship and indicates that AA is playing an important independent role in helping African Americans gain high levels of employment.

Not surprisingly, employer commitments to AA are not significantly related in the path models to blacks holding skilled/semiskilled or unskilled jobs. These positions are relatively plentiful and lesser-skilled blacks need no assistance in gaining this lower-level work. Moreover, AA policies in general do not emphasize jobs in which blacks have traditionally been employed.

This advocacy measure of AA is also a moderately significant explanatory variable for black applicants in the path model (chapter 3; fig. 3.1) for total black employment. Firms that are known to practice AA are considered "black friendly," and tend to attract black job seekers (Holzer and Newmark 2000). Table 6.1 depicts this trend. For businesses that show support (either "somewhat" or "very much") for job preferences for minorities, black applicants average 38 percent, while firms expressing no sense of obligation to minorities average 27 percent. At the total employment level, AA has both a direct and indirect effect on African American workers.

Affirmative action has developed a constituency among some employers and human resource personnel (Kelly and Dobbin 2001). Such AA advocates have stressed the value of diversity in employment because of demographic changes that have altered labor and consumer markets. These employers have maintained support for affirmative action, ensuring that their firms will continue basic affirmative action practices even without government regulations. Known as "diversity management," the repackaged affirmative action measures respond to demographic changes that are creating new business markets (Skrentny 2001), as well as to a personal commitment to social justice.

What kinds of businesses are most likely to advocate employment preferences for blacks and women? To find out, we performed a regression analysis that included contextual variables likely to influence whether a business practices AA or not (Moss and Tilly 2001). Controlling for other factors, four variables are significant: larger, national or regional firms, businesses located near black neighborhoods, and firms found in cities with sizable black populations (table 6.4). Many larger businesses (those with one hundred or more employees) and those with federal contracts (which tend to be larger firms) are required to practice affirmative action (Reskin 1998). National or regional firms also have greater visibility and use management approaches that are more professionalized and concerned with diversity. Contextual factors such as location near black residential areas and in communities with somewhat larger black populations also influence employers' hiring practices. Such factors provide larger numbers of potential black workers while also creating pressure, and a sense of obligation, for employers to hire more black employees.

Employers who have adopted an AA policy were queried about their specific AA elements or practices (table 6.5). Most AA employers emphasize recruitment of minorities. Special recruitment strategies include ads in minority newspapers and other published outlets, notification of employment agencies, and word of mouth through minority employees. A few firms send representatives to predominantly black colleges in the state. The second-most common AA practice is to establish goals for hiring and promoting minorities. Employers typically explained to us that these "goals" are not rigid "quotas," but that such goals help to inform supervisors and

TABLE 6.4 Indicators of Employer Support for Affirmative Action

Independent Variables	Regression Coefficients (Unstandardized Coefficients with Standard Errors in Parentheses)
TYPE of firm	.125** (.062)
LOCATION	.169* (.106)
KIND of firm	−.031 (.025)
AGE of firm	.003 (.003)
SIZE of firm	.059* (.038)
% BLACK CUSTOMERS	.001 (.002)
% BLACK POPULATION	.004* (.003)
Constant	.722*** (.213)
Adj R^2	.110

* p < .10; ** p < .05; *** p < .01.

TABLE 6.5 Affirmative Action Practices by Employers with Affirmative Action Policy

Practice	Number and Percent of Responses
Recruitment	19 (61%)
Set goals in hiring and/or promotion	10 (32%)
Special ads in minority newspapers, publications	6 (19%)
Job training	4 (13%)
No quotas in hiring	2 (6%)
Education	1 (3%)

NOTE: A total of thirty-one employers reported that their business had a formal affirmative action policy.

others in higher-level positions about the employment emphases and needs of the firm. Other important incentives for minority hiring/promotion, such as job training, education, mentoring, visiting job fairs, and outreach to minority neighborhoods and institutions (black churches, for example), are only rarely practiced. As a result, many blacks and other minorities lack important job information and an opportunity to upgrade their skills to become employable.

Training Programs

Cultural diversity and sexual harassment training are direct responses to more diverse workforces. They are also programs that have typically been included as part of comprehensive affirmative action programs. Promoting greater employee efficiency and social comfort in the workplace are goals of many businesses (Jackson et al. 1992). However, many white male workers believe such programs are unnecessary, while women and minorities often claim that diversity and sexual harassment training are infrequent and ineffective. Yet such training, when well executed and carried out regularly with the strong endorsement of employers, has proved to be helpful in "raising sensitivities to race and gender differences" (Lynch 1997, 194).

The amount of cultural diversity and sexual harassment training offered in our sample of businesses is summarized in table 6.6. Eighty percent of businesses provide no diversity training, and another 7 percent offer training for only managers and supervisors. Only twenty-one firms (13 percent) have diversity training for employees, although usually it is provided one time during job orientation or infrequently. There is not a strong business com-

TABLE 6.6 Degree of Race/Gender Sensitivity Training

Sensitivity Training	Number and Percent of Responses
Cultural diversity training	
None	134 (80%)
Yes, managers only	12 (7%)
Yes, at orientation or infrequently	16 (10%)
Yes, regularly	5 (3%)
Sexual harassment/antidiscrimination training	
None	80 (48%)
Yes, managers only	16 (9%)
Yes, at orientation or infrequently	51 (31%)
Yes, regularly	21 (12%)

mitment to these programs. As one might expect, such sensitivity training is most evident in larger, nationally or regionally based firms that support affirmative action.

Most of the diversity and antisexual harassment programs consist of a one-time (or infrequent) session that focuses on the legality and nature of the firm's EEOC, antidiscrimination, and sexual harassment policies. This training can help prevent expensive lawsuits (Lynch 1997), which is often the primary rationale for these programs, but they have little effect beyond this (the next section, on workers' perceptions, strongly supports this claim). According to employers, sexual harassment and discrimination complaints are more common than racial discrimination allegations. Businesses therefore have become embroiled in a growing number of sex discrimination mediations and lawsuits as female workers have increased in numbers and become more willing to file formal charges. Thus, of all diversity programs, sexual harassment training is most prevalent, with 52 percent of businesses offering such training (see table 6.6). Yet employers often claim these programs are inadequate. "Sexual harassment is a big issue here and in many businesses, but it has been left unnoticed for too long," stated a Daytona restaurant manager. "We had a lot of sex harassment complaints here in the last year, particularly improper jokes by employees. Litigation costs money and time." This business had just recently initiated sex harassment training. In addition, the personnel director of a large firm in Titusville claimed, "We have diversity and antiharassment training at orientation, regular retraining for managers and most employees, antidiscrimination and harassment policies, and a hotline for reporting incidents. Yet we still have race and sex incidents here, especially at lower levels where there is lots of diversity among workers. Sex harassment in particular is a problem."

Enforcement of Affirmative Action

The EEOC has primary responsibility for enforcement of AA policies; however, firms with federal contracts must follow the Office of Federal Contract Compliance, the enforcement agency. Beginning with the Reagan administration, EEOC budgets and number of personnel have declined. Between 1980 and 1997, the number of positions in EEOC dropped by about 1,200 from an agency high of 3,777 personnel in 1980. Concurrently, employee charges of race discrimination nationwide increased from 44,436 in 1980 to 50,879 in 1995. However, much larger increases in sex, age, and disability claims replaced race on the EEOC agenda. In 1980, 61 percent of all EEOC cases involved race issues, but by 1995, race-related charges accounted for only 31 percent (Smith 2001). Trends in the courts reinforced these changes in EEOC. In the early years, plaintiffs in race discrimination cases were winning most courtroom battles. By the 1990s, firms, dedicating greater resources toward winning such cases, were victorious in three times as many cases as plaintiffs as courts began to show less tolerance for race-conscious programs (Smith 2001; Kelly and Dobbin 2001).

More currently, an EEOC regional director in Florida claims that because of the agency's dwindling resources only the most serious charges of discrimination are investigated. Since the burden of proof is on the plaintiff, it is difficult to substantiate discrimination charges that may be subtle and institutionalized. In addition, employers are sophisticated and conscious of the way they treat African Americans and other employees. Therefore, 65 percent of claims are dismissed, based on a finding of "no reasonable cause," and most other cases are settled through arbitration. Although all businesses with one hundred or more employees are required to file EEO-1 forms detailing their AA plans, hiring goals, and timetables, EEOC does not have the resources to check these forms or their filings. In the attempt to be more proactive, EEOC in Florida is doing more outreach and educational programs, explaining to local government and business employers, as well as minority interest groups (NAACP, Southern Christian Leadership Conference, League of United Latin American Citizens, and the National Organization for Women), their legal rights, and their obligations. Lack of funding, however, limits these activities as well.

With large numbers of immigrant and migrant farmworkers in the state, EEOC is also targeting these groups and other low-wage earners. This leaves time and resources for the agency to investigate only the most egregious race relations and sexual harassment cases, such as recent reports of hangman's nooses being put in the lockers of black employees. In the regional director's words, "Enforcement of AA is impossible; we simply do not have the resources to do so, and the change in politics in Washington does not allow us to enforce a policy that is so disliked."

Workers' Perspectives on Affirmative Action

Public opinion polls indicate that blacks are more supportive of affirmative action than whites (Kluegel and Smith 1986; Bobo 2001b; Sniderman and Piazza 1993). Depending on the question and particular AA policy, most blacks advocate such policies, while most whites are oppose such policies, although neither group is universal in their perceptions (Bobo 2001a).

Our focus groups with black workers captured a range of views on AA, although most favor AA and think this policy, when implemented and enforced, is beneficial. "AA is always helpful," claimed a black mechanic in Daytona. "If the playing field was level, we wouldn't need it, but it's not, and AA has definitely helped in education and jobs. It's gotten scholarships and jobs for people that otherwise wouldn't have had a chance. Other than the military, it's one of the better programs. It has helped to level out the playing field, though it's not level yet." Most other black employees agreed. "If AA was not in place, businesses wouldn't have employed blacks," stated a Lake City business employee. "In my job, there is no formal AA policy, but they have made an effort to place minorities in management. They felt pressured as federal guidelines filtered down to local businesses. AA helps blacks get better jobs, including me."

However, not all African Americans think that AA has functioned effectively in boosting opportunities for blacks. According to a black truck driver in Lake City, "AA in itself was a good idea, but it's no longer used by many companies, including where I work. If it had been applied, I would've been promoted by now." Others saw criticisms of AA as a political strategy that used blacks as scapegoats. "AA used to help lots of guys get jobs," declared a Daytona restaurant employee. "But now it's become a political thing, which is not meant to really help anyone. Politicians are using it to blame blacks for problems." Other blacks view the entrenched good old boy system as an implacable barrier to AA. In the words of a Lake City worker, "AA could help minorities a great deal, but the good ol' boy system outweighs AA in this city. They hire their friends and relatives, and people without degrees who end up supervising others without degrees. AA doesn't open that big door to jobs and promotions."

A few black employees support the American's Creed and the merit system, believing that if they worked hard and proved themselves, good job opportunities would be available to them even without AA. According to a black Lake City business owner, "It's an economic issue, not a racial one. We need to be self-motivated to make money. We need to stop selling ourselves short and settling for less. Despite the good ol' boy system, I can strive to be anything I want . . . just need to have and get an education. And if the system is closed or limited, you need to leave town, change companies, or change careers. We need to figure out ways to get what we want, and stop worrying about other people or issues, especially race."

Other black workers stress the necessity to help one another to overcome difficulties in the job market. "Once a black man has been hired, we need to support him and he'll eventually be in a position to bring other blacks in," stated a Daytona businessman. "We sometimes oppose each other, but we need to support one another. We shouldn't be at the bottom of the totem pole." Finally, there is some sentiment among African Americans that blacks are not always taking advantage of the opportunities offered to them. In the words of a Lake City grocery market employee, "Blacks need to take advantage of AA and set-aside programs. Some businesses don't have these policies, but some blacks don't apply because they're not aware, feel they're not qualified, or don't like AA . . . see it as a handout. Other blacks just feel they can make it on their own, but often they can't."

White men, in contrast to black workers, express strong disapproval of AA. Surveys have shown that whites in general disapprove of AA in employment for various reasons, including charges of reverse discrimination, supposed use of rigid "quotas," its inconsistency with meritocracy, and the divisiveness of a policy that exacerbates conflict between the races (Reskin 1998; Steeh and Krysan 1996; Sniderman and Piazza 1993).

The views of white workers, often spoken with visible concern and even anger, tend to echo these survey findings. "I have strong feelings about AA . . . it's really an injustice in my mind," asserted a banker in Daytona Beach. "The whole civil rights thing was to give minorities an equal shot based on qualifications, training, and skills, not looking at just color or race. But AA is still looking at race, and that's not solving the problem. In the past, I can see where there needed to be racial reparations, and AA might have been a good temporary solution, but it should not be a permanent thing. We need to get past looking at the color thing."

Whites' beliefs about AA tap into feelings about race as well as a "broader set of convictions about fairness and fair play that make up the American creed" (Sniderman and Piazza 1993, 176). Preferential treatment for blacks produces resentment among whites because it is perceived as unfair and unequal treatment that is in direct conflict with the creed. In this vein, a Daytona social services (private) employee protested, "AA promotes reverse discrimination. I work with a company that takes bids. We bend over to help certified minority vendors, but I could've gotten goods and services done a lot cheaper if I'd been able to hire others, not minorities. . . . I don't think it's fair." Similarly, a white restaurant worker in Lake City declared, "Job competition is awarded [on the basis of] race, not on merit. I've seen where we couldn't hire the most qualified person because he was not the right race. It's a disservice. I haven't seen any good come from it."

Bobo (2001b) contends that while there may be important objections by whites to AA based on principles and race, there are also strong feelings of entitlement among whites to valued resources and privileges, and blacks are perceived as a threat to these entitlements. Therefore, many whites oppose AA because it boosts blacks' opportunities in the competitive quest for good jobs. "There's a white backlash against AA now," stated a white female medical center employee from Lake City. "White males are furious and feel their employment chances are limited. This feeling may work against opportunities for blacks and women."

Most black and white jobholders also perceive as ineffective the cultural diversity and sex discrimination/harassment training components of AA. Workers claim that while such training is important because of continuing incidents of discriminatory behavior and harassment, most diversity workshops are too infrequent, poorly planned and executed, and thus ineffective in creating greater awareness and tolerance of cultural differences. "We had several diversity classes in order to report that the company was one of 'good will,'" explained a white male beverage company employee in Daytona Beach. "Low-level workers had to attend the workshops, which were mainly watching videos, but supervisors did not [have to attend]. The training was pretty poor . . . many workers paid no attention to it. I learned much more by working in a black neighborhood." Similarly, a black Lake City truck driver claimed, "Our company launched a diversity program . . . it's a worldwide business with many ethnic groups. The training consisted of video and audiotapes with Q and A. It had no direct results, however. The company was doing this training that they understood they had to or should do. They were doing it to say they addressed the issues. But they did nothing to increase diversity in the company here [which has few minorities]."

Workers argue that sensitivity workshops are rare and typically implemented only if mandated by government or in response to expensive discrimination lawsuits. "The only time businesses have cultural diversity and sexual harassment training is if they're pushed by the federal or state government," asserted a black auto dealer in Lake City. "There's no pressure from local governments to do so, so most businesses don't. But if the business is getting federal funding or has a government contract, diversity training is mandated. Even then, business leaders think that one session, one day a year, has met the government requirements. It's hard to get people to understand that diversity and gender training is a long-term program." Similarly, a white female employed at a medical facility in Lake City stated that diversity programs began "only after a race discrimination lawsuit was filed. The training was somewhat helpful in getting us to understand differences among us. But racial attitudes are too deeply ingrained here for training to have much effect, except for those who are already somewhat tolerant."

Employers claim that sexual harassment workshops have increased because of the growing number of female complaints and lawsuits. "After a number of harassment incidents, we began sexual harassment training," reported a white woman who works at a hospice in Daytona Beach. "A one-hour session alone is not enough however. We need to understand others' differences as well as similarities. And harassment is not always clear-cut; it's a matter of what offends you." Harassment training, much like diversity programs, tends to emphasize the company's antiharassment policy (most businesses had one) and the complaint process. Explaining clearly what constitutes harassment, and what the harassment penalties are, proved beneficial to both women and men and reduced the number of incidents. Yet some female workers are cautious because of the repercussions often involved in the complaint process. "If you get enough people that aren't afraid to say what happened, you can win the case," stated a black female department store employee in Lake city. "But I've complained about harassment to my supervisor, and he just tells me to 'shrug it off.' I've also encountered problems on the job after I complained."

Affirmative Action in City Departments

The initial Executive Orders 11246 (1965) and 11748 (1969) relating to AA instructed federal government employers to practice affirmative action. Title VII of the Civil Rights Act of 1964 established the EEOC to enforce employment nondiscrimination, and later, EEOC was expected to oversee AA implementation in employment as well (Smelser, Wilson, and Mitchell 2001). Since these executive orders also barred discrimination based on factors not relevant to job performance, it is difficult to separate the effects of antidiscrimination and AA provisions. In 1972, the Equal Employment Opportunity Act extended AA employment coverage to state and local governments as well as to various other major institutions. The act also strengthened the agency's enforcement powers by giving it the right to go to court (Benokraitis and Feagin 1978). From the beginning, however, affirmative action was plagued by ambiguity concerning the concept and enforcement (Reskin 1998; Swain, Greene, and Wotipka 2001).

At the federal level, where AA was first implemented to increase minority, particularly black, government employment, the results proved modest. The proportion of black federal employees increased only 2 percent over the first decade (from 13.9 percent in 1966 to 15.9 percent by 1975; Benokraitis and Feagin 1978). In later decades, this trend continued as African Americans' share of federal jobs rose by 1.6 percent between 1982 and 1995. However, the higher-level federal positions occupied by blacks and white women improved more impressively. In 1970, 2 percent to 4 percent of blacks and women held managerial positions (compared with 10 percent of white men). By 1990, some 15 percent of African American and 21 percent of white female federal employees were managers compared with 19 percent of white males (Reskin and Roos 1990).

Women and minorities also expanded their numbers at the state and local levels following the 1972 act. Between 1973 and 1993, black and Hispanic workers each grew 5 percent, and women increased by 9 percent. White men, however, declined by 5 percent or more in every region of the country but maintained their dominant presence in the composition of state and almost all local government workforces (McCabe and Stream 2000).

Although these figures show increasingly diverse public employees at the federal, state, and local levels over the past several decades, the numbers tell nothing about the factors that have transformed government workforces. In particular, has affirmative action played an important role in increasing the share of minorities, especially of African Americans, in government jobs?

At the local level, we have seen that a number of scholars have examined the various demographic, political, and structural characteristics of government that influence the racial composition of municipal workforces. Nevertheless, few investigations have included city affirmative action policies as one of these independent factors. Although cities have been required since 1972 to have AA programs to increase the employment of women and minorities, the federal enforcement of this directive has been ambivalent (Miller 1978). Further, lawsuits on behalf of minority litigants have been limited by the tremendous backlog of cases at EEOC and the sluggishness of the judicial process (Stein 1986). Politically, the retrenchment on AA by the Reagan administration and the growing antiaffirmative action sentiments by many politicians and white citizens also served to reduce initial commitments to the program (Smith 2001).

Given these considerations, it is not surprising that several systematic studies have found that AA policies have little or no effect on the racial makeup of city workforces. Stein's (1986) investigation of 134 large cities found that autonomous civil service commissions were seemingly not influenced by the standards of AA, and thus minority hiring was unaffected by AA policies. Similarly, in a representative sample of 281 municipal police departments, Zhao and Lovrich (1998) reported that when controlling for other theoretically important variables, affirmative action was not a statistically significant factor in explaining the representation of black police officers.

Nevertheless, other studies have suggested that municipal affirmative action programs that focus on specific goals and timetables for qualified minority applicants are often successful (Martin 1991; Steel and Lovrich 1987). Some of these programs were formally adopted while others were instituted under court order. The factors that proved helpful in increasing black hiring under AA were a critical mass of minority residents who generated support-ive attitudes of city officials toward AA, and the presence of elected and ap-pointed black officials to enforce AA goals (Lewis 1989; Slack 1987).

Determinants of Affirmative Action

Our initial look at affirmative action in these municipalities is to explore the determinants of AA efforts. Table 6.7 presents a summary of our vari-ous measures of AA over time (1960–2000). Shortly after the 1972 Equal Employment Opportunity Act, these cities began to adopt formal AA plans. By 1978, five of the six cities had formal policies, and by the 1990s, in accor-dance with federal grant requirements, all cities had a plan. Nonetheless, not all cities had equally effective AA policies, nor did all departments support their city's plan to the same degree.

The effectiveness of AA policies at the city level was measured in terms of number of specific components or actions, such as special recruiting ef-forts, training programs, or promotion efforts. As shown in table 6.7, the mean city effectiveness rating peaks in 1980 and then slowly declines there-after. This coincides with the Reagan presidency, which clearly signaled the demise of affirmative action efforts with cutbacks in EEOC and reduced enforcement of AA programs. Rising black political power also reduced city AA efforts, as black elected officials were able to pressure city administrators and department heads to hire and promote more African Americans. Many black officeholders, particularly in the Deep South, perceived affirmative ac-tion as too cumbersome, slow, and controversial to be effective.

The heads of departments also varied in the support of AA for blacks (table 6.7). Most supportive were black department heads, who were found only in majority-black cities, and a few white progressive chiefs located in the New South. Departmental emphasis on hiring African Americans was greatest in the police departments because of the public visibility of the police and their recognized need for minorities to justly enforce the law in black neighborhoods. Other department heads expressed little interest in AA either because they already had significant black representation, as in public works and recreation departments, or they strongly opposed AA policies, as in most fire departments.

So what factors explain the degree of AA efforts in a city when we com-bine these various measures? Slack (1987) and Santoro (1995) found that the

TABLE 6.7 Measures of Affirmative Action in the Public Sector

Year	No. of Cities with Formal AA Plan	Mean City Effectiveness of AA Plans[a]	Dept. Mean Support for Black Hiring			
			Police[b]	Fire	Recreation	Public Works
1960	0	0	0	0	0	0
1965	0	0	0	0	0	0
1970	0	0	0	0	0	1.00
1975	2	1.00	1.00	1.00	0	1.00
1980	5	2.00	1.00	1.00	0	0
1985	5	1.75	1.20	1.00	0	1.00
1990	6	1.50	1.20	1.00	1.00	1.00
1995	6	1.10	1.17	1.00	1.00	1.00
2000	5	1.08	1.25	1.00	1.00	1.00

[a]Scaled from 0 to 3 for each city depending on number of affirmative action components (special minority recruiting effort, minority training program, special promotion effort, etc.) in that year. Data were collected from chief executive officer (mayor or city manager) and city records.
[b]Scaled from 0 to 2 for each department based on number of programs designed to increase black hiring as mentioned by the department head that year.

presence of large black populations exerts political pressure on elected city officials to adopt affirmative action policies. However, no major studies look beyond the adoption of such plans to assess the totality of AA effort, which includes scope of the policy (number of components) and the degree of enforcement, both by high-level city officials and by department heads.

To explain factor scores that combined these various aspects of affirmative action for each department, we used regression analysis with four independent variables. As suggested by previous studies, we hypothesized that black political power, which includes black population size and black officials and department heads, would be an important factor. We also thought that larger cities (population size) with more financial resources (measured as black median family income, which is highly associated with median family income generally) would be significant predictors. The presence of a city manager was the fourth variable, reflecting indications that public administrators have developed a strong ethic of social equity (Frederickson 1990) and would therefore support AA efforts.

Table 6.8 presents the regression results for each department. The results vary only slightly by department. Larger cities with more resources are the most significant explanatory variables of AA effort in every department. The larger and more affluent municipalities are the progressive New South cities. Compared with the smaller, more traditional, and poorer Old South com-

TABLE 6.8 Factors Explaining Affirmative Action Efforts

Independent Variables	Regression Coefficients by Department (Unstandardized Coefficients with Standard Errors in Parentheses)			
	Police	Fire	Recreation	Public Works
City population size	.000***	.000***	.000***	.000***
	(.000)	(.000)	(.000)	(.000)
Median black family income	.000***	.000***	.000***	.000***
	(.000)	(.000)	(.000)	(.000)
Presence of city manager	.005	−.079	.013	−.425**
	(.207)	(.196)	(.206)	(.198)
Black political power	−.187**	−.217**	−.257***	−.087
	(.096)	(.093)	(.097)	(.092)
Constant	−1.54***	−1.57***	−1.63***	−1.39***
	(.181)	(.174)	(.191)	(.173)
Adj R^2	.640	.679	.658	.671

* $p < .10$; ** $p < .05$; *** $p < .01$.

munities, New South cities have more job openings for minorities and more progressive city managers. These cities also have separate human resource (or personnel) departments that develop comprehensive AA plans and oversee their enforcement, among other responsibilities. Human resource departments proved to be a major advantage in AA efforts. Our results show, however, that the presence of a city manager alone is not sufficient to influence AA. Two of the three Deep South cities have city managers, but their concerns for social equity in employment have not been sufficiently strong to overcome the overwhelming resistance to AA from other city officials.

A surprising finding in table 6.8 is that black political power is significantly but *negatively* related to AA efforts in three of the four departments. This suggests that sizable black populations and numbers of black officials exert their own direct influence on local governments to employ more African Americans. As one black councilman in Daytona Beach noted, "We encourage businesses and the city to break barriers to hire blacks. We're the messengers who state the city has not met its goals in minority hiring . . . we continually bring this issue to the fore." In these situations, there is no need for AA plans. Indeed, in majority-black communities, affirmative action policies were typically ignored when black officials ruled city hall and determined their own independent minority hiring priorities. Even when whites were in political control in these mostly black cities, they refused to implement AA for fear that the city departments would be flooded with black applicants and city workers would become majority black.

Effect on Black City Employment

Beyond the determinants of AA efforts, we are interested in the effect of this program on black city employment. We had expected that affirmative action, either as a formal plan or informally implemented by city executives, would have a positive effect on black public employment. Our findings in chapter 4, however, indicate no such effect. Regression analyses show that the factor scores that combine all measures of affirmative action for each department are not statistically significant variables in explaining the proportion of black city workers or supervisors. While studies suggest that affirmative action assisted blacks in gaining public jobs initially in the 1970s and in the early 1980s, the reduced emphasis on and lessened enforcement of this program beginning with the Reagan administration decreased its effectiveness locally (Reskin 1998). Similarly, most white men have strongly resisted affirmative action. Finally, as we have shown, black political power overwhelms most other factors in predicting black city employment and supervisors.

Nevertheless, our qualitative data show that affirmative action was well implemented and influenced black jobholders in two cities. Daytona Beach and Titusville, relatively progressive New South communities, were the first of our six cities to implement formal AA plans.

In Daytona Beach, the mayor appointed a mixed-race special committee in 1970 to investigate minority needs, particularly in employment. The committee claimed that racial discrimination and culturally biased entrance exams were the primary barriers to black city employment. With the urging of top city officials, Daytona revised its civil service exams to remove possible racial bias. At the same time, the federal Office of Revenue Sharing, acting on an NAACP complaint, investigated the city's minority employment record and found the city in noncompliance with federal employment guidelines. As a result, the Office of Revenue Sharing threatened to terminate federal funding. Reacting to federal pressure as well as to the special committee report, Daytona implemented its relatively new affirmative action plan more aggressively (Doig 1977; Desiderio 1978). Minority recruitment efforts were increased, including contacts with black organizations and ministers, newspaper ads, classes on test taking, and the use of black recruiters. In addition, a "rule of three" requirement was instituted, whereby the highest exam–scoring black applicant was added to the two finalists for a job or promotion if an African American was not already one of the final three. There was no mandate to hire the black finalist, but this requirement did boost the employment and promotion potential for African Americans. These actions resulted in improved black city employment, up from 16.6 percent of the city's workforce in 1976 to 24 percent by the early 1980s (City of Daytona Beach 1981).

Affirmative action efforts continued to help increase black city workers in Daytona through the 1980s. By the early 1990s, however, the emphasis on affirmative action began to wane. Several white males filed reverse discrimination lawsuits in the late 1980s, and while the city successfully defended its AA efforts, court suits resulted in more restrictions on AA to lessen possible discrimination against white males. The rule of three was modified so that a black would no longer necessarily appear among the three job finalists. At the same time, Daytona's activist city manager, a strong proponent of AA, resigned to take a job elsewhere. The new city manager gave less attention to affirmative action, as did most department heads. In the 1990s, large numbers of white females began to compete with blacks for city jobs, making it more difficult for blacks to gain positions in nearly every department. Increasingly, blacks perceived AA as a liability at times, attaching a "stigma" to black employees as unqualified. As one department head stated, "Many blacks are embarrassed by AA. . . . They feel they can qualify themselves without AA. They don't like to think they need a crutch." With more modest AA efforts, the number of black city employees increased only slightly as many qualified minorities were attracted to better-paying jobs at the space center or in metropolitan Orlando.

As in Daytona, the implementation of AA in Titusville peaked during the 1980s and early 1990s. Black employment at city hall improved somewhat in the early 1980s, primarily because of a progressive AA program and a progressive city manager. The police department initiated a special training program to attract minorities who did not meet the regular entrance requirements, and the city began a release-time educational program to upgrade the skills of minority employees. Titusville expanded its recruitment efforts to include Bethune-Cookman College and other historically black colleges, black churches, community organizations, and word of mouth through African American leaders and ministers. However, the city's special training program for minorities was cut in 1990 as a response to the serious budget constraints caused by the economic recession of that decade. Titusville's affirmative action plan was also altered so that its hiring goals included a variety of minorities in the area, not only African Americans. This resulted in greater emphasis on recruiting and employing women and Hispanics. With less enforcement of AA by the federal government, the city reduced its AA efforts in general. These developments resulted in fewer black applicants for city jobs, and by 2000, white females and Hispanics outnumbered the small proportion of blacks in both the police and the fire departments. Only in public works, where low-skill, low-paying jobs are plentiful and there is little competition, have blacks maintained their numerical superiority in Titusville departments.

In compliance with federal law and grant guidelines, most cities had an AA plan, at least in form, by 1978, and these cities filed the required minority employment progress reports (EEO-4 forms) annually. Nevertheless, beyond Daytona Beach and Titusville, no communities fully implemented their affirmative action policies. This lack of AA effort was particularly apparent in the Deep South cities. In these communities, public officials viewed AA as an unnecessary intrusion of the federal government into local affairs and believed that there was little chance that federal officials would enforce affirmative action requirements. As a Lake City official put it, "This city doesn't want anyone telling them what to do, and we realize the 'Feds' won't enforce an affirmative action plan anyway. They aren't going to bother with a small city like this."

The majority-black cities of Quincy and Riviera Beach also saw little reason to enforce their AA plans. With whites still in political power through much of the 1970s and 1980s, there was stiff resistance to affirmative action. White officials feared AA would open the floodgates to black job applicants, most of whom whites believed to be incompetent. Indeed, the lack of black applicants and the poor performance of blacks on civil service exams (labeled as "culturally biased" by many minorities) were major reasons for the low number of African Americans in city jobs. As blacks gained greater political power in these minority-dominant cities, however, they were able to appoint more African American department heads, revise entrance exams, and attract more blacks to municipal work.

City Employees' Views of Affirmative Action

As with the American population, the opinions of affirmative action expressed by the municipal employees we interviewed varied greatly. Differences in levels of support for AA stem largely from the myriad understandings of what constitutes AA and its basic purposes. As we have seen from the comments voiced in focus groups of private sector workers, blacks tend to see AA as an important policy to prevent discrimination, whereas whites (men in particular) perceive it as a boost to the unqualified. City employees expressed similar perspectives that differed by race.

We discovered, however, that municipal workers' perceptions of AA also varied by department. As depicted in table 6.9, employees of traditional departments, such as police and firefighters, which maintained relatively higher job qualifications, status, and pay, communicate less overall support for AA than other departments. Those interviewed in police and fire positions split evenly by race in their degree of support for AA, with blacks strongly supportive (88 percent) and white males equally opposed (82 percent). Notably, white females and Hispanics are almost evenly divided in their perceptions about AA. Even though both groups, especially females, claim to experience discrimination on the job in these patriarchal departments, they do not connect this discrimination to the need for AA. This finding seems to confirm previous research that suggests that women are more likely than blacks to feel unfairly helped by AA and to be more susceptible to negative self-evaluations due to AA (Eberhardt and Fiske 1994).

In contrast, employees in the departments of recreation and public works are much more diverse by race and gender and consequently less dominated by white males. These departments have fewer job requirements and pay less

TABLE 6.9 Summary of City Workers' Perspectives on Affirmative Action

	Number of Employees Supporting AA		
Departments	Yes	No	Don't Know
Police and Fire			
White females	6	8	0
White males	6	28	0
Black females	6	2	1
Black males	22	2	0
Hispanics	2	2	1
N	42	42	2
Recreation and Public Works			
White females	8	13	1
White males	4	11	3
Black females	6	1	0
Black males	24	3	2
Hispanics	1	1	0
N	43	29	6

NOTE: Question asked of all city worker interviewees: "Do you think affirmative action as a policy to give preferences to blacks and females in hiring and promotion should be supported or not?" Responses of department heads are not included here.

than police and fire, and thus blacks and white females encounter less competition from white males for jobs. In addition, recreation departments stress diversity in workforces since they provide services to multiracial and mixed -gender clientele. Predictably, there is greater support for AA among those interviewed in these departments. Of seventy-eight interviewees, forty-three (or 55 percent) support affirmative action, with six "don't knows." In terms of race, 83 percent of blacks favor AA, while 30 percent of whites advocate this policy (and another 10 percent declare that they "don't know"). There is more support among whites for AA than in the police and fire departments, largely because of the sizable number of white females in recreation. Yet even white males tend to favor this policy more so than in the protective services, with seven of the eighteen respondents (39 percent) either declaring support or answering "don't know."

Thus, the most vitriolic antiaffirmative action comments come from white policemen and firemen, particularly those from the Deep South cities. The most common concern is that AA results in the forced employment of less competent minorities. "I don't like affirmative action . . . it forces us to hire minorities and balance the department regardless of qualifications," claimed a high-ranking white fireman in Lake City. "I don't like that because it takes a special person to be a good firefighter and we need to hire the best qualified, regardless of sex or race." A white female police officer in Crestview echoed this sentiment: "We need to look for competence . . . we must keep our standards, and this is impossible with AA. Everyone should be treated the same in terms of hiring and promotion; color and gender shouldn't matter." Even though AA quota systems have been illegal since the late 1970s, several white officers still refer to AA in this manner. "I don't want a 'quota' person when they come to put out a fire," stated a Crestview white fireman.

White males also express a great deal of animosity over "reverse discrimination," which they often perceive as the inevitable result of hiring or promoting minorities. "White men suffer much reverse discrimination today,' claimed a Daytona policeman. "It creates anger among white males when females and blacks are booted up on the promotion list." The belief that AA gives African Americans considerably better opportunities in employment than whites is widespread. According to a white policewoman in Riviera Beach, "We should do away with affirmative action . . . minorities should not be hired or promoted just because they're minorities. It's not fair and it builds up a great deal of resentment among whites."

Many whites also believe that racial discrimination in employment no longer exists and thus AA is not necessary. "Blacks used to face discrimination and needed AA," stated a white police officer in Daytona. "But that's no longer the case and blacks don't need assistance in getting jobs anymore." Similarly, a white fireman from Crestview asserted, "Minorities can earn their own way because they face no barriers today. They can get an education and a job if they want to. We all have an equal chance now."

In the recreation and public works departments, there is much less white resentment of affirmative action. In fact, there is relatively little awareness that AA was an operative policy since these departments are so diverse. Those with knowledge of AA policies tend to believe that hiring the best-qualified job candidates should be the guiding principle and that minority status should make no difference in departments with plenty of minorities. "We should hire based on qualifications for the job," stated a high-ranking recreation official in Crestview. "I don't agree with AA and preferences for minorities, but blacks and others deserve a fair shake. If I were short-handed of blacks, I would take race into consideration in hiring. But we have many blacks and women in the department."

African Americans are more supportive of AA than whites across all departments. Many blacks believe that racial discrimination continues to affect numerous areas of employment and that AA is a necessary strategy to overcome this barrier. "Affirmative action gives blacks a fair and equal chance," claimed a black Lake City fireman. "Many whites think blacks are thieves or crackheads and don't give them a fair chance." Even in the New South cities, African Americans perceive discrimination is still a factor in city employment. According to a black police officer in Daytona, "Racism exists. Without AA you wouldn't get anywhere . . . you have to recruit and give preference to minorities. White males still dominate departments."

Furthermore, a number of blacks (and some whites) maintain that city employment should reflect the racial and ethnic makeup of the community. Fairness and the race of city workers were well expressed by a high-ranking black firefighter in Daytona who had assisted in the recruitment and hiring of blacks: "Public jobs are a public resource. The city has a responsibility to share assets among all citizens. Jobs should be distributed equitably. Merit is important, but not the only element in hiring and promotions. Race has some preference in my mind because blacks are underrepresented." Even in Titusville, with a small black population and relatively few black city employees, a high-level white official in the fire department claimed, "Affirmative action helps in terms of recruitment, retention, and promotion of blacks and other minorities. The goal of our workforce is to be reflective of the community. . . . Minorities need to see people (in city jobs) of the same background. It also projects that we have diversity in our workforce."

In addition to this sense of fairness and equity, black employees are perceived as necessary to act as conflict-resolving "cultural brokers" who are able to manage, more effectively than whites, problems involving minority citizens, particularly in tense situations. "I can control situations in the black area," asserted a black police officer in Crestview. "Whites cannot. I know the language and culture. So sometimes it's necessary to hire a black—or a female, to search women without a problem of liability. We need minorities to deal with particular situations."

Municipal Diversity and Sexual Harassment Programs

"Even with the rash of diversity workshops and in-service training programs, most managers and supervisors do not adequately understand the cultural backgrounds or skills of their employees. . . . Relatedly, quick-fix on-the-job training activities merely scratch the surface and, in some instances, do more harm than good" (Henderson 1994, 9). This and other studies of cultural diversity training (Lynch 1997; Mobley and Payne 1992) aptly describe the nature and effects of diversity workshops in these six cities. Furthermore, these findings are similar to those reported earlier for the business sector.

We summarize the extent of city diversity and sexual harassment programs in table 6.10. Most of these programs were initiated in the mid- to late 1990s, prompted by a progressive city manager or mayor or, more typically, by a rash of race or sex discrimination complaints and lawsuits. Sexual harassment and discrimination claims have been most prevalent recently, thus explaining the greater emphasis on these workshops rather than cultural diversity (only occasionally are these two programs combined). Diversity training, moreover, has often been expanded to include minorities other than blacks (Latinos, Asians, the disabled) in attempts to reflect the changing demographics of these communities and city workforces. Within these cities, the police and fire departments, composed mostly of white males with traditional norms, have been the settings for the vast majority of race/sex discrimination claims and consequently the focus of most city workshops.

TABLE 6.10 City Cultural Diversity and Sexual Harassment Training Programs

City	Cultural Diversity	Sexual Harassment
Crestview	None	None
Lake City	A little, each year; supervisors only	Every year; all employees
Quincy	None	Once (1999); supervisors only
Titusville	A little, each year; supervisors only	Every year; all employees
Daytona Beach	A little, occasionally; most employees	Every year; all employees
Riviera Beach	Every year; supervisors only	Every year; most employees

In Lake City, for example, five formal employee complaints of discrimination were filed between 1995 and 2001. Two of these claims involved sexual harassment, and two others alleged racial discrimination; four of the five complaints took place in either the fire or police departments. The sexual harassment charges were settled out of court, with the city paying the two female claimants a total of $115,000. The race discrimination complaints, filed by blacks, went to arbitration where the claims were found to be unjustified, resulting in the dismissal of the two city workers (City of Lake City 2002). According to a high-level Lake City official, "We started annual workshops on sexual harassment after the city went through costly litigation of harassment complaints. This training is mandatory for all city employees. We also developed a sexual harassment policy. There is less diversity training . . . it is one component of a yearly workshop for supervisors only."

As shown in table 6.10, cities in the New South are much more likely than those in the Old South to carry out both cultural diversity and sexual harassment training. New South communities have larger numbers of African Americans and women employees, particularly in police and fire departments, and therefore a greater demand for such workshops. More important, with more minority workers, cities in the New South have faced numerous race and sex discrimination charges. In Riviera Beach, for instance, more than a dozen claims of discrimination were filed during the 1990s, costing the city more than $2 million in legal expenses and settlement fees. In addition, New South cities have more progressive city officials and resources, including human resource or personnel departments, both of which serve to encourage antidiscrimination workshops.

City employees whom we interviewed were nearly unanimous in their beliefs that sexual harassment/discrimination programs have been timely and beneficial, whereas cultural diversity training has been sporadic and ineffective. "Yearly mandatory workshops dealing with sexual harassment have been successful," commented a white policeman in Daytona. "They have helped many officers who didn't understand that certain jokes, comments, and pictures on the wall are unacceptable to most women. We are more sensitive to females now and also realize the costs and liability to the city if we don't act according to the sexual harassment policy."

Assessments of diversity training were somewhat more varied, but few evaluations were positive. According to a black female police officer in Riviera Beach, "The city carries out diversity workshops each year for supervisors, and they are supposed to take this information back to their departments, but few actually do this. The workshops could be effective if taken seriously and practiced day to day, yet not many police are open to new information nor do they put it into practice." A white fireman in Daytona Beach perceived these programs somewhat differently but reached the same conclusion: "Most employees think the [diversity] training is a joke. They only go through the training because they have to and just pretend to be involved. The workshops offer no valuable skills or knowledge but simply teach us that we should 'be nice to others and get along.'"

Beverly Daniel Tatum (1997), a psychologist who has studied race relations in schools, the workplace, and other institutions, contends a code of silence among whites and blacks severely inhibits open discussions of racial issues. The silence is a result of the fears by members of both races (as well as other minorities) that discussions of racism may produce conflict and anger, social ostracism and rejection by those who might be offended, loss of status and privilege for supporting minorities, or clear evidence of one's ignorance and naiveté about such issues. As a result, most individuals avoid open discussions concerning race, especially diversity group workshops, which give rise to many of these fears. For the same reason, many cities, schools, businesses, and other institutions resist developing cultural diversity programs, perceiving that most employees would not take them seriously or participate fully or, in other cases, that racism has already been much discussed and therefore is no longer an issue.

Conclusion

Affirmative action is a controversial, confusing, and highly politicized policy that intends to provide greater equality for African Americans and other minorities. In the workplace, preferential treatment for blacks was deemed necessary to compensate for past (and present) race discrimination. Our survey of private sector employers established that few firms have a formal affirmative action policy. Most employers oppose AA as unnecessary, claiming that qualified blacks are hired and no longer face discrimination. Nevertheless, one-third of employers personally support hiring and promotion preferences for blacks and females to achieve greater equity in the workplace. Most importantly, employer commitment to AA is significantly related to black job holding, particularly at the supervisor or managerial level, even when controlling for other variables. Firms most likely to advocate preferences for black employees tend to be relatively large, nationally or regionally affiliated, and located near black neighborhoods in cities with sizable African American populations.

Business AA practices emphasize special recruitment efforts and goal setting for minority employment. Other potentially important programs, such as job training, mentoring, education, and cultural diversity training, are only occasionally implemented. Moreover, EEOC enforcement of AA has been limited because of a lack of resources and reduced attention to race-related issues.

Black employment in city departments has been less affected by affirmative action than in the private sector. Black political power proved to be the most powerful determinant of African American municipal labor. This was evident from the quantitative analysis we presented in chapter 4 and in our qualitative data. Interviews with city officials revealed that these professionals and politicians work outside of, or in the absence of, affirmative action policies to advance the goals of hiring and promoting minority employees. Only in larger, more affluent cities, like Daytona Beach and Titusville, did AA influence black jobholders and then only for a brief period when the politics of AA were favorable.

In both the private and public sectors, workers' views of AA are similar. Blacks support AA and believe it is necessary to overcome racial discrimination. Nevertheless, they recognize that AA is rarely enforced, and therefore, it is often not an effective policy. White men, particularly in the traditional police and fire departments, strongly oppose AA and view it as a form of reverse discrimination and a violation of the principle of meritocracy. In general, employees, regardless of race, concur that cultural diversity workshops, a potentially important component of AA, have been infrequent and ineffective.

While AA was created to compensate blacks for a history of grievous discrimination, the development, goals, and implementation of this policy have generated tremendous conflict, resentment, and political polarization. This has detracted from the efforts of AA to expand employment for African Americans. Particularly troubling is that many whites either acknowledge or participate in racial stereotyping while soundly rejecting the need for a policy to rectify the persistent discrimination. Despite these limitations, affirmative action, particularly in the private sector, has helped to reduce racial discrimination and open doors of economic opportunity for many blacks. The concluding chapter explores further how affirmative action and related prescriptions for change may advance the goals of racial equality.

7

Promoting Progress in Black Employment

THE QUEST FOR ECONOMIC EQUALITY FOR BLACKS in the South remains an elusive goal. The civil rights laws of the 1960s provided African Americans with significant political and legal powers, and as a result, the walls of racial discrimination began to crumble. Blacks gained elected offices, schools desegregated, and white racial hostility became less severe. There were economic advances for southern blacks due to increased urbanization, industrialization, federal aid, and antidiscrimination efforts. Yet the Reagan era of the early to mid-1980s signaled a change in the march toward racial equality. Federal assistance and affirmative action programs were scaled back, and schools began to resegregate as courts returned autonomy to local officials. In addition, the decline of the civil rights movement reduced the pressure for continuing social and economic change. As a result, many Americans, including large numbers of southerners, continue to be "sharply divided by race in their schools, in their neighborhoods, and in their social lives" (Klinkner and Smith 1999, 323).

The key to economic progress for African Americans is employability, which in turn includes access to decent-paying jobs, the potential for promotion, job security, and a sense of status and respect associated with one's occupation. Respectable employment also helps to provide many greater benefits, such as better housing, the possibility of living in a middle-class neighborhood with improved schools, and an overall higher standard of living.

Major Findings

In the six Florida cities, our survey of businesses shows that most black workers hold lower-skilled service industry jobs with limited upward mobility.
Better job opportunities for African Americans are limited greatly by employer discrimination based on their views that blacks lack a proper work
ethic, appropriate attitudes, and sufficient skills and education. Curiously,
acknowledgments and expressions of racial discrimination often persist alongside the rejection by whites of any need for policies, such as affirmative action, that are designed to combat such prejudices. White managers issued
statements such as "blacks don't want to wait on tables," and acknowledged
that their white employees display racial prejudices, including the use of
the N word. These white managers and many of their white employees also
insisted that affirmative action is an outdated policy that is unnecessarily ob-
structing our society's need to move beyond race.

Our qualitative data confirm, as many studies have, that white Americans
generally oppose preferential treatment for African Americans in employment (Bobo 1998; Krysan 2000; Wilson 2006). Similar to this existing research, our analysis also reveals varying factors underlying that opposition.
We found ample evidence of what has been widely described as "symbolic"
(Sears et al. 1997), or "laissez-faire" (Bobo, Kluegel, and Smith 1997), racism. Although whites rarely proclaim any biological inferiority of blacks, they
frequently maintain that racism is a thing of the past and that any current
demands for "special treatment" on the basis of race are excessive and un-
deserved (Sears et al. 1997). We also found evidence that beyond racial attitudes, whites also oppose affirmative action because they "perceive Blacks
as competitive threats for valued social resources" (Bobo 1998, 989). In the
Florida cities where the black population was small, a perception of threat
on the part of whites was minimal. White racism was most prevalent in the
Deep South and in the communities where African Americans make up more
than 35 percent of the population.

The existence of cultural variation between the Old South and New South
was an assumption that underlay the design and implementation of this
project. The history and geography of the Old South is posited to perpetu-
ate a type of racialized thinking that is less common in the more urban and
cosmopolitan New South (Black and Black 1987; Scher 1997). In line with
existing scholarship, we assumed the presence of greater cultural and political conservatism in the Old South than in the New, and that this would be a

factor influencing economic advancement, or lack thereof, for African Americans. Some of our findings support this hypothesis, and others do not.

Our qualitative data confirm greater political conservatism in the Old South and a more pronounced black-white cultural divide. In the Old South, employers were more likely to attribute to blacks cultural characteristics that negatively affect their economic advancement. It was also in the Old South where business owners and managers were more likely to report animosity between racial groups. White employers and white employees in the Old South expressed greater resistance, and even hostility, toward affirmative action than was evident in the New South, and New South cities were more likely than Old to implement diversity training programs. Our quantitative analysis of municipal employment in chapter 4 also showed that the conservative politics of the Old South worked to depress black public sector employment.

Contrary to our expectations, however, economic opportunities for blacks in the private sector are somewhat better in the Old South than in the New South (with the exception of financial institutions and motels). This outcome may be because blacks in relatively geographically isolated Old South cities face less competition from other job seekers, but our data cannot confirm this hypothesis. The Old/New distinction has been useful for explaining politics in the South (Black and Black 1987; Button 1989; Sher 1997) but may now warrant careful re-examination in light of cultural, demographic, and political changes of the past two decades. As discussed in chapter 2, the current socioeconomic characteristics (high school graduation rates, median household incomes, and poverty rates) of blacks and whites in our six cities point to the attenuation over the past two decades of the Old South–New South distinction. Any future refinements of this cultural and political variable should explore additional methods of measurement. We used percentage of votes for Republican candidates in presidential elections as a measure of political conservatism, but this is a partial measure and current political realignments may further complicate its efficacy.

In the Old South, and to a lesser extent the New South, some employers attributed the economic inequality of blacks to cultural attitudes and behaviors. To what extent these employer perceptions are accurate is not always clear. However, we do know that many blacks are at a disadvantage in the labor market because of inadequate education and basic skills, as well as by increasing competition for jobs from white females. Significant numbers face obstacles, such as lack of transportation, job training, affordable childcare, and other structural factors that make it difficult to compete for and hold decent jobs. For example, earlier studies of the effect of affirmative action on blacks and women found that the policy had not dramatically improved the employment situation of either group, but women had benefited more than blacks because women, with the removal or at least the reduction of overt sex discrimination, were better prepared to move into higher-level positions. Blacks, however, suffered combined racial, economic, and educational discrimination, and efforts focused on removing racial discrimination were less effective (Kellough and Kay 1986; Rosenbloom 1980).

Our study uncovers persistent obstacles to the economic advancement of blacks but also confirms that the effect of these obstacles can be reduced by government and private sector interventions, as well as by the blacks' initiatives. Affirmative action in which employers support a diverse workforce has boosted black employment, particularly opportunities for promotion. The rising numbers of national- and regional-based businesses committed to a greater minority workforce has also increased African American employment. In addition, as minorities gain higher-level positions, they are likely to attract and employ more blacks. Resources that blacks bring to the labor market, including population size, customers, and job applicants, are also important. So too are black self-help efforts, such as completing an education, improving job skills, and promoting business and community network or support groups.

While efficiency and economy are major influences in private sector employment decisions, the public sphere is affected by emphasizing social equity. Thus, blacks have fared relatively well in municipal departments. By 2000, African Americans numbered 20 percent or more in all departments other than traditional, white male–dominated fire departments. Even more important, blacks have gained 25 percent or more of high-level supervisory positions in most departments.

We found that black political power is the strongest predictor of African American municipal employment. The civil rights movement mobilized blacks to gain positions in city government, thus providing blacks with the political force necessary to influence public employment. This is an important finding in terms of attesting to the success of past political mobilization and the promise of future political efforts to bring about greater racial equality in both the public and private sectors. Our findings lend support to the cautious optimism of existing scholarship (Eisinger 1980). For example, Fainstein and Fainstein write (1996, 36), "The example of American cities shows the real but limited possibilities of translating political power into social advancement." Browning, Marshall, and Tabb (1990, 212) concur, if somewhat less optimistically: "Have blacks achieved . . . strong political incorporation? Sometimes. Where incorporation has been achieved, have minority-oriented city governments produced gains for minority people? Yes, in significant, but limited areas. Have these government achieved the goals of the movement that produced them? No."

In these six Florida cities, black political power translates into greater numbers of African American employees and supervisors, but so does the presence of a city manager. This finding warrants further comment in that it contradicts earlier studies that found that unreformed municipal governments—those with a mayor as opposed to council-manager—offered greater hope for minority incorporation than did reformed city governments (Lineberry and Fowler 1967; Stein 1986).

The original argument behind the reform movement was that cities should be run more like businesses. Trained professionals, the reformers argued, as opposed to popularly elected mayors, would have the needed skills and neutrality to bring efficiency and fairness to city government and clean up the political patronage and corruption that had come to characterize many urban regimes (Nalbandian 1990; Ross and Levine 1996). Over time, however, critics of reformed government charged that although it had indeed served to isolate city governments from the politics of everyday life, in doing so it had rendered government less responsive to the public. This lack of responsiveness was particularly acute with regard to minorities and citizens who occupied the lower rungs of the socioeconomic ladder. Much of this critique regarding the implications of reformed city government focused on how at-large elections diluted the voting power of racial minorities (Latimer 1979; Bledsoe 1986). Several studies also maintained, however, that professional city managers were unresponsive to the concerns of their minority constituents in contrast to a popularly elected mayor who could provide firm leadership and greater accountability (Banfield and Wilson 1963; Lineberry and Fowler 1967; Karnig and Welch 1980).

Our finding in this study that the presence of a city manager is positively related to black municipal employment suggests several points for consideration. A solid argument can be made for revisiting the relationship between the form of city government and minority incorporation. The seminal works typically invoked to make the case that a mayor form of government is more responsive to minorities than a council-manager are dated in some cases by

158 ★ BLACKS AND THE QUEST FOR ECONOMIC EQUALITY

forty years (Lineberry and Fowler 1967). Over the past several decades, the profession of city manager has undergone significant transformation, as have the socioeconomic and political contexts in which these and other government officials operate.

The first transformation reveals not only the greater professionalization of city managers but also flaws in the original assumptions underlying the reform movement. "What the reformers failed to realize," Ross and Levine explain, "was that no matter how expert, these specialists could never be neutral" (1996, 205). This acknowledgment of a lack of neutrality is offered less as a critique of city managers than as an explanation for the changing roles they have played. If a particular set of biases on the part of city managers, whether rooted in personal background or professional training, once worked against the economic incorporation of blacks, a different set of personal or professional biases may now work to enhance such incorporation. With regard to professional biases, the city manager has come to incorporate the values of social equity that H. George Frederickson (1990) first put forth in 1968 as the "third pillar" of public administration—joining the more staid focus on efficiency and economy.

Moreover, as professionals, city managers have dispensed with the myth of neutrality, recognizing that politics and administration cannot be viewed as separate spheres (Frederickson 1990; Nalbandian 1990; Ross and Levine 1996). In making the case that the practice of local government professionals continuously adapts to changing political environment, John Nalbandian explains, "Today, the idea of the local government professional as a formally insulated administrative expert whose policy involvement is limited to advising a governing body has given way to the role of broker and negotiator of community interests and builder of policy consensus" (1990, 654). In addition to greater engagement on the part of local professionals, the value of social equity now competes with efficiency as a primary concern of city managers (Nalbandian 1990; Ross and Levine 1996).

Our study confirms that professional city administrators are likely to be committed to norms of social equality, and therefore, they push to hire and promote more minorities. Further research can help establish the extent to which this finding reaches beyond our six Florida cities. Future investigations of the influence of the form of city government on black municipal employment must also explore how the presence and influence of a city manager may affect black employment differentially, depending on the percentage of blacks on the city council. For example, we incorporated into our black political power variable the number of black council members. Given that city managers are hired by and report to city councils, it is likely that the actions of city managers with regard to minority incorporation are influenced by the values and preferences of council members and not solely by professionalization.

Blacks, our research shows, fare better in the public sector than in the private sector, but even in the public sector, this group faces significant obstacles to greater job opportunities. While one would expect less discrimination in the municipal sector, African Americans face both blatant and covert forms of prejudice similar to that found in many businesses. Formal skill and education requirements, civil service exams, the reality and perception of competition from Hispanic and white females, and low pay deny jobs to many blacks and discourage others from applying.

Our analysis also confirms some previous research on interminority job competition, including the generally ambiguous results regarding the precise nature of the competition. In the private sector, blacks and white women covary negatively in the labor market at every level of employment. In municipal employment, however, our quantitative analysis in chapter 4 revealed little, if any, interminority job competition between blacks and white women. Despite the appearance of job competition between blacks and white women in the private sector, our analysis also indicated that white females are more likely to attract and hire blacks than are white male employers. With female and minority managers, mean black employment reached 33 percent. In businesses with white male employers, the average black job rate was only 19 percent. Further complicating the picture on interminority job competition, we also know from previous research that black men are employed at slightly higher levels than black women. In 2000 and 2001, black males with less formal education than black females in these cities had gained somewhat greater employment than African American women (Button, Moore, and Rienzo 2005).

Assessing the extent of job competition between blacks and Latinos in these six cities was difficult because the population of Latinos was small. Nevertheless, the potential for such competition was evident, particularly given that black employment is concentrated in industries where many immigrant laborers find work, namely, restaurants and retail. Irrespective of the small number of Latinos and the lack of definitive job competition, the perception of immigrants as a threat to blacks is present. In certain cases, white employers fuel the perception of competition between the two minority groups. Some employers prefer Latino workers, and one manager referred to in chapter 5 allegedly threatens African American employees with "a list of Mexicans who want their jobs." African American employees expressed concern about potential competition from Hispanics, but some also resisted adopting narrow interpretations of interminority competition that blame immigrants for economic inequalities. As one black worker noted, "The real root of the problem is not Hispanics and others, it's companies and their greed." This view resonates with previous public opinion research that found that the African Americans most likely to experience direct competition with Latino immigrants were actually the most sympathetic toward immigrants. The explanation for this lay in blacks' awareness of the potential value of Latinos as political allies (Pastor and Marcelli 2003). In this regard, and given the proof presented here of the significance of political power, we concur with the conclusion reached by Pastor and Marcelli (2003, 159): "Our main point here is that it is important that African Americans determine a position that does not unnecessarily align with the nativist impulses that emerge more from prejudice than economic rationality."

Prescriptions for Change

Education

Education in this country is often viewed as the "great equalizer," the one public institution that can and should help to bring economically disadvantaged groups into the mainstream. Desegregation of schools, particularly in the South, was a major national effort to provide African Americans with greater equality of opportunity. Most social scientists contend that desegregation has been successful, although perhaps less so than advocates hoped. Compared with those racially isolated schools, black students in desegregated settings are more likely to graduate from high school, go on to college, improve their reading and math test scores relative to white students, and have close friends and casual acquaintances of the other race (Hochschild and Scovronick 2003). By the 1990s, however, school desegregation stopped and was partly reversed in many parts of the country, including the South.

Formal education is a key factor in economic progress, specifically in employability, earnings, overall quality of life, economic mobility, and improved social status. In the six Florida cities, many black youth benefited to some degree from school desegregation. For example, more African Americans stayed in school and earned a high school diploma. Between 1980 and 2000, the average black high school graduation rate (for those age twenty-five and over) rose from 43 percent to 68 percent. This was the greatest rate increase in black education in recent times. Nevertheless, while blacks closed the gap with whites somewhat in high school graduation rates, in 2000, an average 16 percent difference remained, with whites achieving a high school diploma at a mean rate of 84 percent. Moreover, black achievement test scores in reading and math were well below those of whites in 2000 (table 7.1). For college-bound high school graduates, black students on average passed the reading exams at a 69 percent rate and the math exams at 63 percent. The comparable pass rates for white students were 87 percent (reading) and 80 percent (math). Thus, most blacks continue to face an educational disadvantage with whites in competition in the labor market.

School desegregation, however, proved to be less of a panacea for African Americans than many had hoped. As our look at this issue in these communities' racially mixed schools has indicated (chapter 2), many problems continue to plague black students. Racial conflicts, harassment of blacks, protests, and even occasional violence have occurred in many schools, particularly in Old South communities where racial animosity runs deep. Many

TABLE 7.1 High School Achievement Test Scores by Race

City	Reading (% passing)		Mathematics (% passing)	
	Whites	Blacks	Whites	Blacks
Crestview	89	81	83	75
Lake City	82	59	71	41
Quincy	—a	63	—	60
Titusville	85	73	77	80
Daytona Beach	80	56	68	46
Riviera Beach	99	84	99	77
Florida	83	56	77	55

NOTE: These achievement test results are reported for high school graduates who intend to enter, or are already enrolled in, postsecondary education programs. The tests are college entry-level placement exams and are indicators of student postsecondary school readiness. The results are reported for the largest, and in some cases the only, high school in the city. The source is Florida Department of Education, School Council Reports (2000–2001).

aNumber of students is too few to report significant results.

of these conflicts have been the result of black complaints about forms of second-generation discrimination in the schools.

A major grievance is the allegedly unfair treatment of black students by their predominantly white teachers and administrators. For example, African American youth are disproportionately assigned to lower-ability classes, pejoratively termed "educable mentally handicapped" programs in Daytona Beach. This grouping of minority students is carried out under the guise of remedial education, but it actually results in racially segregated classes and an inferior education (McClain and Stewart 2002). In addition, blacks in every city have complained about the lack of African American teachers, counselors, administrators, and athletic head coaches, claiming that white school administrators have not actively recruited minorities who would be more understanding of and helpful to black students. Another substantial criticism by blacks of schools is the much higher suspension, expulsion, and dropout rates of African Americans compared with whites. According to a black school administrator in Titusville, "Most teachers (who are white) still don't know how to relate to or deal with black students. As a result, blacks become discouraged and alienated, and get angry or drop out." Finally, white flight from schools with growing numbers of blacks has resulted in the resegregation of many schools, leaving African American students more isolated and with fewer resources.

Given the importance of education for economic success, we have several suggestions to improve schools for black youth. Most important, schools need to implement multicultural, antiracist education into the curriculum. In American history, literature, and government courses, students should learn about people who are like, and unlike, themselves. Teaching students about one another's values and traditions "enhances a sense of inclusion, creates mutual respect, promotes a common core of knowledge and shared values," and increases students' motivation to learn (Hochschild and Scovronick 2003, 170).

African American teachers and administrators are crucial to the full implementation of multicultural education, the provision of positive role models for black youth, and the understanding and support of black students that is vital to keeping them in school and interested in learning. Yet the number of African American educators is small and dwindling. To help remedy this situation, states, private foundations, and universities need to provide scholarships for black college students to become educators and administrators.

In addition, school districts, with the cooperation of black public officials and white business leaders interested in the development of human capital (Henig et al. 1999), can offer financial incentives to attract minority educators to schools with many black students and few black teachers.

School integration has clearly improved the quality of education for African American students. However, resegregation of schools is rapidly changing the education environment as middle-class whites, the courts, and most politicians perceive integration as a failure and are no longer supportive of the methods used to produce racially mixed schools. Given this new reality, we recommend magnet programs, much like those at Suncoast High School in Riviera Beach, to bring white and black students together. Where such programs are impossible, resegregated black schools must receive their fair share of funding and other resources necessary for a decent and equitable education. Only small amounts of educational funding come from Washington, D.C., so it will be essential to appeal to state legislators and courts and to local school boards for such financial resources. Equitable funding among schools is guaranteed in many state constitutions, and black elected officials at state and local levels have become powerful advocates for equal resources.

To be competitive in the job market, black students must complete high school and, of increasing importance, attain a college degree. Desegregated schools have been shown to improve the chances of black students will receive a high school diploma and attend college. As racially mixed schools decline, however, colleges and universities need to "adopt" predominantly black schools, offering tutoring, mentoring, and limited financial resources to help minority students to graduate from high school. At that point, two- and four-year colleges must actively recruit blacks and provide financial aid for economically disadvantaged minorities to achieve a higher education.

Private foundations and religious groups must assist these educational efforts. National foundations, such as Carnegie, Ford, Kellogg, MacArthur, and Pew, as well as local nonprofit organizations, control sizable resources and have been actively involved in improving education for African Americans (Orr 1996). Church and religious organizations have shown a strong interest in the moral and educational development of youth, including disadvantaged minorities. Churches are able to provide experienced volunteers, monetary resources, and advocates for youth in schools. In African American communities, the roots of the church run deep and make religious institutions the focus of political and other organized activities that often benefit black youth. This neighborhood-based spiritual approach to serving young people and others provides a degree of understanding, dedication, and determined commitment rarely found in secular programs (Schorr 1997).

Job Training

The Workforce 2000 report emphasized the importance of job training by employers and other agencies to prepare workers, especially undereducated race/ethnic minorities, for the technological transformations of the twenty-first century. Advances in communications, information management, and the shift of production from goods to services have led to a "digital revolution," which has left many low-skilled workers ill-prepared for the workplace. As a result, job training, along with further education, to enhance the work skills of minorities is a high priority. In the words of a director of a welfare-to-work program in the Deep South, "Job training is increasingly important for workers with few education credentials and little work experience and skills. Yet not many businesses provide such training."

Our study has found that blacks are particularly impaired by the lack of skills and experience when looking for work. Forty-two percent of surveyed employers claimed that black applicants are often unqualified for basic jobs or promotion. Some of these claims are likely related to the negative views some employers hold of blacks. Nevertheless, our focus groups and interviews with African Americans in the public sector reveal that blacks often lack skills related to literacy and math, computers, work readiness (how to interview, appropriate dress and grooming, punctuality), and interpersonal relations.

Several programs would be helpful in enhancing the employability of low-skilled blacks. School-to-work initiatives can provide work experience along with formal education to increase reading, math, and computer competency. Similarly, two-year (community) colleges frequently offer vocational programs and basic education at a low cost. Both public and private job training and placement programs focus on school dropouts, welfare recipients, immigrants, and displaced workers. In particular, those leaving prison need help with reentering society so that they do not return to criminal activities to support themselves. The most successful jobs programs combine skill training with work experience, job placement, and follow-up and support for workers after placement (Moss and Tilly 2001). Employers are also a growing source of training for minority employees. As businesses commit themselves to "managing diversity" in the new labor market, there is greater emphasis on building job skills and creating a comfortable work environment for blacks and other minorities. This approach typically results in improved worker morale and increased productivity (Henderson 1994).

Reducing Race and Sex Discrimination

A large number of employers in both the private and public sectors of our study claimed that they sought to achieve a more diverse workforce. However, barriers remain in the quest to realize this goal. We found that employers retain subjective biases, even blatant racism, in their hiring practices. Employers often perceive that blacks lack necessary skills and a strong work ethic. While white females are seen as superior to other minorities, employing single mothers is viewed as problematic because of family responsibilities that conflict with work-site demands.

The acquisition of the abilities and behaviors employers desire—interpersonal communication, organization, reliability, computer skills—can be learned. These competencies can be included in training programs rather than used as screening tools. Likewise, managers must be trained to decrease the tendency to stereotype workers by race and gender. Most researchers have debunked the perception that minorities, especially African Americans, do not possess an acceptable work ethic. "Among workers of color suffering the greatest disadvantages in the labor force, the work ethic is neither dramatically different than whites, nor significantly deteriorating over time," concluded Moss and Tilly (2001, 258).

Informal networking, or the good old boy system, deters equitable hiring and promotion practices. Many departments and businesses continue to rely on word of mouth, employee referrals, and walk-ins as their primary recruitment strategies. These methods tend to disadvantage minorities and women, many of whom come from socially isolated neighborhoods or families with few working adults. As more minorities are hired, however, they can establish their own social networks to pass on information about available jobs and "minority-friendly" firms and city departments. Indeed, blacks in our focus groups frequently mentioned that encouraging the development of such informal networks among African Americans is a fruitful for increasing minority hires. In addition, formal methods of recruitment, including newspaper ads and employment services, are much more likely to attract applicants with diverse backgrounds. Additional efforts include recruiting at historically black colleges, working with minority churches and neighborhood organizations, and advertising through media channels that focus on racial and ethnic minority groups.

Strictly screening job applicants (such as testing for drugs, asking about past arrests, and checking criminal records) tends to decrease the likelihood that minority candidates, especially African American males, will apply for jobs or will be hired. This practice is required by police departments but is also used by other public departments and private businesses where the need is less obvious. Respondents noted that asking about "arrests" does not mean the applicant has a criminal record, but the suspicion of criminal activity often prevents applicants from gaining employment.

Black employees in our focus groups suggested several strategies to help applicants who have a criminal record. Employer training and education should emphasize that criminal activity is typically associated with economic disadvantage and that it is important to provide economic opportunities for these individuals, especially those that have only been arrested (not convicted) or are one-time offenders. Furthermore, once employed, former criminals would benefit from counseling provided by employers, as well as from a "buddy system," or peer mentoring program, that would help to keep them focused. African Americans with a substance abuse history would also profit from these programs.

Problems continue for minorities even after they are hired. Many blacks and white women we interviewed indicated they had experienced or observed some form of discrimination on the job. For women, both white and black, sexual harassment continues to be a primary issue in a number of businesses and in police and fire departments. Black employees are often targets of racial epithets and other forms of discriminatory behavior.

Effectively implemented cultural diversity and sexual harassment training workshops can assist in decreasing discriminatory behavior. Many working Americans believe the negative racial, ethnic, and gender stereotypes depicted in the media. These beliefs often lead to discriminatory behaviors, which, if left unchecked, trigger higher levels of conflict in the workplace (Henderson 1994). Diversity-awareness training must encourage employees to talk with other workers about their perceptions and feelings in a nonjudgmental way. Training is most helpful when it incorporates videos, team-building exercises, conflict-resolution programs, experiential and role-playing exercises, and supervised dialogues (Forsythe 2004; Sessa 1992). In addition, according to a white female police captain who has dealt extensively with discrimination claims in the New South, "diversity training needs to be frequent and mandatory for everyone to be helpful. It is also important that those in leadership positions issue departmental policy statements and clear rules about 'biased behavior.' Moreover, there should be a discrimination complaint process that is accessible and fair, and has the support of the department head."

Decisions about hiring and, even more so, promotion are often based largely on evaluation of social skills, such as teamwork, customer service, personality, work ethic, and commitment. Employers tend to measure these skills subjectively, and racial bias may well influence these judgments. These skills, including performance evaluations necessary for promotion, need to be clearly stated and measured more objectively. The city of Daytona Beach uses outside evaluators for the testing process to determine promotions. Some businesses and city departments are making efforts to promote from within and to provide opportunities for their employees, particularly minorities, to gain continuing education to qualify for promotion. Efforts to provide equitable opportunities for advancement are crucial for retaining minorities in an organization.

Enforcement of Antidiscrimination Laws

Racial discrimination in employment is most pervasive in locally based smaller businesses and in municipal police and fire departments. Primarily Equal Employment Opportunity Commission (EEOC) and the Office of Federal Contract Compliance (OFCC) enforce federal antidiscrimination and affirmative action policies. These agencies conduct reviews of businesses and state and local governments to ensure that they comply with federal laws regarding nondiscrimination in the job market. These compliance reviews are a major enforcement mechanism and involve an audit of employers' demographics and personnel procedures with negotiations over suggested changes. This process is considered to be an effective oversight strategy, particularly when it targets establishments with a relatively low percentage of blacks and women, which suggests the presence of discrimination, or when it focuses on institutions in which complaints of racial or gender bias are frequent (Leonard 1990).

EEOC and OFCC are seriously understaffed and face backlogs of thousands of discrimination charges to investigate. While politics in Washington has limited the budgets of these agencies, recent changes in enforcement strategies have enabled EEOC and OFCC to become more efficient and effective. The emphasis on a mediation-based dispute resolution program has resolved alleged discrimination charges quickly and efficaciously. In addition, EEOC has developed a small business initiative that focuses outreach, education, and technical assistance on small and midsized businesses and local governments that often lack the resources to implement significant antidiscrimination measures. Enforcement agencies have also increasingly emphasized outreach and education efforts to encourage and to facilitate voluntary compliance with federal laws. This preventive approach has been productive, reaching smaller businesses, cities, and local minority interest groups such as the NAACP, with information about employers' and workers' rights and obligations under antidiscrimination policies (U.S. Equal Employment Opportunity Commission 2001; Interview, EEOC regional director, 2001).

Affirmative Action

While studies suggest that affirmative action assisted blacks in gaining public jobs initially in the 1970s and early 1980s, the reduced emphasis on and lessened enforcement of this program by the Reagan administration decreased its effectiveness locally. Most white males resist affirmative action as well. Criticisms of affirmative action are often framed in terms of its forcing municipal departments and businesses to hire and promote unqualified personnel. Closely related are concerns that affirmative action means governmental imposition of "quotas" in the employment of minorities.

For affirmative action to be successful, supportive leaders, or "champions of change" (Sessa 1992, 61), are critical. "It's important to have a leader who sets the example and makes it clear that 'these people' [blacks] are alright," stated one black female city official. This is crucial to counteract the tendency for heads of departments to "hire based on what they perceive their workers will accept." We encountered such supportive leaders in this study. They acknowledged race bias issues and reframed them in a way that reflected values of fairness and meritocracy. "We discuss the value of having minorities on the force," stated the chief of police in a New South city. "We also hire white males . . . and we will *not* hire unqualified people. I make this clear—individuals who are hired have to be qualified." The same official stated his strong commitment to diversity in terms of fair representation of minorities in the city. "The [police] force needs to mirror the community, but we can't hire or promote unqualified people. And blacks are substantially qualified generally and they are underrepresented, so they should be hired." This position of equity within meritocracy was received positively, even by many white males.

In the private sector, we found that affirmative action has given a boost to black employment and promotion. As the head of the Chamber of Commerce in a New South city explained, "Affirmative action probably has helped, though I don't like to admit it. I don't like government intervention. But 'Big Brother' has encouraged businesses to look at minorities more closely." Corporations realize that diverse workforces are important not only for marketing to racial and ethnic groups but also for attracting talent from a larger pool of qualified minorities who will increase productivity in the long run. Approximately $600 billion in consumer spending is generated annually by minorities, and more than one-third of new entrants into the workforce are persons of color (Forsythe 2004).

An important component of successful affirmative action programs is the implementation of utilization analyses of minorities and women at every level of the organization. African Americans and females are typically found to be most underrepresented in higher-level positions. When underutilization of minorities is apparent, establishing goals and timetables for hiring and promoting women and people of color are useful. Both approaches have been recommended by the EEOC, the oversight agency for affirmative action in employment (Benokraitis and Feagin 1978). In the words of the personnel director for an aerospace firm with a progressive affirmative action policy in the Deep South, "We look closely at the numbers of minorities . . . an availability analysis . . . and we set annual hiring goals. This really helps us to employ more minorities . . . without it we wouldn't make as much progress."

The recruitment of minorities, particularly African Americans, remains a core issue in the traditionally white male police and fire departments. Blacks continue to be wary of working for the police force because of its tradition of antagonism and oppression of African Americans. One successful recruitment approach of blacks is in Titusville, where city officials hold town hall meetings in black neighborhoods and solicit candidates for the police force. "We try to hire locally to keep them," stated one Titusville official. "It's important to get black police to ask blacks to apply. We have paid scholarships to send blacks to the police academy." Offering scholarships or loans to poorer minority candidates that allow them to gain certification and training in police and fire departments is helpful. Candidates receiving such financial assistance must commit to a specified number of years with the department. Providing opportunities for further training and development has also been effective in preparing employees for promotion in both the public and private sectors. This financial assistance and training are necessary not only to better prepare disadvantaged minority individuals but also for municipal departments to compete successfully with the higher-paying private sector.

The fire chief in the New South cited minority recruitment as a primary benefit of having blacks and females on staff. "We can't have all white males in the department, or blacks and women will not be interested. Females and blacks help a lot with recruitment." Another benefit of having blacks in various city departments and businesses is projecting an image of a city that is fair and equitable and provides better, culturally sensitive services. "The city is viewed as more inclusionary and cosmopolitan," stated one high-level Daytona official in explaining the effects of having minorities employed.

Mutual engagement across races also breaks down stereotypes and helps to promote better work relationships. "We can't understand blacks without having blacks on the force," claimed one police chief. "It helps us to deal with a culture we [whites] don't understand. . . . Blacks can be loud, boisterous, and in your face," he explained. "Most white officers don't understand this and can misinterpret this as a problem where there is none." Another example repeated by virtually every protective service officer is the value of having female staff for creating a better understanding of domestic violence, rape, and other "female issues."

Blacks and women in high-profile positions also provide positive role models for others of the same race or gender. Thus, unless minorities "see themselves reflected in leadership and professional roles, they are unlikely to put in the hard work and effort required to attain these positions" (Kahlenberg 1996, 38). Furthermore, minority role models demonstrate that race and sex discrimination barriers can be overcome and are not sufficient to prevent qualified women and people of color from achieving high-level positions. Role models are particularly beneficial in police and fire departments and in historically traditional businesses, where blacks and females perceive they are not wanted or cannot gain upward mobility.

Several police departments have developed programs that focus on minority youth. In Daytona Beach and Titusville, the police developed cadet or explorer clubs for teens to initiate and to recruit youth, some of them blacks, into police work. Police athletic leagues are active in most cities, with police interacting with young people, largely minority, in a nonthreatening environment. Similarly, law enforcement officers, particularly blacks and women, have carried out educational programs in the schools to modify the traditional and often negative views of the police that many youth hold. Each of these programs, when continued or repeated over a number of years, has proved to be helpful in recruiting minority (as well as other) youth.

Some larger businesses also emphasize high schools and colleges as places to educate and attract minority employees. Job fairs are common at historically black colleges, and businesses are increasingly presenting fairs at majority-minority high schools as well. Firms with federal contracts are under pressure to recruit African Americans, and many of these businesses perceive that secondary schools are an ideal place to identify promising minorities and provide them with assistance and incentives that will ultimately lead to employment. In Daytona, an electronics firm that performs work for the government offers college loans and scholarships for minority high school students who perform well in pre-engineering coursework and aptitude tests. In return for financial assistance, minority students must commit to working for the company for a specified number of years after achieving a college degree. This firm has also developed a summer internship program to attract and train students of color. While these efforts proved successful, few businesses have the necessary resources or commitment to diversity to implement such programs.

Self-Help Efforts

Employers frequently criticized blacks for their lack of discipline, motivation, and work ethic. "Black culture is just different [from whites]," claimed the human resources director of a large firm in Quincy. "Blacks are not taught to do a good job or be on time. From the cradle on up, they haven't learned to be responsible." Employers blamed these inadequacies on a variety of cultural conditions, including family breakdown, welfare dependency, ghetto neighborhoods, few role models, and lack of self-esteem. While many sociologists argue that structural conditions such as discrimination and inadequate schools are better explanations of poor job performance by blacks, cultural factors also play a role (Wilson 1996).

Black workers that we interviewed believe that lack of a proper work ethnic is a problem for many African Americans. They also suggested a number of self-help efforts to improve this condition. As stated by a hospice employee in Daytona Beach, "Black working parents must take responsibility for teaching their children that they can dream high about what they want to be, but they must work hard to achieve this." If parents need help or are unable to fulfill this responsibility, they need to enlist other possible mentors and role models for black youth and young adults.

On the job, African Americans have found it useful to develop formal or informal networks. These black support groups meet periodically to discuss work issues, barriers they confront, and ways to deal effectively with job-related problems. Daytona boasts a black police officers' association that functions effectively as a support group, a mentoring system, and a way to channel grievances to the chief of police. In addition, single black mothers need childcare assistance from family, friends, or public and business daycare so that they can continue their education or job training to improve work performance.

Labor training programs are also beneficial when they stress work-oriented values such as pride, discipline, motivation, and self-esteem. Emphasis on these values by community institutions and organizations, including churches, the NAACP, and other local groups, helps to instill positive work attitudes. For example, Quincy's Men of Action association, composed of some forty black professionals, provides mentoring, tutoring, and educational scholarships for black youth. This organization also has mobilized greater community involvement in education and crime prevention, particularly drug trafficking.

Given government's benign neglect of minority workers' issues, it has become increasingly important that blacks use their own resources to improve labor market opportunities. In his keynote address at the 2004 Democratic National Convention, President Barack Obama, then a U.S. Senator from Illinois, stated, "Go into any inner-city neighborhood and folks will tell you that government alone can't teach kids to learn. They know that parents have to parent, that children can't achieve unless we raise their expectations. . . . Making it requires diligent effort and deferred gratification" (Gates 2004, op-ed page). These sentiments are widely shared among blacks. Although structural forces limit job opportunities for African Americans, behavioral factors such as self-destructive life choices and personal habits constrict labor market advancements as well. Moreover, blacks can control their own behavioral or cultural conditions.

Other Remedies

Creative methods to address race equity issues emerged in some of our cities' public departments and private businesses. Recognizing the problems inherent in living within low-income neighborhoods, Daytona Beach invested in "incubators" to enable black businesses to become established by subsidizing rent and providing tax breaks. Black-owned businesses are likely to hire and to create a comfortable work atmosphere for African American workers. The need to affect broader change is reflected in two programs introduced in our cities. The mayor of Titusville instituted a Character First program in city government. He asserted that its intention, "to recognize you for who you are," would do more than affirmative action because it "focuses on building good character in everyone and to change the way people think [about diversity]." In Daytona Beach, Bridge Builders was established by the city's Human Relations Board to enable blacks and whites to socialize together, such as having dinner at one another's homes, thus creating greater empathy and cooperation and breaking down racial stereotypes. In addition, the Daytona city manager regularly brings together black and white leaders to talk about race issues and what can be done to improve relations.

Many minorities are locked into low-level jobs because they lack the experience, knowledge, and background necessary for promotion. Moreover, women and minorities are often excluded from on-the-job training and employer-supported education programs that may lead to promotion because of their low-skill positions that do not require additional training (Henderson 1994). To improve this situation for minority groups, several organizations in our study have implemented formal or informal mentoring programs, whereby employees can learn higher-level skills and share information and experiences. These programs are particularly helpful for minorities who may not know other blacks or females with experience in their department or business to call on for professional help. Mentors are invaluable for shepherding isolated blacks and women through the system and for providing them with the informal training necessary for promotion. Similarly, a liaison officer, responsible for addressing concerns of minority (mainly female) employees, has been instituted in the Daytona Beach police department and was cited as an especially fruitful method for addressing recruitment and retention issues. The liaison officer is a ranking minority member who is trusted by both the department leaders and other minority officers. Particular benefits reaped from this position included developing changes in policy, programs, and materials that met the diverse needs of minorities, such as the purchase of belts and holsters in sizes that fit women's bodies and institutionalizing a site where concerns and complaints regarding mistreatment could be mediated.

Initiatives that some major American corporations have instituted to build collegial interdependent relationships among racially diverse employees are found in a few of our surveyed businesses. Such programs attempt to emphasize the positive nature of difference, to increase employees' comfort level with their differences, and to "capitalize on differences as a major asset to the company's productivity" (Walker and Hanson 1992, 120). Underlying these experiences is an emphasis on nonjudgmental dialogue in which personal attitudes and beliefs can be examined, perhaps changed if desired, to increase the ability to trust and to share power with one another. In addition to awareness and skill training, programs instituted under this philosophical base include multiple cultural events (such as Black History Month) that celebrate different traditions, efficacy training (how to operate effectively within the dominant culture), and minority support groups that meet regularly to discuss issues. For example, larger businesses increasingly support caucus groups composed of minorities that serve to inform management of their needs and supply support and professional training for their members (Sessa 1992). What is the benefit to organizations that institute such programs? Several, including building a "solid reputation as one of the best places to work—not just for women and minorities—but for everyone" (Walker and Hanson 1992, 135), which in turn enables corporations to attract the best employees. Another major advantage is empowered employees who produce higher-quality work and greater innovation.

We have also found that black elected officials; local civil rights organizations, such as the NAACP and the Southern Christian Leadership Conference; and black leaders have proved useful in pressuring businesses and municipal departments to recruit, to hire, and to promote African Americans. In Lake City, for instance, the NAACP, led by a black activist, continually encourages sizable firms to employ larger numbers of blacks. The NAACP also solicits qualified African Americans to apply for available jobs, particularly in the police department and businesses that historically shunned blacks. In Daytona Beach, "black elected officials and leaders are very important to minority hiring, and the black community can be organized, even beyond churches," claimed an African American city official. "We have the NAACP, a black newspaper, a black radio station, and black grassroots organizations. Having strong leaders [from] Bethune-Cookman College helps too."

Lack of adequate and inexpensive transportation to places of employment is a problem for many black workers in each of these cities and especially acute in the rural Deep South communities that have no public transportation and where blacks often face long commutes to jobs. In Quincy, for example, there is no bus system, and many blacks have no cars, but most decent-paying employment is found twenty-five miles away in Tallahassee. Workforce development agencies and several black leaders and city officials advocate reduced-fare public transit for economically disadvantaged workers. In New South cities with municipal transportation, the recommendation is for more extensive and less expensive services. In some instances in which blacks lack transportation to their jobs, businesses themselves provide transportation.

Women, particularly black women, in the focus groups stated that childcare responsibilities are a barrier to employment. Mothers of young children are increasingly seeking paid work, partly because of welfare reform requirements. In other instances, poorer mothers are trying to gain more education or job training to attain better-paying jobs. Recommendations to help alleviate childcare constraints include greater welfare transition funding for low-income single mothers and public daycare facilities at reduced costs for poor mothers who work. Some businesses also provide inexpensive, on-site childcare for employed mothers.

A Final Word

Achieving a decent job with all the economic and social benefits that go with it is still a difficult task for many blacks living in the South. The roots of racism and discrimination run deep, and the cumulative effect over generations of both blatant and covert oppression of blacks is a barrier to equality of opportunity. Yet most whites, including those in positions of political and economic power, believe that antiblack discrimination is no longer widespread. Whites thus conclude that African Americans, like white immigrant groups before them, are now able to make progress in the economic realm if they are willing to work hard.

Despite what whites believe, the struggle for economic equality for blacks in the South is not over. Three initiatives are essential for African Americans to make greater progress in employment and the economic sphere more generally. First, government must ensure that discrimination against blacks, women, and disadvantaged groups is strictly constrained so that these groups have a greater chance to get ahead. Second, public policies need to be enacted that will provide people of color with good education, adequate shelter and food, and decent jobs for those who want them. The private sector and community organizations should also help to secure those basic benefits for the disadvantaged.

Finally, blacks have an important role to play in making economic improvements. The systemic limitations of American society are significant but do not negate the important element of human agency. The promise of a mutually reinforcing combination of government and personal actions is eloquently summarized by Jennifer Hochschild (1995, xiv): "The genius of the ideology of the American Dream is the balance it creates—between, on the one hand, what the polity must do because individuals cannot and, on the other hand, what individuals must do because the polity cannot. The polity must provide the means to success for all; individuals must pursue that success as best they can."

The recent dominance of conservative Republicans at the national level as well as in many states resulted in a growing disregard for the needs of African Americans and other disadvantaged groups. In addition, racial antagonisms so deeply embedded in southern culture continue to thwart the efforts of many blacks. Yet, with the changing demographics, progressive states, municipalities, businesses, and other private sector organizations are actively promoting opportunities for people of color. Ultimately, it is hoped, the basic goodness and sense of fair play of southerners (and other Americans) will successfully confront the American Dilemma and create a more egalitarian society.

Municipal Employment

We used multiple indicators, both qualitative and quantitative, to explore the changes in black city employment in the police, fire, recreation, and public works departments. Our assumption was that no single method of investigation seemed adequate and that a battery of research strategies, each with its own strengths and weaknesses, would provide greater confidence in our ultimate conclusions.

To chart African American jobholding from 1960 to 2000, we relied on city records, newspaper reports, and interviews with department heads every fifth year from 1975 to 2000. To assess current employment issues, we relied heavily on in-depth interviews with a sample of city employees. These interviewees were selected randomly from a list of departmental workers, with an oversampling of black employees and of workers with more than a brief tenure in the department. The authors and well-trained graduate students carried out these interviews between May 2000 and September 2001. One hundred seventy municipal employees were interviewed; table A.1 details the numbers by department, race/ethnicity, and gender. With a letter of support from the mayor and the approval of our proposed interviews from each department head, we encountered almost no resistance to this research approach. Appendix B provides the questionnaire used in these interviews.

Face-to-face, open-ended interviews with the promise of anonymity for respondents generated rich, detailed information about both public and private sector employment. The informal, conversational tone of the interviews helped to gain the involvement and interest of interviewees. The structure and tone of the interviews, which were held in a private setting, created an atmosphere in which respondents often spoke freely about sensitive issues such as race.

TABLE A.I Number of Municipal Department Employee Interviews by Race/Ethnicity and Gender

Employee Groups	Police Department	Fire Department	Recreation Department	Public Works Department
Black males	13	11	15	14
Black females	7	1	6	2
White females	9	9	11	7
White males	19	19	8	13
Hispanics	2	3	0	1
Total	50	43	40	37

Focus Groups

To gain insights on employment issues from workers in the private sector, we carried out focus groups in Lake City and Daytona Beach. Resources did not allow us to do this in every city, so we selected one Deep South and one New South community, where the black population was roughly equivalent to that in other southern cities (20–45 percent African American). In each city, we hired a labor consultant, usually from a job-training or employment agency, to recruit workers to participate in the focus groups. Participants were primarily selected from the kinds of businesses that we had surveyed, including retail stores, restaurants, industries, financial institutions, motels and hotels, and recreational establishments. Each participant received $25 in remuneration. Focus groups offer several advantages in addressing sensitive issues such as race. Unlike most surveys, focus groups allow participants to explain in detail not only what they think but also how and why they hold such beliefs. Focus groups also afford the opportunity for interaction among those involved, often creating a synergy that generates new perceptions. The result is a richness of information that adds much to our understanding of controversial topics (Krueger 1994).

Community Respondents

In addition to interview surveys of businesses and in-depth analyses of municipal departments, we interviewed citizens who were identified as well informed generally about issues of race and employment. Names of such citizens were chosen based on newspaper reports and those nominated by business and municipal leaders. Community respondents, 60 percent of whom were white and 40 percent black, averaged ten per city and consisted primarily of major business owners, high-level city officials, including council members, employment agency directors, heads of the Chamber of Commerce, the NAACP, and other black interest group leaders, and educators.

Business Employment

The questionnaire used with employers in the private sector was pretested in several businesses in a nearby community. Appendix C provides this questionnaire.

OLS regressions and path analysis were used to test predictors of black employment. On the basis of literature review in chapter 3, we developed the hypothesized path model shown below (fig. A.1).

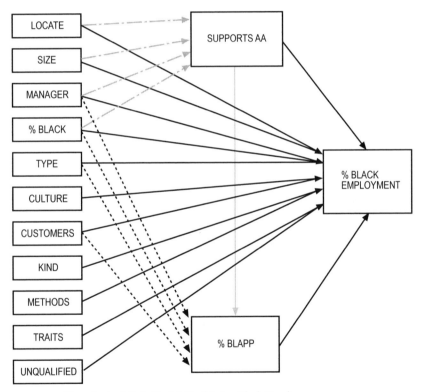

FIGURE A.1 Hypothesized Path Model: Explaining Black Employment

Interview: Department Employees

Position _____ Race/Gender _____ Date _____
City _____

1. How long have you been an employee in this department?

2. How did you first hear about this job?

3. Do you know if the department has been going out of its way the last few years to hire minorities and women? If so, why?
   • Specifically, what has the department been doing to try to employ more minorities?

4. How successful has each of these approaches been in terms of improving minority hiring?

5. In getting this job, did you receive any preferential treatment because you are a minority?

6. Have you attempted to gain promotion in this department? If so, explain. Were you successful? What did you do? etc.

7. Do you think that minorities in this department have a fair chance of promotion or not?

8. Have you received any special mentoring or training as a minority or female employee to help you perform better or to better prepare you for a chance of promotion? If so, describe it.

9. Have there been any complaints by white men, or by any others in the department, about the emphasis on hiring or promoting minorities and women? If so, describe them. If not, why not do you think?

10. Have there been any issues between you and white men in this department? If so, describe what they are and how you've attempted to deal with them.

11. Are there any other problems that you have faced as a black or female employee? If so, how have you attempted to deal with these problems?

12. Have you heard about any racial/gender issues that other minorities or women have faced here?

13. Does the department have a formal affirmative action policy or not? If so, please describe it.
    - Do you personally support such a policy or not? How might it be improved?

14. Does this department carry out any cultural diversity training or workshops for employees?

Sexual harassment workshops? If so, what kind and how often?

15. Have any black organizations, like the NAACP, or black individuals urged your department to hire or promote blacks?

Women's groups for women?

16. Have any black elected officials or black city administrators urged your department to hire or promote blacks?

Women officials or administrators for women?

17. Are there any other factors that influence the hiring or promotion of minorities in this department?

18. Do blacks and women generally socialize separately or with other department members in city-sponsored activities or programs? If so, why do you think this is?

19. Are the jobs within this department generally integrated or blacks and whites/males and females perform for different types of jobs within this organization?

20. Do blacks or women have their separate formal work associations or not?

21. Are employees in this department unionized or not? If so, does the union support the hiring and promotion of minorities or not?

22. What have been the effects, if any, of having blacks working in this organization (department)? Women?

23. Why do you think there aren't more blacks working in this department? Women?

24. What do you think this department should do in order to hire and promote more blacks? Women?

25. Within this department, do you think today there is more, less, or about the same amount of antiblack feeling as compared with four or five years ago? Explain.

    How about general feelings toward women, have they changed or not? Explain.

26. Within the department (for white interviewees), what do most whites think of blacks today? Explain.

    (For black interviewees) What do most blacks think of whites today? Explain.

Appendix C

Questionnaire for Business Owners/ Managers

1. How long has this business been here? _____ As an employer in this city, what have been your major problems?

2. How many full-time employees does your business presently have? _____

   Has this number increased, decreased, or remained the same over the past five years or so? _____ If changed, how much?

3. How do you usually go about getting new workers?

4. How do you choose new employees from among applicants? What characteristics do you usually regard as most important?

   How do you usually go about promoting employees?

5. Do you get any black applicants for jobs here? _____ any women? _____

   If so, what would you estimate the proportion of job applicants who are black in the last year? _____ what is your estimate of proportion of women? _____

6. What is the **percentage** (*#/total # in that level of position*) of blacks among your employees:

   In professional and managerial positions? _____

   In skilled or semiskilled positions? _____

   In unskilled or menial positions? _____

7. **a. What is the percentage of females among your employees:**

In professional and managerial positions? _____

In skilled or semiskilled positions? _____

In unskilled or menial positions? _____

b. What is the percent of black females among your employees:1

in professional and managerial positions? _____

in skilled or semiskilled positions? _____

in unskilled or menial positions? _____

c. What is the percent of Hispanics (male and female):

in professional and managerial positions? _____

in skilled or semiskilled positions? _____

in unskilled or menial positions? _____

8. Has the percentage of black employees at these various levels **changed** or not in the past five years? _____

If so, how much approximately at each level? _____

Why?

9. Has the percentage of female employees at these various levels **changed** or not in the past five years? _____

If so, how much approximately at each level? _____

Why? _____

10. Is there a higher turnover in this business among white or black employees? _____

How high is the annual turnover, typically, for blacks? _____

Do most of these black employees quit, get fired, or retire?

_____

Is there a higher turnover in this business among male or female employees? _____

How high is the annual turnover, typically, for women?

Do most of these female employees quit, get fired, or retire?

11. Some companies have been going out of their way lately to hire and promote more blacks. Is this true or not of this business? Why or why not? If yes, what **specifically** do you do?

12. Have you been going out of your way lately to hire or promote more women or not? Why or why not? If yes, what do you do **specifically**?

13. Some businesses that have tried to hire blacks have given up because their workers objected so strongly to working with or being supervised by blacks. How have your employees reacted to this here? Explain.

How about for women?

14. Other businesses that have tried to hire or promote blacks have found that there are very few qualified blacks. Has this been true here or not?

How about for women?

15. Do you have a formal affirmative action policy or plan for this business? _____

If so, how long have you had such a policy? _____

Why do you have such a policy?

Describe the policy/plan:

16. Do you personally think affirmative action as a policy to give preferences to blacks and females for hiring and promotions should be supported or not? Why or why not?

17. Does your business carry out any cultural diversity training or workshops for employees? _____ Sexual harassment workshops? _____

If so, are they required? _____

How often?

Describe these workshops:

18. Have any local groups, like the NAACP or women's organizations, or individuals, including minority public officials, urged you to hire or promote blacks? or women? Explain.

19. Why do you think there aren't more blacks working in this business? Women?

20. What do you think this business should do to hire and promote more blacks? Women?

21. What have been the effects, if any, of having black employees in this business?

    Women?

22. (For businesses with customers, i.e., restaurants, motels) About what percent of your customers are blacks? _____ Women? _____

23. Some managers or owners of businesses complain that blacks are more likely to be involved in shoplifting and vandalism than whites, and therefore it is necessary to keep a watchful eye on them when they are in the establishment. Do you agree or disagree with this statement? (strongly agree/disagree?) Why?

24. Among businesspeople you know in this city,

    (For white interviewees) What do most whites think of blacks today? Explain.

    (For black interviewees) What do most blacks think of whites today? Explain.

References

Alozie, Nicholas O., and Enrique J. Ramirez. 1999. "'A Piece of the Pie' and More: Competition and Hispanic Employment on Urban Police Forces." *Urban Affairs Review* 34 (3): 456–75.

Aoki, Elizabeth. 1991. "Riviera's Broadway Fights for Economic Survival." *Palm Beach Post,* May 12.

Associated Press. 1999. "Ex-Principal Denied Teaching Job." *Gainesville Sun,* January 13.

Bean, Frank, B. Lindsay Lowell, and Lowell Taylor. 1988. "Undocumented Mexican Immigrants and the Earnings of Other Workers in the United States." *Demography* 25 (1): 35–52.

Beeler, Leslie. 1994a. "Lack of Minority Hiring Frustrates Group." *Lake City Reporter,* December 2.

———. 1994b. "School Board Adopts Policy on the Hiring of Minorities." *Lake City Reporter,* December 14.

Benokraitis, Nijole V., and Joe R. Feagin. 1978. *Affirmative Action and Equal Opportunity: Action, Inaction, Reaction.* Boulder, Colo.: Westview Press.

Bernstein, Aaron. 2001. "Racism in the Workplace." *Business Week,* July 30, 64–68.

Black, Earl, and Merle Black. 1987. *Politics and Society in the South.* Cambridge: Harvard University Press.

Bledsoe, Timothy. 1986. "A Research Note on the Impact of District/At-Large Elections on Black Political Efficacy." *Urban Affairs Quarterly* 22 (1): 166–74.

Bobo, Lawrence D. 1998. "Race, Interests, and Belief About Affirmative Action." *American Behavioral Scientist* 41 (7): 985–1003.

———. 2001a. "Race, Interests, and Beliefs About Affirmative Action: Unanswered Questions and New Directions." In *Color Lines: Affirmative Action, Immigration, and Civil Rights Options for America,* ed. John David Skrentny. Chicago: University of Chicago Press.

———. 2001b. "Racial Attitudes and Relations at the Close of the Twentieth Century." In *America Becoming: Racial Trends and Their Consequences.* Vol. 1, ed. Neil J. Smelser, William Julius Wilson, and Faith Mitchell. Washington, D.C.: National Academies Press.

Bobo, Lawrence, James R. Kluegel, and Ryan A. Smith. 1997. "Laissez-faire Racism: The Crystallization of a 'Kinder, Gentler' Anti-black Ideology." In *Racial Attitudes in the 1990s: Continuity and Change,* ed. Steven A. Tuch and Jack K. Martin. Westport, Conn.: Praeger.

Borjas, George. 1990. *Friends or Strangers.* New York: Basic.

———. 1998. "Do Blacks Gain or Lose from Immigration?" In *Help or Hindrance? The Economic Implications of Immigration for African Americans,* ed. Daniel Hamermesh and Frank Bean. New York: Russell Sage Foundation.

Bozzo, John. 1998. "Panel Set to Recommend BCR Plan." *Daytona Beach News-Journal,* June 29.

———. 2000. "Human Relations Council Launched." *Daytona Beach News-Journal,* September 11.

Bracey, Laurin. 1982. "Two Incumbents Are Ousted; Three Runoffs Set October 5th." *Gadsden County Times,* October 9.

Briggs, Vernon, and Stephen Moore. 1997. "Still an Open Door: U.S. Immigration Policy and the American Economy." In *Immigration: Debating the Issues,* ed. Nicholas Capaldi. New York: Prometheus Books.

Brown, Charles, James Hamilton, and James Medoff. 1990. *Employers Large and Small.* Cambridge: Harvard University Press.

Brown, Rupert. 1995. *Prejudice: Its Social Psychology.* Oxford: Basil Blackwell.

Brownfield, Cindi. 2002. "BCR Settlement Funds Make Their Way to B-CC." *Daytona Beach News-Journal,* March 14.

Browning, Rufus, Dale Marshall, and David Tabb. 1984. *Protest Is Not Enough: The Struggle of Blacks and Hispanics for Equality in Urban Politics.* Berkeley and Los Angeles: University of California Press.

———. 1997. "Mobilization, Incorporation, and Policy in Ten California Cities." In *Racial Politics in American Cities,* ed. Rufus P. Browning, Dale R. Marshall, and David H. Tabb. New York: Longman.

Buccino, Neal. 1998a. "Ex-firefighter Loses Discrimination Suit." *Florida Daily News,* April 30.

———. 1998b. "Ex-firefighter's Lawsuit Against Crestview Begins." *Florida Daily News,* April 28.

Button, James W. 1989. *Blacks and Social Change: Impact of the Civil Rights Movement in Southern Communities.* Princeton: Princeton University Press.

Button, James, and Matthew Corrigan. 1997. "Blacks and the Continuing Quest for Equal Employment in Six Florida Communities." *Journal of the Community Development Society* 28:84–99.

Button, James, Kelli Moore, and Barbara Rienzo. 2005. "Supporting Diversity Works: African American Male and Female Employment in Six Florida Cities" (unpublished manuscript).

Button, James, Scott Richards, and Evelyn Bethune. 1998. A Look at the Second Generation of Black Elected Officials in Florida. *State and Local Government Review* 30 (3): 181–89.

Callahan, Joe. 1992a. "Drive-By Gunfire Scares Columbia Residents." *Gainesville Sun,* December 9.

———. 1992b. "Rumors Create Tension at Middle School." *Lake City Record,* April 7.

Cameron, Charles, David Epstein, and Sharyn O'Holloran. 1996. "Do Majority-Minority Districts Maximize Substantive Black Representation in Congress?" *American Political Science Review* 90:794–812.

Card, David. 1990. "The Impact of the Mariel Boatlift on the Miami Labor Market," *Industrial and Labor Relations Review* 43 (2): 245–57.

Carey, Sarah. 1986. "Board Plans Forum for Parents." *Gadsden County Times,* September 25.

———. 1987a. "Class-Action Suit over Jail Conditions Refiled." *Gadsden County Times,* July 9.

———. 1987b. "School Board Debates Meaning of Test-Taking Statistics." *Gadsden County Times,* October 29.

———. 1988. "Appeals Court Reduces Damages in Hospital Discrimination Suit." *Gadsden County Times,* January 28.

Carmines, Edward, and James Stimson. 1989. *Issue Evolution: Race and Transformation of American Politics.* Princeton: Princeton University Press.

Carter, John. 1992. "Voters OK Single-Member District Plan." *Daytona Beach News-Journal,* November 5.

Cayer, N. Joseph, and Lee Sigelman. 1980. "Minorities and Women in State and Local Government." *Public Administration Review* 40:433–50.

Cherry, Robert. 2001. *Who Gets the Good Jobs? Combating Race and Gender Disparities.* New Brunswick: Rutgers University Press.

Cherry, Robert, and William M. Rodgers III, eds. 2000. *Prosperity for All? The Economic Boom and African Americans.* New York: Russell Sage Foundation.

City of Daytona Beach. 1981. *AA Report,* June 16.

City of Lake City. 2002. *AA Report.*

Clifton, Alexandra Navarro. 1999a. "Mainlanders Wilson, Wade Win." *Palm Beach Post,* March 24.

———. 1999b. "Much-Sued Riviera Beach Sees Insurance Costs Double." *Palm Beach Post,* September 25.

———. 2000. "Riviera Has Plan for Own Cityplace." *Palm Beach Post,* September 28.

Colby, David C. 1985. "Black Power, White Resistance, and Public Policy: Political Power and Poverty Program Grants in Mississippi." *Journal of Politics* 47:579–95.

Cooper, William. 2000. "Riviera Mayor Harboring Big Dreams for City." *Palm Beach Post,* March 1.

Croucher, Sheila. 1997. *Imagining Miami: Ethnic Politics in a Postmodern World.* Charlottesville: University Press of Virginia.

Cruz, Robert. 1991. "The Industry Composition of Production and the Distribution of Income by Race and Ethnicity in Miami." Paper presented at the Joint Meeting of the Association for the Study of the Cuban Economy and the National Association of Cuban American Educators, August 16, Miami, Fla.

Darity, William A., and Patrick L. Mason. 1998. "Evidence on Discrimination in Employment: Codes of Color, Codes of Gender." *Journal of Economic Perspectives* 12 (2): 63–90.

Davidson, Gary. 1989. "County Now Hiring More Firms Run by Women, Minorities." *Daytona Beach News-Journal,* March 7.

Daytona Beach Evening News. 1983. "New Tri-County Jobs Program to Start: County Council OKs Required Phaseout of CETA Program." September 15.

Daytona Beach News and Journal. 1987. "Suggs Is Chosen as Mainland Coach." April 29.

Decker, Susan. 1996. "Police Minority Hiring on Rise." *Florida Today,* April 17.

Deger, Renee. 1991. "Residents, Police Unite to Fight Crime." *Daytona Beach News-Journal,* October 23.

Desiderio, Bob. 1978. "Minority Hiring Record Shows Some Improvement." *Daytona Beach News-Journal,* February 13.

Desmon, Stephanie. 1998a. "Students Rejected to Save Dollars." *Palm Beach Post,* July 20.

———. 1998b. "Where the Magnet Experiment Worked." *Palm Beach Post,* July 19.

Doig, Stephen. 1977. "Minority Hiring Practices Lag Behind Federal Standards." *Daytona Beach News-Journal,* April 11.

Donnelly, Francis X. 1994. "Racial Disparities Emerge from Tough Discipline." *Florida Today,* April 19.

Douthat, Bill, and Dale Fuchs. 1993. "Lawmakers Reject Singer Island Secession Plea." *Palm Beach Post,* November 19.

DuPont, Alice. 1986. "Union Pulls out of Election." *Gadsden County Times,* June 26.

———. 1991. "Quincy Commissioners Discuss Police Department." *Gadsden County Times,* April 26.

———. 1996a. "Farmworkers Arrested During Protest." *Gadsden County Times,* March 21.

———. 1996b. "Farmworkers Demonstrate Wednesday to Form Union." *Gadsden County Times,* March 14.

———. 1996c. "Farmworkers to Be Reinstated." *Gadsden County Times,* September 19.

———. 1998. "City Attorney Fired." *Gadsden County Times,* May 14.

———. 2000. "City, Former Offer Settle." *Gadsden County Times,* August 10.

———. 2002. "Police Chief Moore Resigns." *Gadsden County Times,* August 22.

DuPont-Smith, Alice. 1987a. "Crime and Crack Use in Quincy Are Both on Increase, Show Definite Relationship." *Gadsden County Times,* February 5.

———. 1987b. "Crime Permeates the Gadsden Arms Apartment Complex." *Gadsden County Times,* March 19.

———. 1987c. "25 Workers Walk out at Higdon Grocery Co., Say They Were Unjustly Fired, but Company Officials Disagree." *Gadsden County Times,* March 26.

———. 1988a. "City Department Heads Have Both Triumphs and Troubles." *Gadsden County Times,* July 28.

———. 1988b. "City Manager Fired on 3–2 Commission Vote." *Gadsden County Times,* May 26.

———. 1990. "Two Teachers Assaulted by Students." *Gadsden County Times,* June 7.

———. 1991. "Rotary Club Honors Special Unit with Service Above Self Award." *Gadsden County Times,* April 11.

———. 1993a. "County Manager Fired." *Gadsden County Times,* April 8.

———. 1993b. "Mystery of Dropout Statistics Still Unclear." *Gadsden County Times,* January 7.

Dye, Thomas, and James Renick. 1981. "Political Power and City Jobs: Determinants of Minority Employment." *Social Science Quarterly* 62:475–86.

Eberhardt, Jennifer L., and Susan T. Fiske. 1994. "Affirmative Action in Theory and Practice: Issues of Power, Ambiguity, and Gender Versus Race," *Basic and Applied Social Psychology* 15 (1–2): 201–20.

Ehrenreich, Barbara. 2001. *Nickel and Dimed: On (Not) Getting by in America.* New York: Henry Holt.

Eisinger, Peter K. 1980. *The Politics of Displacement.* New York: Academic Press.

———. 1982. "Black Employment in Municipal Jobs: The Impact of Black Political Power." *American Political Science Review* 76: 380–92.

Engstrom, Richard L., and Michael D. McDonald. 1981. "The Election of Blacks to City Councils." *American Political Science Review* 75:344–54.

Ensley, Gerald. 1998a. "Crash in 1995 Led to Quincy's Tensions." *Tallahassee Democrat,* June 28.

———. 1998b. "Hirings, Firings Unsettle Quincy." *Tallahassee Democrat,* June 10.

Erlich, Reese. 1994. "Study Revives Immigration Debate over Impact on Jobs," *Christian Science Monitor,* May 2, p. 8.

Espenshade, Thomas J., and Tracy A. Goodis. 1985. *Recent Immigrants to Los Angeles: Characteristics and Labor Market Impacts.* Washington, D.C.: Urban Institute Press.

Evans, Chris. 1994. "A Black Voice in Titusville: Publication Blasts Leaders, Cites Unfairness." *Florida Today,* June 6.

———. 1995. "Local NAACP Seeks Fresh Start." *Florida Today,* February 18.

Fainstein, Norman, and Susan Fainstein. 1996. "Urban Regimes and Black Citizens: The Economic and Social Impacts of Black Political Incorporation in U.S. Cities." *International Journal of Urban and Regional Research* 20 (1): 22–37.

Falcon, Angelo. 1988. "Black and Latino Politics in New York City." In *Latinos in the Political System,* ed. F. Chris Garcia. Notre Dame: Notre Dame University Press.

Farley, Reynolds, and Walter R. Allen. 1989. *The Color Line and the Quality of Life in America.* New York: Oxford University Press.

Feagin, Joe, and Claire B. Feagin. 2003. *Racial and Ethnic Relations.* Upper Saddle River, N.J.: Prentice Hall.

Firebaugh, Glenn, and Kenneth Davis. 1988. "Trends in Antiblack Prejudice: 1972–1984 Region and Cohort Effects." *American Journal of Sociology* 94:251–72.

Fix, Michael, and Raymond J. Struyk, eds. 1993. *Clear and Convincing Evidence: Measurement of Discrimination in America.* Washington, D.C.: Urban Institute Press.

Florida Department of Education. 2001. *School Advisory Council Reports,* 2000–2001. Tallahassee, Fla.: Florida Department of Education.

Florida Today. 2000. "Brevard Needs More Diversity in Elected Officials." May 28.

Forst, Lee. 1995. "Black Leaders Call for Community Action." *Florida Daily News,* February 13.

Forsythe, Jason. 2004. "Winning with Diversity." Special Advertising Supplement. *New York Times Magazine,* September 19.

Fox, John. 1997. *Applied Regression Analysis, Linear Models, and Related Methods.* Thousand Oaks, Calif.: Sage.

Frederick, Henry. 1999. "Visitor Dies of Gunshot Wound to Head." *Daytona Beach News-Journal,* April 12.

Frederickson, H. George. 1990. "Public Administration and Social Equity." *Public Administration Review* 50 (2): 228–37.

Fuchs, Dale. 1993. "Police Still Lag in Racial Diversity: The Percentage of Minority Police Officers Is up, but It's Still Below the Population." *Palm Beach Post,* July 18.

———. 1994. "Singer Island Secession Bid Reflects Clash of Cultures." *Palm Beach Post,* July 18.

Furry, Joe. 1991. "Cross Burning Tragic for Long." *Okaloosa News Journal,* September 18.

———. 1992. "Crestview High Officials Suspend Nine Students After Friday Brawl." *Okaloosa News Journal,* March 25.

Gadsden County Times. 1970. "Violence Flares in City Saturday as Result of Negro Being Wounded." October 15.

———. 1975. "Blacks Win Two of Five Posts, Another in Run-Off." March 27.

———. 1977. "City Commissioners Leon Weaver and Melvin Barber, Jr. Sworn into Office." April 21.

Gainesville Iguana. 1997. "Unionists from Around the South March with Quincy Mushroom Workers." July/August.

Gates, Henry Louis. 2004. "Breaking the Silence." *New York Times,* August 1.

Gienger, Viola. 1990a. "Few Blacks Enrolled in Magnet Programs: NAACP Fears New Form of Segregation." *Palm Beach Post,* October 12.

———. 1990b. "Ministers Will Mediate Differences Between Blacks, School District." *Palm Beach Post,* July 11.

————. 1994. "Magnet Plan OK'd with Reservations." *Palm Beach Post,* December 13.

Gilsenan, Patrick. 1996. "Confederate Flag Torn by Modern Flap." *Florida Daily News,* March 31.

Gleckman, Howard, Tim Smart, Paula Dwyer, Troy Segal, and Joseph Weber. 1991. "The 'Other Minorities' Demand Their Due." *Business Week,* July 8, 50–63.

Glisch, J. 2000. "Comments Force Area to Reevaluate Race Relations." *Florida Today,* March 23.

Golden, Pam. 1996a. "Former Firefighter Suing Crestview." *Florida Daily News,* July 24.

————. 1996b. "Group Claims Police Abuses." *Florida Daily News,* January 23.

Goldfield, David R. 1990. *Black, White, and Southern: Race Relations and Southern Culture 1940 to the Present.* Baton Rouge: Louisiana State University Press.

Graham, Hugh Davis. 1990. *The Civil Rights Era.* New York: Oxford University Press.

Grimison, Matt. 2002. "Business Practices to Be Observed." *Daytona Beach News-Journal,* April 11.

Hall, Grace, and Alan Saltzstein. 1975. "Equal Employment Opportunity for Minorities in Municipal Government." *Public Personnel Management* 4:386–93.

————. 1977. "Equal Employment Opportunity for Minorities in Municipal Government." *Social Science Quarterly* 57:864–72.

Harper, Jack. 1991a. "Falling Test Scores Have Officials Still Looking for Answers." *Gadsden County Times,* May 9.

————. 1991b. "School Violence Upsets Board Member." *Gadsden County Times,* January 24.

Hawthorne, Michael. 1990. "Officer Suspended for Using Excess Force." *Daytona Beach News-Journal,* November 16.

————. 1991. "Blacks Still Fight to Overcome: Dream of Full Equality Unfulfilled." *Daytona Beach News-Journal,* October 20.

Heckman, James, and Brook Payner. 1989. "Determining the Impact of Federal Antidiscrimination Policy on the Economic Status of Blacks." *American Economic Review* 65:158–68.

Heinz, Catia. 1995. "More New Jobs Are Coming to the Crestview Area." *Crestview News Leader,* September 27.

Henderson, George. 1994. *Cultural Diversity in the Workplace: Issues and Strategies.* Westport, Conn.: Quorum Books.

Henig, Jeffrey R., Richard C. Hula, Marion Orr, and Desiree S. Pedescleaux. 1999. *The Color of School Reform: Race, Politics, and the Challenge of Urban Education.* Princeton: Princeton University Press.

Hibbs, Douglas A. 1974. "Problems of Statistical Estimation and Causal Inference in Time Series Regression Models." *Sociological Methodology* 5:252–308.

Hill, William D. A. 1990. "Black Leaders Charge Actual Culprits in Detainee's Beating Going Unpunished." *Daytona Beach News and Journal,* November 16.

Hochschild, Jennifer L. 1995. *Facing up to the American Dream: Race, Class, and the Soul of the Nation.* Princeton: Princeton University Press.

————. 1998. "Affirmative Action as Culture War." In *Race and Representation: Affirmative Action,* ed. Robert Post and Michael Rogin. New York: Zone Books.

————. 2004. "Three Puzzles in Search of an Answer from Political Scientists (with Apologies to Pirandello)." *PS: Political Science and Politics* 37 (2): 225–29.

Hochschild, Jennifer, and Nathan Scovronick. 2003. *The American Dream and the Public Schools.* New York: Oxford University Press.

Hogan, Dennis P., and David L. Feathermann. 1977. "Racial Stratification and Socio-economic Change in the American North and South." *American Journal of Sociology* 83:100–126.

Holland, Elizabethe. 1992. "Klan Stages Rally in Milligan." *Florida Daily News,* March 29.

Holland, John. 1994. "Rally Planners Say Minorities Overlooked for Volusia Posts." *Daytona Beach News-Journal,* October 19.

Holloway, Lynette. 1989a. "McGann Returned to Riviera Council At-Large Seat Gives Panel a White Majority." *Palm Beach Post,* April 19.

———. 1989b. "Race Key Issue in Riviera Council Majority May See Change." *Palm Beach Post,* April 18.

———. 1990. "Ministers Give Mills Year to Improve Schools for Blacks." *Palm Beach Post,* July 12.

———. 1992. "Deadline for Desegregation Strategy to Limit Busing Is Going Nowhere Fast." *Palm Beach Post,* April 19.

Holzer, Harry J. 1996. *What Employers Want: Job Prospects for Less-Educated Workers.* New York: Russell Sage Foundation.

———. 1998. "Employer Hiring Decisions and Antidiscrimination Policy." In *Generating Jobs: How to Increase Demand for Less-Skilled Workers,* ed. Richard Freeman and Peter Gottschalk. New York: Russell Sage Foundation.

Holzer, Harry J., and David Newmark. 2000. "What Does Affirmative Action Do?" *Industrial and Labor Relations Review* 53:240–71.

Holzer, Harry J., and Paul Offner. 2004. "The Puzzle of Black Male Unemployment." *The Public Interest* 154:74–84.

Huckfeldt, Robert, and Carol Kohfeld. 1989. *Race and the Decline of Class in American Politics.* Chicago: University of Illinois Press.

Huffman, Matt L. 1999. "Who's in Charge? Organizational Influences on Women's Representation in Managerial Positions." *Social Science Quarterly* 80:738–56.

Ives, Millard K. 1999a. "2 Local Women Part of Lawsuit: Cracker Barrel Accused of Racism." *Lake City Reporter,* October 7.

———. 1999b. "Supervisor: Complaint Led to Problems at VA." *Lake City Reporter,* August 27.

Jackson, Susan E., and Associates. 1992. *Diversity in the Workplace: Human Resources Initiatives.* New York: Guilford Press.

Jencks, Christopher, and Susan Mayer. 1990. "Residential Segregation, Job Proximity, and Black Job Opportunities." In *Inner City Poverty in the United States,* ed. Laurence E. Lind and Michael McGeary. Washington, D.C.: National Academies Press.

Justice, Molly. 1999a. "Feds Sue Adam's Mark Chain Complaints During Black College Reunion Help Spark Justice Department Probe of Hotels." *Daytona Beach News-Journal,* December 17.

———. 1999b. "Judge Strikes Down BCR Traffic Plan." *Daytona Beach News-Journal,* April 9.

———. 1999c. "Suit Claims Adam's Mark Discriminated During BCR Guests: Higher Room Rates, Fewer Amenities." *Daytona Beach News-Journal,* May 21.

Kahlenberg, Richard D. 1996. *The Remedy: Class, Race, and Affirmative Action.* New York: Basic Books.

Karnig, Albert K., and Susan Welch. 1980. *Black Representation and Urban Policy.* Chicago: University of Chicago Press.

Keech, William R. 1968. *The Impact of Negro Voting.* Chicago: Rand McNally.

Kellough, James, and Susan A. Kay. 1986. "Affirmative Action in the Federal Bureaucracy: An Impact Assessment." *Review of Public Personnel Administration* 6 (2): 1–13.

Kelly, Erin, and Frank Dobbin. 2001. "How Affirmative Action Became Diversity Management: Employer Response to Antidiscrimination Law, 1961–1996." In *Color Lines: Affirmative Action, Immigration, and Civil Rights Options for America,* ed. John D. Skrentny. Chicago: University of Chicago Press.

Kenon, Ruben. 1992. "Crisis of Confidence." *Lake City Reporter,* July 20.

Kerr, Brinck, and Kenneth Mladenka. 1994. "Does Politics Matter? A Time-Series Analysis of Minority Employment Patterns." *American Journal of Political Science* 38 (4): 918–43.

Key, V. O. 1949. *Southern Politics.* New York: Vintage.

King, Martin Luther, Jr. 1976. *Where Do We Go from Here: Chaos or Community?* New York: Bantam.

Kirschenman, Joleen, and Kathryn M. Neckerman. 1991. "'We'd Love to Hire Them, But . . .': The Meaning of Race for Employers." In *The Urban Underclass,* ed. Christopher Jencks and Paul E. Peterson. Washington, D.C.: Brookings Institution Press.

Klinkner, Philip A., and Rogers M. Smith. 1999. *The Unsteady March: The Rise and Decline of Racial Equality in America.* Chicago: University of Chicago Press.

Kluegel, James R., and Eliot R. Smith. 1986. *Beliefs About Inequality: Americans' Views of What Is and What Ought to Be.* New York: Aldine.

Krueger, Richard A. 1994. *Focus Groups: A Practical Guide for Applied Research.* Thousand Oaks, Calif.: Sage.

Krysan, Maria. 2000. "Prejudice, Politics, and Public Opinion: Understanding the Sources of Racial Policy Attitudes." *Annual Review of Sociology* 26:135–68.

Kuhn, Ed. 1990. "NAACP Files Complaint over Hiring." *Lake City Reporter,* June 26.

———. 1991. "Baumgardner Trying to Change Klan Image." *Lake City Reporter,* November 11.

———. 1994. "County Work Detoured by KKK Cross." *Lake City Reporter,* May 25.

Kuklinski, James H., and Michael D. Cobb. 1997. "Racial Attitudes and the 'New South.'" *Journal of Politics* 59 (2): 323–49.

Kweit, Robert, and Mary G. Kweit. 1999. *People and Politics in Urban America.* New York: Garland.

Latimer, Margaret. 1979. "Black Political Representation in Southern Cities." *Urban Affairs Quarterly* 15 (1): 65–86.

Lee, Jennifer. 1998. "Cultural Brokers: Race-Based Hiring in Inner-City Neighborhoods." *American Behavioral Scientist* 41:927–37.

Leigh, Wilhelmina A. 1998. "Into the Millennium (1994–2005): Employment Patterns and Likely Opportunities for Blacks and Whites." In *Job Creation: Prospects and Strategies,* ed. Wilhelmina A. Leigh and Margaret C. Simms. Washington, D.C.: Joint Center for Political and Economic Studies.

Lennard, James R. 1994. "Hiring Practices Aired." *Crestview News Leader,* April 20.

Leonard, Jonathan S. 1984. "The Impact of Affirmative Action on Employment." *Journal of Labor Economics* 2:439–63.

———. 1990. "The Impact of Affirmative Action Regulation and Equal Employment Law on Black Employment," *Journal of Economic Perspectives* 4 (4): 47–63.

Lewis, William G. 1989. "Toward Representative Bureaucracy: Blacks in City Police Organizations, 1975–1985." *Public Administration Review* (May/June): 257–68.

Lineberry, Robert, and Edmond Fowler. 1967. "Reformism and Public Politics in American Cities." *American Political Science Review* 61:701–16.

Lynch, Frederick R. 1997. *The Diversity Machine: The Drive to Change the "White Male Workplace."* New York: Free Press.

MacLeod, Jay. 1995. *Ain't No Makin' It: Aspirations and Attainment in a Low-Income Neighborhood.* Boulder, Colo.: Westview Press.

Manolatos, Tony. 2001. "Racial Lines Still Divide Brevard." *Florida Today,* April 7.

Martin, Doug. 1995. "Firing of Erie Wilson, Dropping Basketball Top Stories at LCCC." *Lake City Reporter,* December 29.

Martin, Susan E. 1991. "The Effectiveness of Affirmative Action: The Case of Women in Policing." *Justice Quarterly* 8:489–504.

Martinez, Ray. 1994. "Crestview Riot Leaves Six Injured." *Florida Daily News,* August 12.

Matthews, Donald R., and James W. Prothro. 1966. *Negroes and New Southern Politics.* New York: Harcourt, Brace and World.

McAleean, John. 1995. "Roots of Racial Division Run Deep." *Florida Today,* October 5.

McCabe, Barbara C., and Christopher Stream. 2000. "Diversity by the Numbers: Changes in State and Local Workforces, 1980–1995." *Public Personnel Management* 29:93–106.

McClain, Paula D. 1993. "The Changing Dynamics of Urban Politics: Blacks and Hispanic Municipal Employment—Is There Competition?" *Journal of Politics* 55 (2): 399–414.

McClain, Paula D., and Albert Karnig. 1990. "Black and Hispanic Socioeconomic and Political Competition." *American Political Science Review* 84 (2): 535–45.

McClain, Paula D., and Joseph Stewart Jr. 2002. *"Can We All Get Along?" Racial and Ethnic Minorities in American Politics.* Boulder, Colo.: Westview Press.

McClain, Paula D., and Steven C. Tauber. 1998. "Black and Latino Socioeconomic and Political Competition: Has a Decade Made a Difference?" *American Politics Quarterly* 26:237–52.

McConahay, John B. 1986. "Modern Racism, Ambivalence, and the Modern Racism Scale." In *Prejudice, Discrimination, and Racism,* ed. John F. Dovidio and Samuel L. Gaertner. New York: Academic Press.

McGlen, Nancy E., and Karen O'Connor. 1998. *Women, Politics, and American Society.* New York: Longman.

Meyer, Marilyn. 2000. "Titusville High Reopens After Threat of Violence." *Florida Today,* February 15.

Miller, Mary Lenn. 1978. "Implementation of Federal Policy at the Local Level: A Study of Affirmative Action in Municipal Governments." Presented at the annual meeting of the Southwestern Political Science Association, Houston, Tex.

Mladenka, Kenneth R. 1989. "Blacks and Hispanics in Urban Politics." *American Political Science Review* 83 (1): 165–91.

Mobley, M., and T. Payne. 1992. "Backlash! The Challenge to Diversity Training." *Training and Development* 46:45–52.

Moore, David. 1993. "City Approves Minority Hiring Plan." *Lake City Reporter,* May 18.

Moore, Steve. 1990. "Jackie Robinson: A Hero Honored." *Daytona Beach News-Journal,* September 16.

Moss, Philip, and Chris Tilly. 1996. "'Soft' Skills and Race: An Investigation of Black Men's Employment Problems." *Work and Occupations* 23 (3): 252–76.

———. 2001. *Stories Employers Tell: Race, Skill, and Hiring in America.* New York: Russell Sage Foundation.

Muller, Thomas. 1993. *Immigrants and the American City.* New York: New York University Press.

Muth, R. F. 1971. "Migration: Chicken or Egg?" *Southern Economic Journal* 37 (1): 295–306.

Myrdal, Gunnar. 1944. *An American Dilemma: The Negro Problem and Modern Democracy.* New York: Pantheon.

Nalbandian, John. 1990. "Tenets of Contemporary Professionalism in Local Government." *Public Administration Review* 50 (6):654–62.

———. 1991. *Professionalism in Local Government: Transformations in the Roles, Responsibilities, and Values of City Managers.* San Francisco: Jossey-Bass.

National Urban League. 2002. *The State of Black America, 2002.* Washington, D.C.: National Urban League.

Navarro, Mireya. 1996. "Florida Farm a Labor Battleground." *New York Times,* April 11.

Neckerman, Kathryn M., and Joleen Kirschenman. 1991. "Hiring Strategies, Racial Bias, and Inner City Workers." *Social Problems* 38:433–47.

Norton, Eleanor Holmes. 1996. "Affirmative Action in the Workplace." In *The Affirmative Action Debate,* ed. George E. Curry. Reading, Mass.: Addison-Wesley.

Ocker, Lisa. 1986. "City's Goal: Revitalized Downtown." *Palm Beach Post,* November 25.

Ocker, Lisa, and Stephen Pounds. 1986. "Upheaval Hurts as City Woos Investors." *Palm Beach Post,* November 23.

O'Halloran, Michael. 1998. "Police Chief Out; Fire Chief Gone." *Gadsden County Times,* June 11.

———. 2000. "Quincy's Finances $1.3 Million in Red." *Gadsden County Times,* July 27.

Okaloosa News Journal. 1989. "Local Man Arrested for Cross Burning." August 2.

———. 1991. "Firebomb Suspect Arrested for Arson and Hate Crimes." August 7.

Orr, Marion. 1996. "Urban Politics and School Reform: The Case of Baltimore." *Urban Affairs Review* 31 (3): 314–45.

O'Toole, Denise. 1991. "Disparities Tarnish School Advances." *Daytona Beach News-Journal,* October 26.

Ouder, Paula, and Bob Arndorfer. 2002. "Confederate Battle Flag Raised over I-75." *Gainesville Sun,* February 16.

Pallesen, Tim. 1992a. "Delay Urged in Crime Crackdown: Black Leaders Ask Counseling First for Drive-By Suspects." *Palm Beach Post,* April 2.

———. 1992b. "Police to Crack Down on Drive-By Shootings: County Unit to Get Federal Help." *Palm Beach Post,* March 24.

Palm Beach Post. 1990. "Magnet Schools' Draw Shows They Are Working." December 11.

———. 1991. "The Busing Stops Here." March 20.

———. 2001. "3 Riviera Officers Ordered Reinstated." January 17.

Pastor, Manuel, Jr., and Enrico Marcelli. 2003. "Somewhere over the Rainbow? African Americans, Unauthorized Mexican Immigration, and Coalition Building." *Review of Black Political Economy* 21 (1–2): 125–55.

Pfankuch, Thomas B. 1998. "Quincy Watches Power Shift." *Jacksonville Times Union,* November 15.

Piore, Michael. 1979. *Birds of Passage.* New York: Cambridge University Press.

Portes, Alejandro. 1987. "The Social Origins of the Cuban Enclave Economy." *Sociological Perspectives* 30 (4): 340–72.

Portes, Alejandro, and Alex Stepick. 1993. *City on the Edge: Miami and the Immigrants.* Berkeley and Los Angeles: University of California Press.

Pounds, Stephen. 1986. "Coalition Seeks to Replace Racial Politics." *Palm Beach Post,* November 24.

Putnam, Robert D. 2003. "APSA Presidential Address: The Public Role of Political Science." *Perspectives on Politics* I (2): 249–56.

Raines, Franklin D. 2002. "What Equality Would Look Like: Reflections on the Past, Present and Future." In *Black America: Opportunity and Equality = One America.* New York: National Urban League.

Reskin, Barbara F. 1998. *The Realities of Affirmative Action in Employment.* Washington, D.C.: American Sociological Association.

Reskin, Barbara F., and Patricia Roos. 1990. *Job Queues, Gender Queues.* Philadelphia: Temple University Press.

Roberts, Leslie. 1995. "Columbia Bands out of Step with MLK Parade." *Lake City Reporter,* January 18.

Rodgers, Harrell R., and Charles S. Bullock. 1972. *Law and Social Change: Civil Rights Laws and Their Consequences.* New York: McGraw-Hill.

Rosenbloom, D. H. 1980. "The Federal Affirmative Action Policy." In *The Practice of Policy Evaluation,* ed. D. Nachmias. New York: St. Martin's Press.

Ross, Bernard, and Myron Levine. 1996. *Urban Politics: Power in Metropolitan America.* 5th ed. Itasca, Ill.: F. E. Peacock.

———. 2001. *Urban Politics: Power in Metropolitan America.* 6th ed. Itasca, Ill.: F. E. Peacock.

Rowland, Ashley. 2002. "Lake City Logo Spurs Protest." *Gainesville Sun,* February 17.

Royce, David. 2000. "Black Voters Rally to Support Moore." *Gadsden County Times,* September 3.

Saltzstein, Grace Hall. 1989. "Black Mayors and Police Policies." *Journal of Politics* 51 (3): 525–44.

Santoro, Wayne A. 1995. "Black Politics and Employment Policies: The Determinants of Local Government Affirmative Action." *Social Science Quarterly* 76:794–806.

Scher, Richard K. 1997. *Politics in the New South: Republicanism, Race and Leadership in the Twentieth Century.* Armonk, N.Y.: M. E. Sharpe.

Schiller, Bradley R. 2001. *The Economics of Poverty and Discrimination.* Upper Saddle River, N.J.: Prentice Hall.

Schorr, Lisbeth B. 1997. *Common Purpose: Strengthening Families and Neighborhoods to Rebuild America.* New York: Doubleday.

Schuman, Howard, and Lawrence Bobo. 1988. "Survey-Based Experiments on White Racial Attitudes Toward Residential Integration." *American Journal of Sociology* 94:273–99.

Schuman, Howard, Charlotte Steeh, Lawrence Bobo, and Maria Krysan. 1997. *Racial Attitudes in America: Trends and Interpretations.* Cambridge: Harvard University Press.

Sears, David O. 1988. "Symbolic Racism: Profiles in Controversy." In *Eliminating Racism,* ed. Phyllis A. Katz and Dalmas A. Taylor. New York: Praeger.

Sears, David, Collette Van Laar, Mary Carrillo, and Rick Klosterman. 1997. "Is It Really Racism? The Origins of White Americans' Opposition to Race-Targeted Policies." *Public Opinion Quarterly* 61:16–53.

Sessa, Valerie I. 1992. "Managing Diversity at the Xerox Corporation: Balanced Workforce Goals and Caucus Groups." In *Diversity in the Workplace: Human Resource Initiatives,* ed. Susan E. Jackson and Associates. New York: Guilford Press.

Sher, Richard. 1997. *Politics in the New South: Republicanism, Race, and Leadership in the Twentieth Century.* Armonk, N.Y.: M.E. Sharpe.

Simon, Julian. 1999. *The Economic Consequences of Immigration.* Ann Arbor: University of Michigan Press.

Sitkoff, Harvard. 1981. *The Struggle for Black Equality: 1954–1980.* New York: Hill and Wang.

Skrentny, John David. 1996. *The Ironies of Affirmative Action: Politics, Culture, and Justice in America.* Chicago: University of Chicago Press.

———, ed. 2001. *Color Lines: Affirmative Action, Immigration, and Civil Rights Options for America.* Chicago: University of Chicago Press.

Slack, James D. 1987. "City Managers, Police Chiefs, and Fire Chiefs in the South: Testing for Determinants and Impact of Attitudes Toward Affirmative Action." *Review of Public Personnel Administration* 8:11–32.

Smelser, Neil J., William Julius Wilson, and Faith Mitchell, eds. 2001. *America Becoming: Racial Trends and Their Consequences.* Vol. 1. Washington, D.C.: National Academies Press.

Smith, Barbara McClure. 1992a. "Charges May Be Made in CHS Fight; Principal Vows No More Violence at CHS." *Okaloosa News Journal,* September 23.

———. 1992b. "CHS Students Charged." *Okaloosa News Journal,* October 14.

Smith, Brendan. 1996. "'Plain Fun' for a Weekend: Party Gains Momentum as Crowds Begin to Roll In." *Daytona Beach News-Journal,* April 13.

Smith, James P. 2001. "Race and Ethnicity in the Labor Market: Trends over the Short and Long Term." In *American Becoming: Racial Trends and Their Consequences.* Vol. 2, ed. Neil J. Smelser, William Julius Wilson, and Faith Mitchell. Washington, D.C.: National Academies Press.

Smith, James P., and Finis Welch. 1989. "Affirmative Action and Labor Markets." *Journal of Labor Economics* 2:269–301.

Sniderman, Paul M., and Thomas Piazza. 1993. *The Scar of Race.* Cambridge: Harvard University Press.

Snowden, William. 1992. "Public Works Director Suspended Amid Allegations." *Gadsden County Times,* March 26.

Solomon, Jolie. 1996. "Texaco's Troubles." *Newsweek,* November 25, 48–55.

Spriggs, William E., and Rhonda M. Williams. 2000. "What Do We Need to Explain About African-American Unemployment?" In *Prosperity for All? The Economic Boom and African Americans,* ed. Robert Cherry and William M. Rodgers. New York: Russell Sage Foundation.

Steeh, Charlotte, and Maria Krysan. 1996. "The Polls—Trends: Affirmative Action and the Public, 1970–1995." *Public Opinion Quarterly* 60:128–58.

Steel, Brent, and Nicholas Lovrich. 1987. "Comparable Worth: The Problematic Politicization of a Public Personnel Issue." *Public Personnel Management* 16 (Spring): 23–36.

Stein, Lana. 1986. "Representative Local Government: Minorities in the Municipal Work Force." *Journal of Politics* 48 (3): 694–713.

Stoll, Michael, Edwin Melendez, and Abel Valenzuela. 2002. "Spatial Job Search and Job Competition Among Immigrant and Native Groups in Los Angeles." *Regional Studies* 36 (2): 97–112.

Sullivan, Bartholomew. 1987. "'Reform' Promise Could Mean Rough Road for Riviera." *Palm Beach Post,* April 20.

Swain, Carol M., Kyra R. Greene, and Christine Min Wotipka. 2001. "Understanding Racial Polarization on Affirmative Action: The View from Focus Groups." In *Color*

Lines: Affirmative Action, Immigration, and Civil Rights Options for America, ed. John David Skrentny. Chicago: University of Chicago Press.

Swirko, Cindy. 1991a. "Blacks Picket over Columbia Principal." *Lake City Reporter,* July 24.

———. 1991b. "Columbia Panel Denies Pleas About Principal." *Lake City Reporter,* July 10.

———. 1991c. "NAACP Boycott Gains Support." *Gainesville Sun,* August 22.

Tatum, Beverly Daniel. 1997. *"Why Are All the Black Kids Sitting Together in the Cafeteria?" and Other Conversations About Race.* New York: Basic Books.

Thompson, A. P. 2000a. "Battle of the Flag." *Gainesville Sun,* February 18.

———. 2000b. "NAACP Requests Removal of Confederate Flag." *Gainesville Sun,* December 15.

———. 2001. "Lake City's New Logo Attracting Criticism." *Gainesville Sun,* March 7.

Tomaskovic-Devey, Donald. 1993. *Gender and Inequality at Work: The Sources and Consequences of Job Segregation.* Ithaca, N.Y.: ILR Press.

Trontz, Ian. 1997. "Plot to Oust Riviera Police Chief Nearly Succeeded." *Palm Beach Post,* April 13.

U.S. Department of Labor. 1989. *The Effects of Immigration on the U.S. Economy and Labor Market.* Washington, D.C.: Bureau of International Labor Affairs.

U.S. Equal Employment Opportunity Commission. 2001. *EEOC Enforcement Activities.* Washington, D.C.: U.S. Equal Employment Opportunity Commission. www.eeoc.gov/enforce.html (accessed December 19, 2001).

Verhovek, Sam Howe. 1997. "In Poll, Americans Reject Means but Not Ends of Racial Diversity." *New York Times,* December 14, 1, 32.

Waldinger, Roger. 1997. "Black/ Immigrant Competition Re-assessed: New Evidence from Los Angeles." *Sociological Perspectives* 40:365–86.

Walker, Barbara A., and William C. Hanson. 1992. "Valuing Differences at Digital Equipment Corporation." In *Diversity in the Workplace: Human Resource Initiatives,* ed. Susan E. Jackson and Associates. New York: Guilford Press.

Walker, Samuel, Cassia Spohn, and Miriam DeLone. 1996. *The Color of Justice: Race, Ethnicity, and Crime in America.* Belmont, Calif.: Wadsworth.

Ward, Steven. 1997. "Woman Scared After Racial Incident: Slur-Laced Note Thrown Through Window, Graffiti Found on Street." *Lake City Reporter,* July 11.

Washington Post/Kaiser Family Foundation/Harvard University. 2001. *Race and Ethnicity in 2001: Attitudes, Perceptions and Experiences.* Special Report. Washington, D.C.: Kaiser Family Foundation.

White, George. 2001. "Group Suggests Targeting 'Hidden Racism.'" *Star Advocate,* August 1.

Whitney, Valerie. 1992a. "Black College Reunion Packs Them In." *Daytona Beach News and Journal,* April 15.

———. 1992b. "Police Program Helps Change Children's Lives." *Daytona Beach News-Journal,* January 13.

———. 2000. "Minorities: Bush's Plan Still Unproven." *Daytona Beach News-Journal,* October 1.

Wilks, Ed. 1999. "'God Squad' to Spread Good Will During BCR." *Daytona Beach News-Journal,* April 5.

Wilson, Thomas. 2006. "Whites' Opposition to Affirmative Action: Rejection of Group-Based Preferences as Well as Rejection of Blacks." *Social Forces* 85 (1): 111–20.

Wilson, William Julius. 1996. *When Work Disappears: The World of the New Urban Poor.* New York: Knopf.

Wirt, Frederick M. 1970. *Politics of Southern Equality: Law and Social Change in a Mississippi County.* Chicago: Aldine.

———. 1997. *"We Ain't What We Was": Civil Rights in the New South.* Durham: Duke University Press.

Wisniewski, John. 1990. "Black Daytona Beach Residents Claim Unfair Treatment by City." *Daytona Beach News-Journal,* March 22.

Wolf, Karen. 1992. "Tensions at Crestview High Erupt in Lunchtime Brawl." *Florida Daily News,* March 21.

———. 1993. "Feds Investigate Racism Charges." *Florida Daily News,* April 23.

Zhao, Jihong, and Nicholas Lovrich. 1998. "Determinants of Minority Employment in American Municipal Police Agencies: The Representation of African American Officers." *Journal of Criminal Justice* 26 (4): 267–77.

Zuckerman, Laura. 2001. "Adam's Mark Settles Lawsuit." *Daytona Beach News-Journal,* December 4.

Index